JOHN GLOAG ON INDUSTRIAL DESIGN

Volume 9

THE ENGLISHMAN'S CHAIR

THE ENGLISHMAN'S CHAIR

Origins, Design, and Social History of Seat Furniture in England

JOHN GLOAG

Routledge
Taylor & Francis Group

LONDON AND NEW YORK

First published in 1964 by George Allen & Unwin Ltd.

This edition first published in 2023
by Routledge
4 Park Square, Milton Park, Abingdon, Oxon OX14 4RN

and by Routledge
605 Third Avenue, New York, NY 10158

Routledge is an imprint of the Taylor & Francis Group, an informa business

British Library Cataloguing in Publication Data
A catalogue record for this book is available from the British Library

ISBN: 978-1-032-36309-7 (Set)
ISBN: 978-1-032-36725-5 (Volume 9) (hbk)
ISBN: 978-1-032-36760-6 (Volume 9) (pbk)
ISBN: 978-1-003-33362-3 (Volume 9) (ebk)

DOI: 10.4324/9781003333623

Publisher's Note
The publisher has gone to great lengths to ensure the quality of this reprint but points out that some imperfections in the original copies may be apparent.

Disclaimer
The publisher has made every effort to trace copyright holders and would welcome correspondence from those they have been unable to trace.

THE
ENGLISHMAN'S
CHAIR

ORIGINS, DESIGN, AND SOCIAL HISTORY
OF SEAT FURNITURE IN ENGLAND

BY

JOHN GLOAG

F.S.A., Hon.A.R.I.B.A.

London
GEORGE ALLEN & UNWIN LTD
RUSKIN HOUSE MUSEUM STREET

PRINTED IN GREAT BRITAIN
in 11 point Baskerville type
BY UNWIN BROTHERS LTD
WOKING AND LONDON

DEDICATED TO
ELISE AND JULIAN GLOAG

CONTENTS

ILLUSTRATIONS IN THE TEXT

LIST OF PLATES

REFERENCES AND ACKNOWLEDGEMENTS

Footnotes have been avoided. Books and other sources that are quoted or referred to in the text are listed under chapters, beginning on page 269. Acknowledgements to the sources of illustrations are given in the captions.

THE ENGLISHMAN'S CHAIR

ISTORICAL accounts of chair-making and design have been incorporated in many works on English furniture, and of these the most comprehensive appears under the entry *Chair* in Volume One of *The Dictionary of English Furniture*, in the edition enlarged and revised by Mr Ralph Edwards in 1954. An instructive description of the methods and materials used by joiners and chair-makers is included in Chapter Three of *Furniture Making in Seventeenth and Eighteenth Century England*, by the late Robert Wemyss Symonds; and a short, compact and excellent book on the subject is *The English Chair*, originally issued in 1937 by M. Harris and Sons, and since reprinted. The works mentioned cover the history of chairs up to the end of the Georgian period, and for their next phase of development we may consult such authoritative studies as *Victorian Furniture*, by R. W. Symonds and B. B. Whineray, and *English Cottage Furniture* and *Victorian Furniture* by F. Gordon Roe.

In this book I have attempted to write a short history of English chairs as a continuous story, from the fifteenth century, when a recognizable native style appeared, to the genesis and development of the modern movement in design. For five centuries the character of chair design—and indeed of nearly all furniture—has been directly connected with or influenced by architecture. For example, when English architects in the 1920s and '30s were preoccupied with what Geoffrey Scott called "The Mechanical Fallacy", and the *avant-garde* gave honour to the so-called "international style", chairs of tubular metal and fabric were designed with all traces of national distinctiveness conscientiously erased. Since the Second World War, the English tradition has reasserted an individuality that was too strong to be permanently submerged in the prosaic anonymity of barren functionalism. That grisly phrase: "A house is a machine for living in", was supplemented by another: "An armchair is a machine for sitting in and so on". M. Le Corbusier, who coined both, exercised a potent influence on the growth and development of the modern movement, not only through his revolutionary book, *Towards A New Architecture*, in which those phrases appeared, but by the consistent logic of his teaching and the vitality of his work as an architect. The modern movement has outgrown the calculated austerity of its bleak period between the wars; its manifestations in architecture and the industrial arts have mellowed, like many of its ardent missionaries; and materials, manufacturing techniques, and the general approach to furniture design have changed more in the last forty years than in the previous four hundred. Because we are still in this period of change, I have made no attempt to assess or describe the character of contemporary work. I am fully aware of new graces in the seat-furniture of the present day, of a gay inventiveness, of light and elegant shapes that make the tubular metal chairs of the 1920s seem as crude as the first bi-plane flown by the Wright Brothers compared with the latest super-sonic jet; but even so, I realize that before the end of the twentieth century furniture designers may be saying about the chairs made now very much what Hepplewhite said in *The Cabinet-Maker and Upholsterer's Guide* about the work of his predecessors, and what Sheraton said about Hepplewhite.

March 1964   JOHN GLOAG

CHAPTER I

POSTURE AND DESIGN

T HE ancestry of the English chair is as mixed as that of the English people, and though far-distant pre-Christian origins have affected the character of design and decoration, costume and manners have often determined the shape not only of seats but the posture of those seated. The vast spread of the farthingale, worn by women of fashion in the late sixteenth and seventeenth centuries, was accommodated by the broad-seated back-stool, the so-called farthingale chair, and the Victorian crinoline inspired the production of the lady's easy chair, low-seated, with an upright shell back and vestigial arms; while for centuries the hardness of flat uncushioned seats was minimized by the voluminous clothes of those who used them—even a monk's habit could be bunched up to soften the surface of a stall or the cutting edge of a misericord. Seats of almost any kind, fixed or movable, reveal the posture and carriage of the men and women for whom they were made, and chairs show more faithfully than any other article of furniture the importance accorded to dignity, elegance or comfort, thus supplementing the comprehensive disclosures made by architecture about life in any period. Chairs indicate whether social life was formal and rigid, gracefully relaxed, casual and careless, austere, voluptuous, romantic, imitative, democratically standardised, affluent, vulgar, indifferent to art, dull, snobbish, or poor.

The design and social character of chairs in England, from the Middle Ages to the twentieth century, is the subject of this book. The history of the English chair begins with the late mediaeval period, when an individual native style in architecture and the crafts became recognizable. Other forms of seat furniture are included, for although the chair occasionally developed in isolation, it was often related to architecture, and had sometimes emerged as an independent entity from a group of seating units that was part of an architectural concept. Thus ancient Greek chairs may have derived their initial form from the tiers of shaped marble seats in an open-air theatre just as some fifteenth-century chairs derived theirs from choir stalls. This evolutionary process was reversed in the second half of the seventeenth century, when chairs were extended laterally to form double or triple seats— the so-called love-seat and the settee—with the chair back, unaltered in shape or decoration, used in duplicate or triplicate.

The study of chair-making in England would be incomplete without some reference to the skilled crafts, the structural inventions, and the ornamental forms that were developed originally in the ancient world—in Egypt, the empires of the Middle East, and the Graeco-Roman civilization. Techniques, like turning and joinery, were known and practised many centuries before Christ, and while civilizations collapsed and were followed by dark ages of barbarism when the refinements of life were forgotten, crafts were transplanted to other countries where they flourished, so technical knowledge survived, for it was not persecuted or forbidden like other forms of knowledge when the Age of Reason was replaced by the Age of Faith. The survival power of ornament was considerable, and motifs that had first appeared as early as the Fourth Dynasty in Egypt (2900–2750 BC), could reappear in France and England during the late eighteenth and early nineteenth centuries, while ornament associated with or derived from the classic orders of architecture, perfected in Greece and adapted and used throughout the Roman Empire, exerted an influence on the decoration and subsequently on the form of English furniture after the late sixteenth century. A Roman patrician would have found many familiar shapes in the furniture of a Georgian gentleman's house, and the sabre-legged Greek Revival chairs of the Regency would have been equally familiar to Pericles or Plato.

The design of seats partly depends on the postures adopted for dignity or comfort. Different races have characteristic ways of sitting which seem to have a cultural derivation and have not arisen because of any anatomical differences between Asiatics,

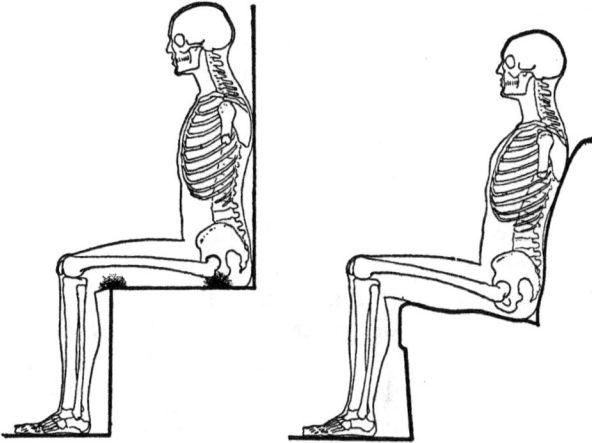

Left: The back is completely vertical, with the result that the head is thrown off balance, the back left unsupported, and the sitting posture becomes penitential as the flat seat is not shaped to the body or tilted and is the wrong height from the ground. These strictures would apply to the chairs on plate 1, on which an Egyptian noble and his wife sit with patient dignity, though slight concessions have been made to the contours of the human body by a barely perceptible inclination of the back, and a curved junction with the seat, which has a shallow dip. *Right:* The seat is the right height, and, like the back, is shaped to the body and tilted to provide a comfortable sitting position. (Reproduced from *Furniture from Machines* by permission of the author, Gordon Logie, and the publishers, George Allen and Unwin Ltd.)

Negroes and whites. The Chinese, Japanese, Burmese, Indonesian, Hindu, and some of the Middle Eastern nations like the Turks, sit comfortably with the lower limbs arranged horizontally; a posture that has been described as the hieratic or Buddha position, and is usually depicted in paintings and sculptured figures of Buddha and adopted by Buddhist priests. This sitting position has for many centuries influenced the design of Oriental furniture, and by lowering the eye level has lowered the height of seats and tables, which, by comparison with European seats and tables, seem very close to the floor. In the Middle and Far East mats or cushions placed directly on the floor are often used instead of stools and chairs. A less serene and dignified position is squatting with the legs disposed vertically, the knees brought together below the chin, the spine curved forwards, and the arms extended, resting on the knees or clasped about them. There are two distinct variations of squatting: in the first, used by Negroes in a primitive, tribal state of civilization, the buttocks rest on the ground with the back supported by some vertical prop—a tree trunk, a wall or a fence. In the second, the individual squats on his heels or hams, with the buttocks clear of the ground—a position often shown in Ancient Egyptian paintings and sculpture, common also in India, and habitual among many African tribes. The Ancient Egyptians sat upright on chairs and stools with seats of varying height, though even a low-seated chair, like the example in acacia wood, *circa* 1250 B C, on plate 3, was higher than anything Oriental, for the sitting positions of the Egyptian upper classes were the same as those of all classes in Europe: the Fellahin, peasants and slaves, might squat, but the Pharaoh and his court officials and the horde of well-housed bureaucrats sat with well-drilled dignity.

The Greeks and the Romans reclined on low couches when they dined, and the Greeks had recognized the importance of a curved, comfortable support for the back when they sat on chairs. A flat seat and a completely vertical back throw the head off balance and give no support to the small of the back, as the diagrams on page 3 of good and bad profiles of seats show very clearly; but for thousands of years the claims of dignity have excluded comfort, though the Greeks proved that dignity and comfort were not incompatible in chair design. (Plates 6 and 7.) Asiatic peoples had combined dignity with comfort in their habitual sitting positions; Europeans, who preferred to sit upright, were prepared to sacrifice comfort, and retained the unyielding, vertical chair back until the sixteenth century. Today the science of anthropometrics, which concerns the measurements of the human body, is making fresh contributions to the study of comfort, though the basic needs of support and muscular relaxation remain unchanged.

In simple tribal communities, a seat just high enough to allow the chief to look down on his squatting tribesmen was all that dignity demanded: a block of wood or stone, or as technical skill advanced, a low stool, were the predecessors of the throne. In all ages authority has required the enhancement of superior height: thrones rested on a platform ascended by steps, judges were enthroned above the level of their courts, prelates and the Masters of mediaeval guilds also sat on thrones, and the seats occupied by the feudal lord, his relatives and special guests were set on a raised daïs at one end of the great hall. *Inferior* had a physical as well as a social meaning: the lower orders were literally at a lower level when in the presence of their lords and masters who always looked down on them from a height, from a chair of state or the back of a horse. In the presence of kings, princes of the church and great noblemen, not only serfs and servants, but the lesser nobility and gentry were obliged to show their respect by kneeling. In England the chair has for centuries been a symbol of authority, even when no chair is in use. The account of the election in *The Pickwick Papers* records a vote of thanks that was moved to the Mayor of Eatanswill "for his able conduct in the chair; and the mayor devoutly wishing that he had had a chair to display his able conduct in (for he had been standing during the whole proceedings) returned thanks". Chairman has become a title, invested with power, and though the chair as a material symbol has become less important, it still figures prominently in the halls and council chambers of City Companies, learned societies, universities and many professional bodies, while in monarchies the throne is emblematic of royal supremacy.

This traditional association of chairs with an upright, dignified bearing was not overcome until the late seventeenth century when the easy chair was invented, and though nobody at the time suspected what this invention would do to good manners, it was the starting point of a slow but continuous decline of dignity. By increasing standards of comfort, chair-makers and upholsterers began to change posture through design, thus unwittingly changing the character of manners, which became less formal, easier, and in many ways happier, while dignity was relegated to Royal and official functions. The gradual decay of elegance and the ultimate triumph of comfort are recorded by the chairs and seats in use throughout the Georgian and Victorian periods and by those we use today.

Painting of chair with X-shaped underframe, from the tomb of Nebamun, Thebes, *circa* 1400 BC. The legs appear to terminate in claw-and-ball feet, but the ball may be the end section of cylindrical rests, like those on the folding stool shown on the upper part of plate 3. The curved members of this chair are unrelated; the underframing looks clumsy and even unstable, partly because the slight curve of the legs disrupts the line of the back and they cross at an angle that makes them appear structurally unsound, for the seat is not braced by a curve that is intentionally inclined to support weight but by one that sags ominously. Reproduced from *The British Museum: Egyptian Antiquities* (London: M. A. Nattali, 1846), Volume II, page 64.

CHAPTER 2

ORIGINS IN THE ANCIENT WORLD
AND EARLY MIDDLE AGES
3400 BC–AD 1300

IDEAS that now seem commonplace to us once had an incandescent originality that blinded and bewildered or provoked the hostility of those who heard them propounded or saw them demonstrated. In architecture there were structural inventions: somebody thought of putting a horizontal cross-piece above two uprights of equal length, so post-and-lintel construction arrived. Chair-making began when somebody, several thousand years ago, suggested that a piece of flat wood laid on top of three or four stones of approximately equal height would provide a movable seat. Collecting a few stones of about the same size was a simple job compared with shifting a solid block of wood or stone from place to place, when the tribe was on the move. No doubt there was resistance to the innovation: conservative-minded tribesmen may have held that it was improper for anybody below the rank of chief or medicine-man to have a seat at all, and anyway the official seat should always remain in one place, while movable seats would only encourage ambitious young upstarts to sit like their betters instead of squatting like humble subjects. New ideas are usually condemned as irreverent, subservient, and lacking in respect for authority; and they have to be fought for by those who believe in them. Change was resisted among primitive peoples because they lived in a traditional framework of habit and custom, from which they feared to escape, in case they offended the gods, the spirits of their ancestors, or their own rulers

7

and priests. (Perhaps the only new idea that ever became popular at once was the invention of fermented drinks, though maybe a few congenital Puritans objected even in Neolithic times.) Resting a trimmed and smoothed board on stones was the first stage in the evolution of a free-standing, movable seat; the next, which must have taken many generations to reach, was to fit three or four legs to the board, plugging them into holes bored or scraped out on the under-side, and producing as a result something that was stable, and saved the trouble of searching for supporting stones.

As skill in woodworking improved, the crude upright supports for seats were carved, for primitive and civilized people alike have a deep need for and love of ornament, and as craftsmen generally go to nature for models, some of the earliest examples represent the legs of animals. Breasted mentions stools supported on carved ivory legs, representing those of a bull, in the First and Second Dynasties of Ancient Egypt, 3400–2980 BC, and for centuries the placid, unchanging Egyptian civilization developed the art of furnishing, evolving a stylised fauna and flora for thrones, chairs and stools, and perfecting such structural inventions as the folding stool and the braced frame. The folding wooden stool, *circa* 1300 BC, on plate 3 has duck's head terminals, inlaid with ivory and ebony, the beaks butting against turned rests, and the seat supports dipped to allow the leather or fabric slung from them to provide a hollow seat. The statue of the Egyptian noble and his wife, *circa* 1450 BC, illustrated on plate 1, shows two chairs, side by side, though the back is represented as continuous, perhaps because the sculptor forgot to carve a vertical division. The legs and paws of a lion are accurately and boldly carved; the seats are dipped, curving up to join the back, which is slightly inclined. Such small concessions to comfort do not diminish the dignity of the aristocratic couple who sit bolt upright, their arms formally disposed, the husband's left hand resting lightly, in a gesture of possessive but carefully controlled affection, on his wife's hands, which are clasped on her knees. Their feet point straight before them.

The chairs which are engraved on the stele, reproduced on the upper part of plate 2, have low backs and very slender legs, which may have been turned. The date is about 1200 BC, but turning was known in Egypt much earlier, so was joinery. A

The Assyrian King Sennacherib seated on a throne that looks more comfortable, despite a rigid back, than the cushioned stool of King Ashurnasirpal, shown on plate 4. The throne rests on turned cones, the footstool has paw feet in front, and twelve bearded figures are arranged in three tiers on the sides. This dates from the eighth century BC, and the stool on plate 4, *circa* 1260 BC, is a simpler and better design, which suggests that Assyrian art had declined during the intervening centuries. Reproduced from Layard's *Discoveries in the Ruins of Ninevah and Babylon* (1853), Chapter VI, page 150.

painting from the tomb of Nebamun and Ipuky, Thebes, *circa* 1380 BC, shows goldsmiths and joiners busy in their workshops. Turning is an ancient art, and though lost or in abeyance during periods of decline and chaos, it has always been recovered. H. P. Shapland has suggested in *The Practical Decoration of Furniture* that "the trunks of saplings or the smaller branches of trees provided primitive man with the prototype of the turned handle for his implements and weapons. The rings or annulets cut on the haft of the axe or club in order to give a firm grip, and which took, as civilization progressed, a decorative form, may be regarded as the earliest essays in the treatment of circular shafts which culminated in elaborate lathe work." Wood has been shaped by cutting tools on a rotating surface since very early times, but there is no record of when or where the first lathe was invented. It was used by the Egyptians, Assyrians, Greeks and Romans, in the Byzantine

Grecian sphinx guarding a cinerary urn. Sphinxes are used to support the arms of the chair carved on the Parthenon frieze, reproduced on plate 5, and sometimes flanked the seat of a marble chair in the same position as the owls flanking the chair on plate 8. The Greek sphinx flew across the centuries to alight on furniture designed by Robert Adam and Thomas Hope. Two recumbent sphinxes adorn the chair on plate 47, designed by Robert Adam for the bed chamber at Osterly House, Middlesex, in 1777; with wings upraised, they support the oval chair back, and are far less intimidating than the lion-headed type used by Thomas Hope as seat-ends in the interior shown on page 180.

(The engraving is reproduced from *The Antiquities of Athens*, by Stuart and Revett, Vol. IV.)

Empire and throughout the Romanesque period; but Egyptian work was far more accomplished than the much later Byzantine and Romanesque turning. The legs of the furniture made in Ancient Egypt had greater precision, and careful attention was given to the outline of the shafts; possibly because furniture design was developing concurrently with architecture, and woodworkers were transferring to a more tractable material the lessons learnt the hard way with granite or limestone. There was an interchange between forms evolved for wood and stone: masons often borrowed and gave permanence to ideas originated by woodworkers.

The Egyptian craftsman, whether he worked with stone, pottery or wood, had a totally different approach to materials from his mediaeval European successors. Sir William Flinders Petrie remarked on "the base imitation of nature in copying the grain of wood", which was practised as early as the Fourth Dynasty (2900–2750 BC); stone was imitated too by painting, and pottery vases were painted to simulate valuable stone. "The imitation of nature was the standpoint from which he started," wrote Petrie, "and he had no objection to carry out that imitation with paint or otherwise; our abstract standpoint of an artistic effect which must never involve falsity, but which may have little or nothing to do with nature, was altogether outside of his aesthetic."

Egyptian artists sometimes escaped from the inert symbolism that imprisoned inspiration and restricted experiments and innovations, and such transient freedom was marked when they depicted lively scenes from life, like the fight of the boatmen, that famous piece of relief sculpture in the Cairo Museum dating from the Fifth Dynasty (2750–2625 BC), or the much later painting of fowling in the marshes, from the Tomb of Nebamun, Thebes, *circa* 1400 BC, in the British Museum. Domestic scenes, or royal and religious ceremonies are nearly always static; guests at a banquet, even when watching dancing girls, are frozen in identical attitudes of polite attention, and the chairs they use seem to be part of the formal pattern of manners that directed the life of the upper classes. Among the paintings in the British Museum is one of a banquet, also from the tomb of Nebamun at Thebes, with the guests seated on chairs that have lion's legs and paws, some coloured yellow, which suggests gilding, others black that

Detail of seats in the Theatre of Dionysos, Athens, 340 BC. The rising tiers of seats in the Greek theatre were components of an architectural concept, which may have developed originally from flights of steps. For magistrates and priests, marble thrones were provided, with curved legs and paw feet, forerunners of the cabriole leg that became fashionable in Europe some two thousand years later. (See plate 6.) Here the concave leg is indicated, comparable with the chair leg depicted on the grave-stone of Xanthippos. (See plate 7.) (Drawn by Hilton Wright, and reproduced from *Guide to Western Architecture*, by permission of the artist and the publishers George Allen and Unwin Ltd.)

may indicate either paint or ebony. The seats have flat cushions with various patterns on a white ground: thin red lines crossing at right angles, or linked diamond shapes, red or blue. Some other tomb paintings from Thebes of the same date show seats with scroll feet curving inwards and resting on turned bases.

Structural inventions, like joinery, led to the making of chairs of the type illustrated on the lower part of plates 2 and 3, which both date from the Nineteenth Dynasty, when Rameses II was Pharaoh (1292–1225 BC). The example with the high, open back, filled by four flat vertical uprights, has the seat-frame socketed into the legs, with the ends of the tenons visible; while the stretchers that link front legs and back legs are socketed into the thickness of the wood. Egyptian woodworkers used, and probably invented, the mortice and tenon joint, which consists of a cavity, the mortice, cut into a piece of wood to receive the tenon, a projection cut on another piece of wood to fit into it exactly: a structural technique unknown to English chair-makers before the sixteenth century AD. The high inclined back and the yielding seat of woven string, resembling cane-work, gave far more comfort than the low-backed chairs shown on the stele on the upper part of plate 2 or those of the noble and his wife on plate 1, but comfort has been achieved without any softening grace of line. Skill is apparent; art is absent. A similar lack of grace marks the design of the low chair on plate 3, which is made of acacia wood with a panelled and inlaid back, clumsy legs terminating in lion's paws that rest on turned and grooved bases, and a curved member uniting back and seat frames. Both chairs are crude by comparison with the elegant lines of the folding stool on the upper part of plate 3, which is designed with a thorough understanding of the subtle relationship between the concavity of the seat, the delicate sweep of the legs with their duck's head terminals, and the cylindrical turned rests. The significance of such curvilinear relationships has been missed in the X-shaped chair reproduced on page 6. This example, from the tomb of Nebamun at Thebes, *circa* 1400 BC, shows the owner of the tomb seated. The chair back, which ascends in a gentle curve to a rudimentary scroll, is coloured black, with a thin red line; the legs, banded in red on the upper part, have traces of yellow or gold where they cross, and are elsewhere painted black. What appears to be a claw-and-ball device is used for the feet, the ball painted yellow and outlined in red, which may indicate gilding, but the ball could be the circular end of a turned rest. The seat is draped with a material that resembles leopard skin. The under-framing appears clumsy and even unstable, partly because the slight curve of the legs disrupts the line of the back and they cross at an angle that makes them appear structurally unsound, for instead of being braced by an upward curve to support the weight on the seat, the curve sags ominously.

Like the Victorian furniture makers, the Egyptians seemed to believe that the artistic quality of work was derived from the abundance and impressiveness of ornamentation. Rich effects were desired and secured. The art of beating gold into a thin skin and spreading it over wood or metal was known, perhaps as early as the Twelfth Dynasty (2000–1788 BC), and the use of gilding heightened the appearance of lavish wealth, an impression enhanced by employing materials such as ebony and ivory, not only for inlaid ornament, but for the legs of chairs and stools. The crude and barbarically vulgar design of many Egyptian chairs and other articles of furniture is concealed from the unobservant by opulent decoration.

Among the stylised natural forms employed by Egyptian painters and carvers and bequeathed to later civilizations were the lotus flower and bud, and one of the many variations of that flower, with curled-over sides and projecting centre, is the ancestor of the *fleur-de-lys*. As many animals and birds had some religious significance, they never appeared in their complete form on chairs and stools—only their legs and paws, talons and beaks were used. The paw foot was passed on to Assyria and both paw and hoof to the Graeco-Roman civilization. The Egyptians invented the hybrid monster, which the Greeks named the sphinx, a recumbent lion with a wigged human head, that sometimes portrayed the features of the reigning Pharaoh, or had, instead of a human head, that of a ram—the sacred animal of Ammon—or a falcon. The sphinx was often a unit in some large-scale architectural complex of avenues, courts and temples; a royal or religious symbol that was never used ornamentally. In France during the reign of Louis XVI there was a short-lived fashion for ornamenting furniture and chairs with the heads of sphinxes; in Napoleon's Empire the sphinx reappeared with other Egyptian motifs; while in England Thomas Hope used variations of the Egyptian and Greek sphinx in his influential book of designs, *Household Furniture and Interior Decoration*, published in 1807. Such decorative uses would have seemed sacrilegious in Ancient Egypt.

The Assyrians adopted the sphinx, bringing it to its feet so that it stood, tensed and alert, with the body of a lion or a bull, from which great wings swept back, and a human head with a long rippling beard asserted a virile masculinity. (A variation of this form was used by the Hittites.) By the seventh century BC the Assyrian sphinx occasionally changed its sex, and a woman's head appeared on a winged, recumbent body. The more delicate Greek version, as shown on plate 5 and page 10, was a winged lion with the head and bust of a serene and beautiful woman—a type used

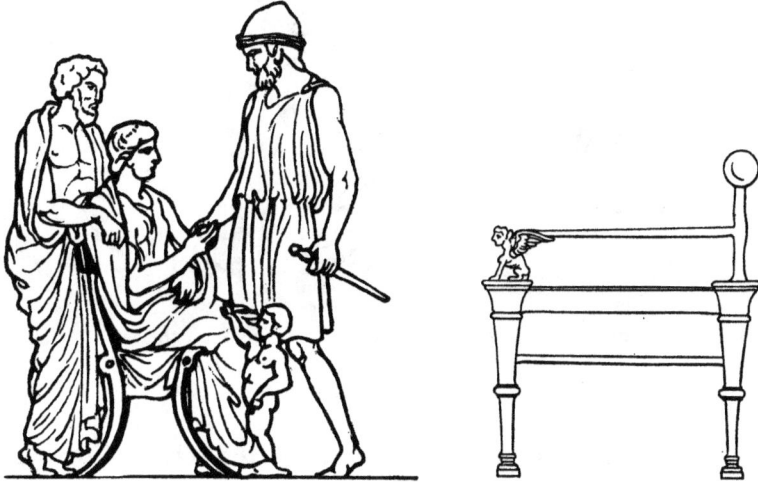

Left: The *klismos*, "a Greek invention, being derived," according to Dr
G. M. A. Richter, "from no Egyptian or Assyrian prototype, but apparently
evolved from the simpler type of throne". The concave legs splayed outwards,
the uprights crossed by a shallow concave back-rest allowed a free, natural
position for those seated. The *klismos*, Dr Richter concludes, "is certainly one
of the most graceful creations in furniture, combining comfort with elegance.
For sheer beauty of line it has few rivals". The Athenian sepulchral urn from
which this is drawn is included on plate 7, together with another example of
the *klismos* from the grave-stone of Xanthippos. *Right:* Archaic rigidity is still
apparent in this chair from the Parthenon frieze. (See plate 5.) *Below:* Early
nineteenth century chair, with lines inspired by the *klismos*. The concave sabre
or scimitar legs are modified versions of prototypes from the fifth and fourth
centuries BC. Unlike Thomas Hope's version on plate 7, continuity of line
between the back legs and back uprights has been preserved.

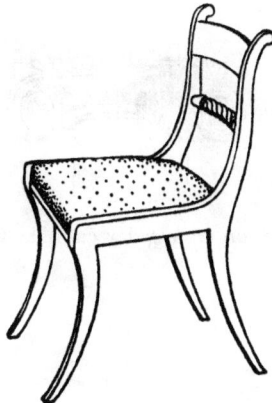

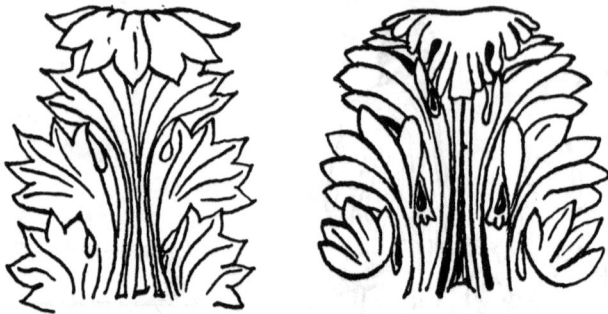

Two variations of the formalized acanthus leaf: Greek on the left, Roman on the right. *Drawn by Hilton Wright.*

in pairs to support the arms or to flank the seat of Greek and Roman chairs.

Seats depicted on Assyrian bas-reliefs have an unvarying stiffness of line, and although Assyrian craftsmen may have invented the forerunner of the armchair, their work showed no advance on Egyptian standards of design and execution. The examples on plate 4 and page 9 are regal seats, separated in time by five centuries, and comparison between them suggests that during that period Assyrian art had declined. King Ashurnasirpal, *circa* 1260 B C, is shown on plate 4, enthroned on a cushioned stool that has a slightly dipped seat decorated with crisply carved ram's heads; the legs, splayed outwards at a barely perceptible angle, are braced by a stretcher, decorated with volutes, and the feet turned and ornamented with rings. The king's footstool has lion's paws.

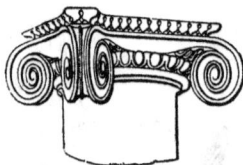

Ionic volutes on an angular capital. *After Nicholson.*

The drawing on page 9 shows King Sennacherib, *circa* 705 B C, on a throne with an exceptionally high seat, curved arms, and a straight back. The open sides and the space between seat and stretcher are filled by twelve bearded figures, supporting with upraised arms the horizontal members of the frame; the legs rest on high turned cones decorated with a pattern of scales, and the front legs of the footstool have paw feet resting on smaller cones. The complexity of the design emphasizes its clumsiness. The designer of the much earlier stool on plate 4 modified stiffness of line by a sparing use of ornament.

Some of the early Greek stools and chairs resemble Egyptian models, with seats supported by X-shaped folding underframes or lion's legs. Many are shown on Greek pottery. Among the Attic black figured vases in the British Museum is a black and red neck-amphora, *circa* 540 B C, with a scene showing Zeus with other gods, seated on a stool with a seat ending in volutes and an X-shaped underframe, so slender that the crossed legs appear to be thin, bent metal rods. In the Golonos Group, *circa* 500 B C, a horizontal panel on an epinetron shows women and youths sitting on X-shaped folding stools, supported on lion's legs, turned inwards. There is also a chair with a high back, curving over to end in a swan's neck and head.

Turned legs, tapering towards the foot, sometimes ended in paws or hooves. Ball turning was known, and is illustrated by the chair on plate 5, reproduced from a Macedonian medal. An armchair, carved on the Parthenon frieze, with arms supported by sphinxes, also appears on plate 5. Both are examples of the archaic, upright type; but Greek designers soon surpassed such static forms and devised the *klismos*, a chair with concave legs splayed outwards and uprights crossed by a shallow concave back-rest, that allowed people to sit freely in a natural position. The examples on plate 7 from an Athenian grave stone, *circa* 430 B C, and a panel from a sepulchral marble urn, also Athenian and about the same date, demonstrate the visual superiority of Greek design— a superiority indicative of a civilization where art and life were inseparable, and the sense of sight consistently honoured. Comfort and elegance are united in the *klismos*. Comparable examples appear on some of the Attic black figured vases in the British Museum, notably a scene showing Dionysos with maenads and a

The influence of Roman orders on the turned legs of mid-seventeenth-century chairs. *Left:* Tuscan. *Right:* Doric. (*After Rickman.*) Base, shaft and capital are reproduced in the chair legs on the extreme right, also on the front legs of the chair on page 57. Doric and Tuscan columns had been copied in the late sixteenth century, not very happily when turners and carvers tried to improve on the original, and produced versions like the front legs of the joined chair on plate 18.

satyr, on a Bell-Krater found at Capua, *circa* 420–400 B C, where a chair appears with very emphatic concave legs, of the type descriptively called "sabre" legs in the early nineteenth century, the curve of the back leg flowing into that of the back to form an elongated S-profile. The concave horizontal back-rest fits the shoulders. The close kinship between free-standing chairs with concave legs and the privileged seats in the rising tiers of the Greek theatre is apparent when the chairs on plate 7 are compared with the seats in the Theatre of Dionysos at Athens shown on plate 6 and by the drawing on page 12. The tiers of seats in a theatre may have developed originally from flights of steps; they were continuous, spectators sat on them side by side, bringing their own cushions or strips of fabric, while magistrates and priests had special seats, marble thrones with curved scroll legs and paw feet, forerunners of the cabriole leg that became fashionable in western Europe some two thousand years later. Architectural affinities are apparent in the marble chair with a concave back, serpentine arms ending in scrolls, and a pair of owls below the scroll terminals, illustrated on plate 8.

The relationship between architecture and chair design, established in Greece, has never been broken off, and the Greek discovery of a natural and graceful form for chairs is characteristic of the people who perfected the Doric, Ionic, and Corinthian orders of architecture, and created the system that governed the proportions of each. Whether a chair was carved from marble, cast in bronze, or constructed of wood, the skill of the craftsman who made it was directed by the most exacting standards of design, amounting to a demand for perfection. The three Greek orders of architecture were adapted by the Romans, who added two others: the Tuscan and the Composite. The Roman Doric and Tuscan orders, shown on page 18, influenced the ideas of turners over a thousand years after the Roman Empire had ended. Their columns and capitals were often reproduced with variations by English chair-makers of the late sixteenth and early seventeenth centuries, and the legs of the joined chair on the lower part of plate 18 illustrate how far those Elizabethan and Jacobean craftsmen could stray from the original, while the "farthingale" chair on page 57 and the profiles of mid-seventeenth-century chair legs on page 18 show how turners eventually mastered the correct proportions. Ionic volutes, detached from their capitals, were also used ornamentally on the cresting and underframing of seventeenth-century English chairs, mingled with other versions of the spiral scroll. The volute, which may have been suggested by the shape of the nautilus shell, was known and used in Egypt and Assyria long before it appeared on Ionic and Corinthian capitals. (See plate 4 and pages 16 and 23.)

Although nearly all the ornamental motifs used by the Greeks or associated with the classic orders were derived from organic

Above and below: Two variations of the Greek anthemion, honeysuckle or palmette. (*After Nicolson.*) See opposite and page 22 for other examples of Greek ornament.

Right: The anthemion ornament, like the acanthus leaf, persisted as an ornamental motif. During the classical revival in the second half of the eighteenth century, the device was used in a modified form to fill the oval backs of chairs. (See page 161.)

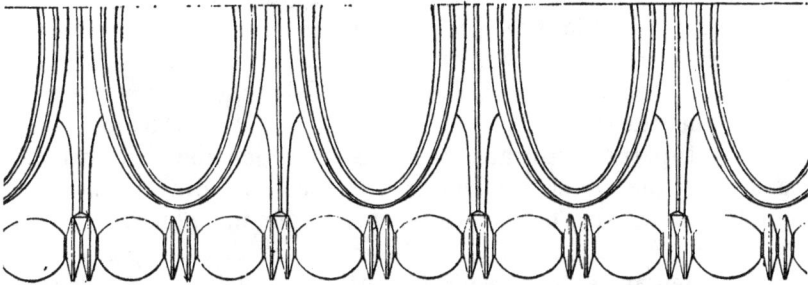

The echinus, or horse-chestnut ornament, also known as egg-and-tongue or egg-and-dart. (*After Nicholson.*) See opposite and page 22 for other examples of Greek ornament.

sources, nature was never copied. The anthemion, known in its simplest form as the honeysuckle or palmette, was a stylised version of a natural prototype; even when the serrated leaves of the vine, interspersed with bunches of grapes, were sculptured on pedestals or panels, they were symmetrically arranged as part of a balanced composition. One of the most characteristic ornaments, the echinus, or horse-chestnut (egg-and-tongue), was regularized, and became as coldly tidy as those inorganic patterns . . . the labyrinth, or Greek fret, the wave scroll, and the bead-and-reel. The most ubiquitous was the formalized acanthus leaf, which not only adorned the capitals of Corinthian columns, but supplied an infinity of scrolls and convolutions. The leaves of the *acanthus mollis* (brank-ursine or bears' breech) were large, deeply cut and hairy; and when their natural, disorderly vigour was subdued by those who carved them in stone or wood, they still retained a tenacious vitality. This motif spread to every part of the Graeco-Roman world, as far as India in the wake of Alexander's conquests and, after the Renaissance, to every continent where Europeans settled or traded. In England, from the sixteenth century to the twentieth, the acanthus leaf has been carved on chairs of every description, enriching knees, elbows, feet, splats, rails, stretchers, aprons, and the cresting or tablets of yoke rails.

The potency and persistence of Greek design were attested early in the nineteenth century by antiquaries and architects like

Thomas Hope, who advocated the study and adoption of Greek ornament. Abundant and accurate records existed; the results of the travels and researches of James Stuart and Nicholas Revett in Greece, sponsored by the Society of Dilettanti, were presented under the title of *The Antiquities of Athens*, between 1762 and 1814 in four superbly illustrated volumes, of which the first was the genesis of the Greek Revival in England. Two others had been published when Thomas Hope wrote the introduction to his *Household Furniture and Interior Decoration*. With lofty pomposity, and in language that reads like a bad anticipation of Henry James, he explained how furniture design might be purged of natural and national characteristics, and why this was desirable.

"I hoped," he wrote, "that the change in all those varied implements of use and comfort which every house of any size required, from a tiresome and monotonous insignificance of form and ornament, to a delightful and varied significance of shape and embellishment, of which I could only set the example in a humble and restricted way, would gradually, by others, be extended to an infinitely greater number and diversity of objects; that thus insensibly the arts of design, applied to every article, and studied in every profession conducive to the comforts of man, would be made to diffuse their beneficial influence throughout the minutest ramifications even of what had hitherto been considered as the exclusive province of the mere mechanic trades; and that consequently almost every production of industry, rescued in some measure from the hands of the mere plodding

Greek fret or labyrinth. From Wornum's *Analysis of Ornament.*

Left: Greek Corinthian capital, from the Choragic Monument of Lysicrates, Athens. *Right:* Roman Corinthian capital from the temple of Mars Ultor. (*After Nicholson.*)

artisan, would be enabled to give some scope to the talent of the professor of the more liberal arts; the draughtsman, the modeller, the painter, and the sculptor."

Those professors of "the more liberal arts" could design neo-Greek chairs that were heavier versions of antique models; and one of them, reproduced from Hope's book, is shown on plate 7 side by side with a *klismos* from an Athenian sepulchral marble vase. Hope's chair with its stuffed upholstered seat was far more comfortable than anything made in the Greek city states during the fifth or fourth centuries B C, and the comfort and the competent use of wood and metal came from the "mere plodding artisan", the chair-maker, with a hundred and fifty years of cumulative skill behind him, and from a technique of upholstery unknown to the ancient world. That skill, taken for granted by drawing-board designers, had been able to accommodate all the lively, eccentric, romantic or severely classical fashions that had attracted the fugitive loyalty of the modish world from the second half of the seventeenth century to the end of the Georgian period; but no English maker ever forgot that chairs were meant to be

B*

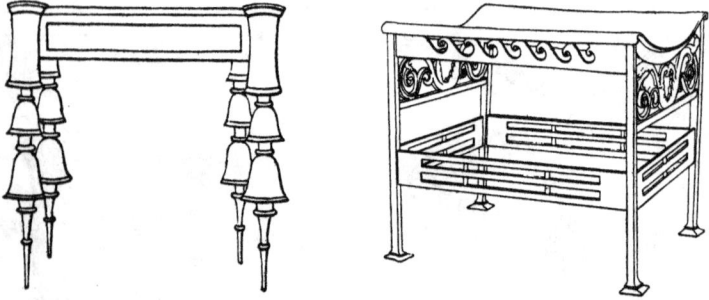

Left: A Roman stool from Herculaneum, with bell turned legs. Such stools cast in bronze were derived from a wooden prototype. (From Edward Trollope's *Illustrations of Ancient Art*.) *Right*: A bronze stool with a dipped seat, 18 inches high, obviously designed for casting and owing nothing to a wooden prototype. An example is in the British Museum. *Drawn by Marcelle Barton.*

sat upon. The attempted reproduction of Greek elegance or Roman grandiosity created something very different in character from the originals; for the subjects imitated were of marble or bronze, and their shapes, transferred to wood, with metal used only for embellishment, disclosed latent graces. These did not survive, as the insistence by leaders of taste on the duty of copying classic prototypes with reverence and fidelity slowly paralysed the adroit interpretive powers of cabinet-makers and chair-makers during the first quarter of the nineteenth century; imitation, unlit by inspiration, debilitated form, debased proportions, and led to Victorian confusion, when ornament was mistaken for design.

The subservient dependence of furniture craftsmen on classic sources was justified with naïve frankness by Richard Brown in *The Rudiments of Drawing Cabinet and Upholstery Furniture*, published some thirteen years after Thomas Hope's book. "Ornaments in their individual parts," he wrote, "must be originally selected from Nature, but Nature presents a wide field, into which, he who enters without a competent preceptor, will be in the utmost danger of losing his way. The works of the ancients should, therefore, be previously studied, as being a kind of map to the study of nature, pointing out what objects should be selected for imita-

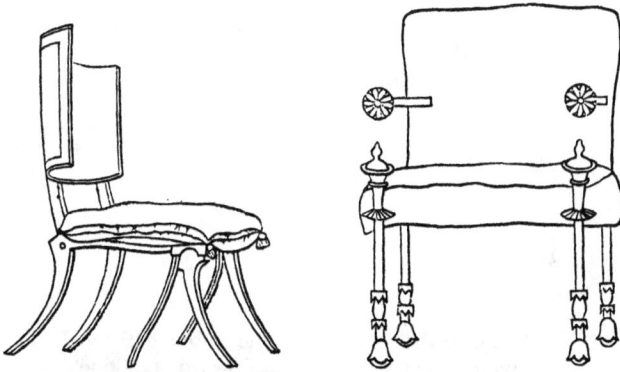

Left: A cushioned chair from Herculaneum, with a concave back-rest, and double legs in front. *Right:* A Roman state armchair from a Pompeian painting. The legs and arms are apparently of metal, the seat is cushioned, and the back stuffed. The arms are simply projecting rods ending in paterae.

A marble seat, supported on lion's legs which rise from a solid base. From a Pompeian painting.

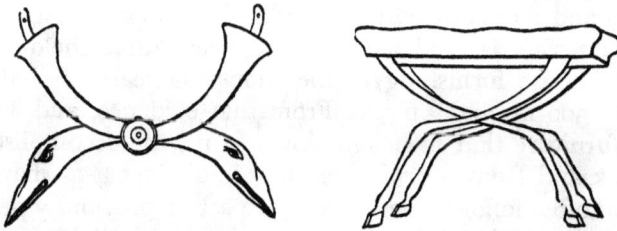

Left: A bronze curule seat, *sella curulis,* 14 inches in height. This was the state stool used by consuls and magistrates. From an example in the Naples Museum. *Right:* A folding stool, for private use, with a cushioned seat. From a painting at Herculaneum. All five subjects reproduced from Edward Trollope's *Illustrations of Ancient Art,* plate XXII.

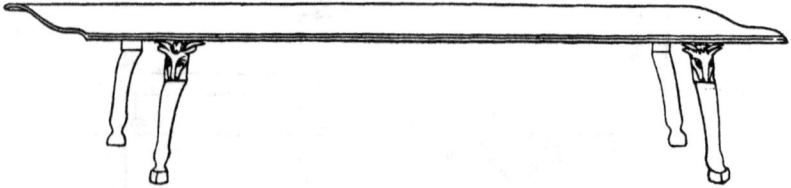

A bronze bench found in the *tepidarium* of the public baths at Pompeii, 6 feet long and 1 foot wide. Reproduced from Edward Trollope's *Illustrations of Ancient Art*, plate XXIII.

tion, and the methods by which such objects may be combined with advantage." He dismissed the common art of the country, exhibiting, like Hope, the arrogant detachment of the man of taste for craftsmen who worked at the bench, and said in the "Preliminary Discourse" of his book, that "Before the cabinet-makers were acquainted with the works of the Greek school, and had acquired a knowledge of drawing, their designs were made up of the most trivial conceits; the artisans being mere plodding mechanics, they went on in one perpetual round of unvarying sameness; their furniture was consequently quite void of taste, and the inanity and tameness of their forms and appendages tired both the eye and the mind, and labour was wasted on transient whims or puerile fashion."

Comparison between the abilities of Greek and Roman wood-workers and those of Georgian England is impossible, as we have to rely on pictorial and sculptural representations for our know-ledge of house furnishing in the thousand years of civilization between 500 BC and AD 500. From that evidence, and from the metal furniture that has come down to us, the accomplishments of Greek and Roman craftsmen may be deduced, as shapes cast in metal often followed very clearly a pattern previously perfected in wood. The bell and ring turning on the stool from Herculaneum on page 24 is an example of this debt to a wooden prototype, though metal has allowed the use of sharp, slender feet that could resist damage far better than wooden members of the same attenuated shape.

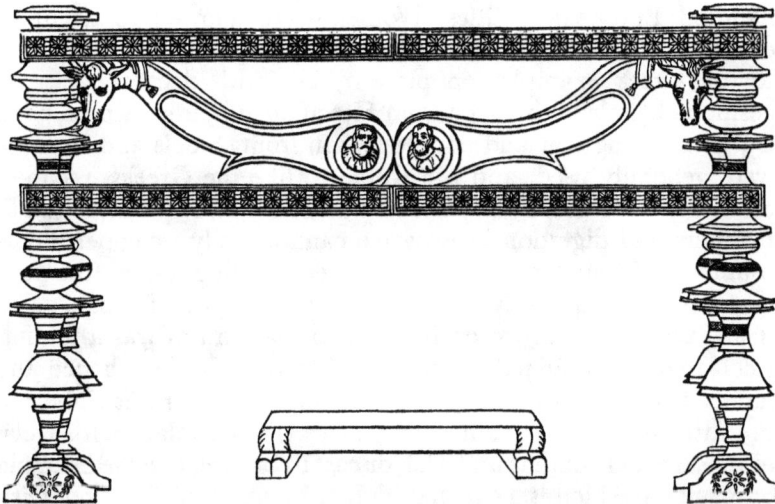

Two examples of Roman seats of state, with footstools. The seat at the top of the page is from a bas-relief on the tomb of Caius Calvetius Quietus. Reproduced from Edward Trollope's *Illustrations of Ancient Art*, plate XXIII.

The influence of Etruscan design is apparent in Roman furniture, for Etruria originally included Italy from the Tiber to the Alps, and the art of that lost civilization strongly affected architecture and the associated crafts during the early life of the Roman Republic: thereafter, as the power of Rome expanded throughout the Mediterranean basin, Greek art and culture exerted a comparable influence. Archaic Greek, Etruscan, and Roman seats had a family likeness; but after the Greeks dispelled rigidity by inventing chairs with curves that supported an easy, natural posture, no fresh structural advances were made to secure comfort until the second half of the seventeenth century AD.

The term *sedilia* covered all types of seats used by the Romans, and of these the state chair alone had a back and arms. Known as the *solium*, and reserved for gods and princes, the memory of its symbolic majesty haunted the palaces and great houses of mediaeval Europe as indefatigably as the ghost of the Roman Empire haunted European politics. Women were allowed to sit upon chairs that had backs, cushioned seats, and no arms, similar to the Greek examples on plate 7, but with deeper backs. A cushioned chair of this type from Herculaneum, is shown on page 25, with a long seat and double legs in front. Stools and benches were generally used, and the Romans, like the Greeks, reclined on couches at meals, a posture that must have affected table manners and digestion in ways we cannot easily imagine. Stools usually had four legs, but there were folding types, the legs crossing to form an X, with a collapsible seat of fabric. The *curule*, the *sella curulis*, used by Roman magistrates was a folding stool that was carried in the magistrate's chariot—hence the name, as *currus* is Latin for chariot. Simple in form but elaborate in finish, the *sella curulis* had curved legs, often inlaid with ivory or made wholly of that material, or cast in bronze, like the example on page 25, which is 14 inches high. The small bronze stool with a dipped seat, 18 inches high, on page 24 was designed for casting: scrollwork, wave ornament, square-sectioned legs and slotted stretchers owe nothing to a wood prototype.

The Roman seat of state, other than the *solium*, was the *bisellium*, a form or stool long enough for two people, though used only by one, for it was intended exclusively for distinguished people. The flat surface was softened by a loose cushion. These seats varied in

Left: A faldestool, or chair of state, with ball and ring turning, X-shaped underframe either bracing the front legs or supporting the seat, and paw feet in front. *Right:* A high-backed chair of state, apparently intended for two people, though the seated figures seem to be sharing it without comfort or dignity. The same form of turned work is used on both examples, which are drawn by F. W. Fairholt from an illuminated manuscript of the Psalms, written by Eadwine, one of the monks of Canterbury, in the first half of the twelfth century, and preserved in the library of Trinity College, Cambridge. Fairholt's drawings are reproduced from *A History of Domestic Manners and Sentiments in England,* by Thomas Wright (1862).

height, according to the rank of those permitted to use them. Marble seats, backless, and supported on the legs of a lion or some other animal, stood permanently in fixed positions, and movable benches of bronze, six feet or more in length with a seat a foot wide, were used in such public places as baths, theatres, and the senate-house. The examples in stone and metal on pages 25 and 26, illustrate their decorative character.

"Under the Roman Empire, the labour of an industrious and ingenious people was variously, but incessantly employed, in the service of the rich," wrote Gibbon. "In their dress, their table,

Paw feet terminating the carved legs of a Norman stool, eleventh century. The seated king is William the Conqueror. Drawn by F. W. Fairholt from an original manuscript by William, Abbot of Jumiéges, preserved at Rouen, and included in *Costume in England* (1860).

their houses, and their furniture, the favourites of fortune united every refinement of convenience, of elegance, and of splendour, whatever could soothe their pride, or gratify their sensuality." Elegance was sometimes obliterated by an excessive regard for magnificence; and the well-proportioned shapes of seats were hidden by draperies, for in Roman as in mediaeval furnishing luxury was identified with the use of rich fabrics. Even in remote provinces like Britain, furniture would follow the prevailing forms, and fragments have been found at Silchester, Dorchester, and other Romano-British sites, usually the legs or feet of tables and seats. From Silchester a turned couch leg has been recovered, made of shale, the bituminous material that resembles slate; in this case, Kimmeridge shale from Dorset. Perishable materials, like wicker, provided comfortable seats; and the basket-work chair on the sepulchral monument to Julia Velva, shown on plate 9, resembles a type common in the second half of the nineteenth century.

Such crafts as basket-making and the simpler forms of wood-work probably survived the general decay of skill that accom-panied the decline and final collapse of the Western Roman Empire. Britain, cut off from the central government early in the fifth century, parted with such luxuries as elegant and comfortable furnishing, imported fabrics, and artistic fashions. As the cities fell into decay, and the big country houses were deserted, the memory of Roman standards of civilization faded; and the most westerly

Above: A high-backed settle, with arms at each end, and the back rising to a point, surmounted by a ball and cross. The seat was long enough to take four people without crowding. The finial on the right hand end was a decorative device that persisted for centuries: such finials appear on the high-backed fifteenth-century settle on plate 14, and on the low-backed example on page 43. Seats in alcoves, ranged along a wall, like those shown *below*, probably originated the idea of a free-standing high-backed seat to accommodate two or more people sitting side by side. Both examples, drawn by F. W. Fairholt from the twelfth-century Psalter at Trinity College, Cambridge, are reproduced from *A History of Domestic Manners and Sentiments in England*, by Thomas Wright (1862).

province of the Empire passed into a period of primitive utility that lasted for five hundred years. Stools, wicker chairs, and benches broad enough to be used as beds by night, replaced the gracefully-formed and agreeably ornamented furniture of the villas and official residences.

In the East Roman Empire the traditions of classical design were preserved for some generations, though they ceased to generate new ideas or exert guidance in the matter of proportions. Under the Byzantine Empire, design lost both inspiration and clarity; craftsmen devoted their skill to elaborate carving, but richness of decoration could not disguise the crudity of the thrones, state chairs and couches that were made between the sixth and the tenth centuries. In Western Europe, Romanesque architecture developed, and from the tenth to the thirteenth century, its characteristic forms were sometimes impressed on furniture, and such borrowed features as columns and arcades appeared in miniature on chairs, above and below the seat, supporting the arms and linking the back legs with the front. The turner transformed such architectural motifs, and by the twelfth century was producing chairs with a sturdy structural unity like the example on plate 10, reproduced from a carving at Chartres Cathedral. Such designs were the progenitors of a long line of turned chairs.

By the thirteenth century, furniture had acquired distinct national characteristics, just as Romanesque architecture had acquired national variations. In Saxon and Norman England there were benches and settles, seats ranged against walls, stools, and chairs of state. Ancient ornamental devices reappeared intermittently; the ball-turning on the early twelfth-century faldestool and the high-backed chair illustrated on page 29 is a refinement of that depicted on the Macedonian coin on plate 5; the front legs of the faldestool rest on paw feet, like the eleventh-century Norman stool on page 30 and some of the chairs and stools that appear in the Bayeux Tapestry. No memory of classical traditions existed in England; furniture, especially chairs and stools, had been purged of refinements in the bleak age of utilitarian design that had passed between the death of Roman Britain and the Norman conquest. Apart from turned work, early mediaeval design had little or no subsequent influence, so the development of the English chair did not begin until the fourteenth century.

CHAPTER 3

THE NATIVE ENGLISH STYLE
1300–1550

O UR knowledge of mediaeval furniture in England is derived largely from examples depicted in paintings and illustrated manuscripts; but some seats have survived, like the mid-fifteenth-century oak chair, once the right hand seat of a triple throne which stood on the daïs of the Great Hall in St Mary's Guildhall, Coventry. That Hall was built for the united guilds of St Mary, St John the Baptist, and St Catherine, in the early part of the fifteenth century. The triple-seated throne was made for the Masters of the guilds, and the surviving seat has the figure of St Mary carved on the side in the spandrel formed by the curve of the arm. Tracery is carved on both surfaces of the back, on the base of the seat, and at the side below the spandrel, reflecting the Perpendicular phase of Gothic architecture, while the finials represent the Royal Lions of England and the arms of Coventry. Detailed drawings of this decoration are shown on pages 34 and 35. An earlier chair, with comparable architectural affinities, appears in the late fourteenth-century portrait of Richard II in Westminster Abbey. The piercing of the arms, the tracery carved on the back, and the high, slender finials with crockets proclaim their relationship with contemporary Gothic. This portrait, by an unknown artist, is reproduced on plate 11.

Earlier still is the Coronation Chair in Westminster Abbey, illustrated on page 37. The design has been attributed to Adam, the King's goldsmith, and the account for the year 1300, which is headed "Account of Adam", suggests that the original intention

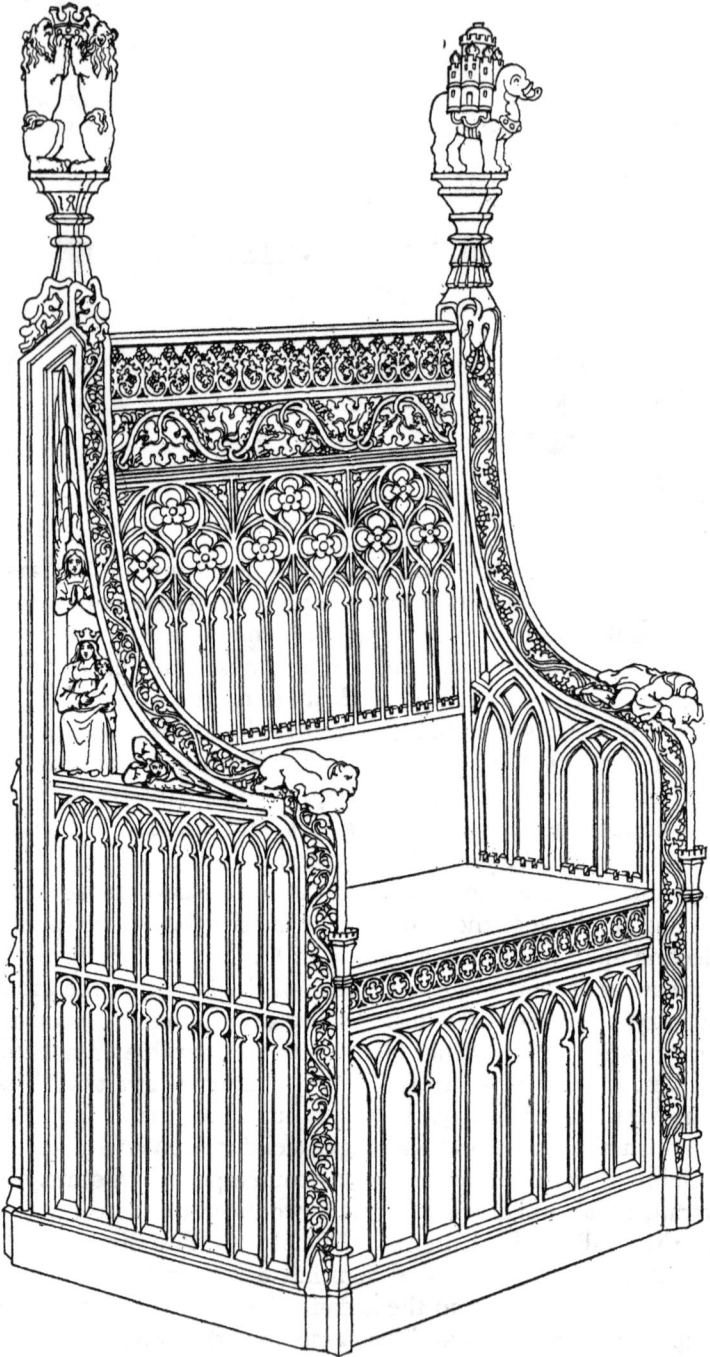

34

Above and opposite: Front and back views of a mid-fifteenth century oak chair, formerly the right-hand seat of a triple throne on the daïs of the Great Hall in St Mary's Guildhall, Coventry. Both drawings reproduced from *Furniture with Candelabra and Interior Decoration,* by Richard Bridgens (London, 1838).

was to cast the chair in bronze; but the idea was abandoned, and an oak chair made instead, at a cost of 100s., without apparently any alteration to a design that had been contrived for metal. Bronze or oak would have been equally suitable for taking the impress of current architectural forms, so what was conceived primarily for execution in stone hardly restricted the English woodworker's gift for humouring his material, and the Coronation Chair represents the translation of the mason's conception by the joiner and carver. The chair combined the functions of state seat and war memorial. Described in the original bill as "a chair for the Scotch stone by the altar and in front of the feretrum", it was designed to display the Stone of Scone, not only as a trophy of Edward I's military prowess, but as a sacred object with a mystical and magical history. It was the "Stone of Destiny"; legends accumulated about its origin, and by the late sixteenth century it was confidently identified as the stone "upon which the patriarch Jacob reposed when he saw the angels ascending and descending a ladder reaching to heaven", as Frederick, Duke of Wirtemberg duly recorded when he visited Westminster Abbey in 1592. (The stone's potency in rousing archaic passions was demonstrated as recently as 1950, when it was stolen by fanatical Scottish Nationalists on Christmas Eve, secreted in Scotland for some months, and returned in April 1951.) The display of the Stone of Scone was a subordinate function; for originally the chair was impressively magnificent, and from the wardrobe accounts of 1300–1 appears to have been the actual work of Master Walter, the "king's painter" to Edward I. The four lions on which the chair rests were much later additions, possibly Elizabethan or Jacobean.

What we see today is a despoiled and mutilated relic of a chair that formerly blazed with gold and colour; for there are indications that the whole surface was covered originally with flat gilded gesso, whereon patterns were incised by dotted lines. The turrets and the leopards that once surmounted the pinnacles at the back, were removed early in the nineteenth century, and for generations destructive nonentities were allowed to carve their initials and names on the woodwork. Nobody at that time seemed to have any respect or sense of responsibility for such survivals of mediaeval craftsmanship. Even that observant and sensitive

The Coronation Chair, in Westminster Abbey, as it now appears. The design has been attributed to Adam, Edward I's goldsmith, though from the wardrobe accounts of 1300–1 the chair appears to have been the work of Master Walter, the "king's painter". The platform below the seat is open in front, with two pierced quatrefoil panels at the sides, to display the Stone of Scone. Originally the pinnacles at the back were surmounted by turrets and leopards, which were removed early in the nineteenth century. The four lions at the base are later additions, late sixteenth or early seventeenth century, though some authorities regard them as Victorian. *Drawn by Marcelle Barton.*

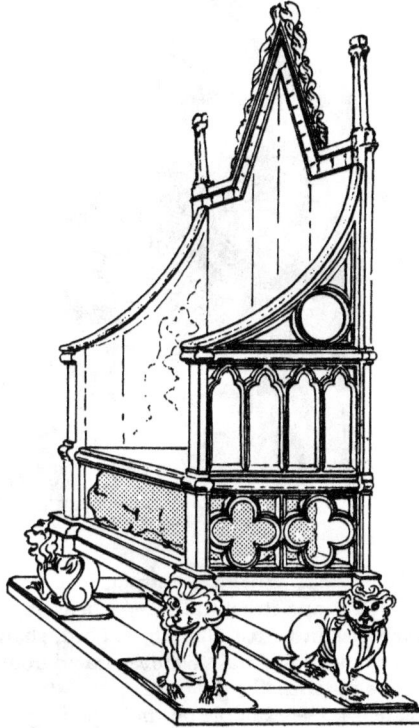

American writer, Washington Irving, could refer to it as "the great chair of coronation, rudely carved in oak, in the barbarous taste of a remote and gothic age", when he described Westminster Abbey in volume one of *The Sketch Book of Geoffrey Crayon Esq.*, which was published in 1820 and dedicated to Sir Walter Scott. (The dedicatee, who had employed Edward Blore to build Abbotsford in the Scottish Baronial style, could hardly have relished this allusion to Gothic taste.)

Some idea of the opulent decoration and colour of a mediaeval chair of state is conveyed by the Throne in the House of Lords, designed by the Gothic revivalist, Augustus Welby Northmore Pugin, about 1846, and shown on plate 13. An architect of genius, his creative gifts reincarnated the spirit of mediaeval design, interpreting afresh the forms that so many of his uninspired con-

Choir stalls, usually constructed in series, were architectural conceptions, related to and structurally dependent on a wall, like the early fifteenth century examples in Christ Church, Oxford, shown above. (From Parker's *Glossary*.) When individual stalls were separated from their place in the series they became chairs in form, like the privileged seats in the Greek theatre. (See page 12 and plate 6.) The example on the opposite page, from the lower part of one of the wooden fourteenth century stalls in the chancel of Nantwich Church, Cheshire, shows how easily the transition from stall to free-standing chair could be made. The hinged seat is turned up, showing the projecting bracket on the underside, the misericord, which was supposed to allow a slightly more restful position for those leaning against it, without actually providing a seat, though the sharp, serrated edge of this particular misericord would discourage anybody from leaning too long. (From Lysons' *Magna Britannia*.) A misericord from Henry VII's Chapel, Westminster Abbey, is shown below. (From Parker's *Glossary*.)

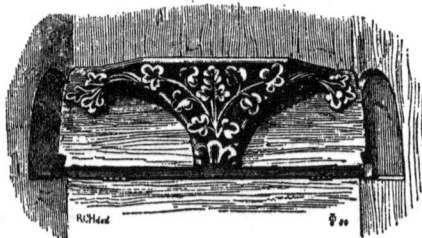

Pew from Steeple Aston, Oxfordshire, *circa* 1500, with blind tracery carved on the end, showing the relationship to Perpendicular architecture. (From Parker's *Glossary*.) Originally the term *pew* or *pue* meant an elevated place or seat, and was later applied to seats or enclosures in churches, used exclusively by high dignitaries or other exalted officials. An early use of the term occurs in the *Vision of Piers Ploughman*, *circa* 1360, in the line "Yparrocked in puwes", which means shut up in pews.

J. P. *del*

temporaries were content to copy with pious diligence. From his work, which had the warmth and fullness of life, we gain our last glimpse of the English Middle Ages. No Georgian antiquary or Victorian "architecturalist", however enthusiastic and intent on conscientiously reproducing what he could measure and record, was able to give the fiery conviction to mediaeval form and colour that Pugin gave to the inside of the Houses of Parliament. "We have," he said, writing about that work, "the arms and badges of a long succession of our kings; images of ecclesiastical, military, and royal personages; appropriate legends in beautiful text run on every scroll: each emblem is characteristic of our country. The internal decoration is to be of a purely national character. . . ." So within the Houses of Parliament, during a century of progress, insurgent inventiveness, expanding material wealth and declining artistic perceptivity, the English native style, through the artificial respiration of Pugin's genius, lived again.

That style had developed during the fourteenth and fifteenth centuries, not only in domestic architecture, but in the furnishing of palaces, and the country and town houses of prosperous merchants and tradesmen. The craftsmen who made or helped to make furniture were carpenters, joiners, carvers, turners, cofferers (or coffer-makers), and, to a limited extent so far as chairs were concerned, upholders (or upholsterers), also broderers (embroiderers). There were no single chairs, that is chairs without arms, in mediaeval England; only armchairs, which were large, massive, and usually occupied a permanent place on the daïs of a great hall or some other important and commanding position. They were seldom moved from that accustomed place: they weighed too much. In a big house there would be one chair for the master and perhaps one for the mistress. The chair was associated with dignity, with formal occasions, with power. The more elaborate throne-like types, which often had a high back from which a canopy projected, were reserved for kings and great lords, judges and the higher ranks of the clergy. Less exalted people sat on much simpler chairs, made from turned spindles or wickerwork, but generally on small, circular-seated stools with three turned legs, splayed outwards. (See plate 12.) The chairs of spindle construction were made by turners, those of wickerwork by basketmakers: both were ancient crafts. Of the two, basket-making was probably the oldest continuously-practised craft in Britain, pre-Roman in origin and never lost, like other crafts. The type of wicker chair carved on the Romano-British monu-ment of Julia Velva, illustrated on plate 9, was so simple and obvious that mediaeval basketmakers may well have produced something very like it. Basketmakers were included in a list of the Crafts of London, mentioned in the books of the Brewers Company in 1422. They were seventy-sixth in order of appearance on that list which was headed: "The titles of divers crafts of old accustomed and still continuing in this the 9th year of Henry V., and here set down in case they may in any manner be of advantage to the Hall and Company of Brewers." (The list was apparently prepared by the Brewers as a guide for letting their hall to Companies and Fraternities without halls of their own.) An Order of Common Council, dated October 12, 1463, restricted basketmakers to the Manor of Blanche Appleton (now the site of Fenchurch Street railway station), owing to the supposed fire risk of their materials, and over a century later, on September 22, 1569, the Company of Basketmakers of the City of London was

Above: A free-standing, low-backed settle, beside a table dormante. Fixed pews in churches may have been the prototypes for such low-backed seats. Drawn by F. W. Fairholt from the fifteenth century illuminated manuscript of the *Roman de la Violette.* Reproduced from *A History of Domestic Manners and Sentiments in England,* by Thomas Wright (1862).

Right: Pews, like stalls, were architectural conceptions, and their form possibly originated the low-backed settle. Compare this example from Headington, Oxfordshire, with the long seat shown above. From Parker's *Glossary.*

A low-backed settle fitting into a corner, and a chair with a concave back. The moulded capping on the back, and the posts crowned with finials, are similar to those of the high-backed settle on plate 14. Drawn by F. W. Fairholt from the illuminated manuscript, *Boccace des Nobles Femmes*. Reproduced from *A History of Domestic Manners and Sentiments in England*, by Thomas Wright (1862).

established by an order in the Court of Mayor and Alderman. Owing to the yielding nature of wickerwork, the basketmakers' chairs were probably the most comfortable, and certainly the cheapest form of seating. The occasional mention of *wanded* chairs in late mediaeval and sixteenth century inventories may refer to chairs of woven wands or withies.

Nearly everybody sat on benches and forms or flat-topped chests, which were ranged against the walls. As chests were heavy, even when empty, and benches were often fixed—"dormante" was the contemporary term—the only easily movable seats were stools. Church stalls and pews were the prototypes of chairs and benches. Stalls were usually constructed in series and, like the triple throne for the Masters in St Mary's Guildhall, Coventry, were architectural conceptions; so were fixed pews with their carved bench ends. Separated from its place in a series, a choir stall becomes a chair in form, like the example from the chancel of Nantwich Church, Cheshire, on page 39. But church stalls were not free-standing; they were often related to and structurally

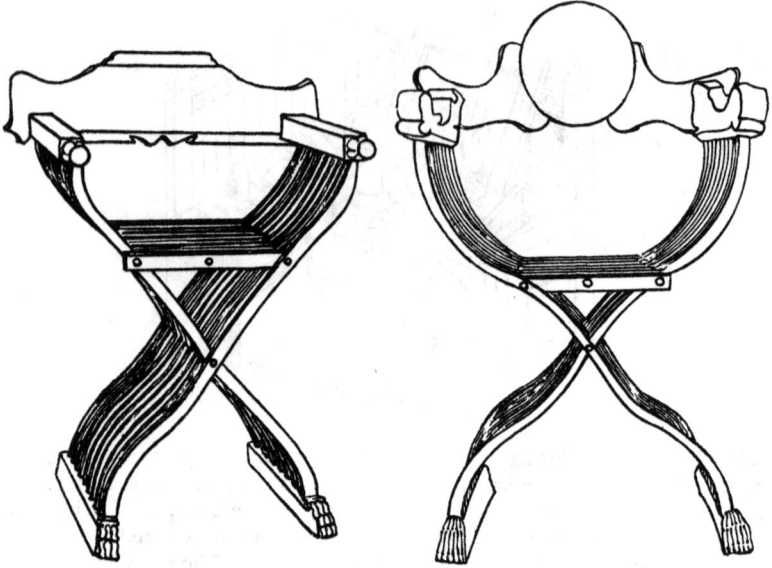

The X-shaped form was handled lightly and gracefully by Italian chair-
makers of the fifteenth and sixteenth centuries; but English makers followed
the sturdier and far clumsier Flemish chairs, depending on the use of rich
fabrics to suggest luxury, and missing the elegance that slender structural lines
conferred on the Italian designs. *Drawn by Marcelle Barton.*

dependent on a wall, such as those in Christ Church, Oxford, on
page 38. The settle was also at first dependent on a wall, with a
high panelled back, sometimes fitting into the corner of a room,
occasionally continuing below a window; a communal seat which
accommodated several people like a pew. When settles became
independent seats, they resembled movable pews; but the chest
was one of their ancestors, as there was nearly always a locker
below for which the hinged seat acted as a lid. Throughout the
Middle Ages the use of wall benches as dining seats followed the
mediaeval habit of sitting on one side only of a dining table; but
the free-standing settle altered that arrangement, so seats could
be moved away from the wall, though until the end of the sixteenth century one side of the dining table was always left free.

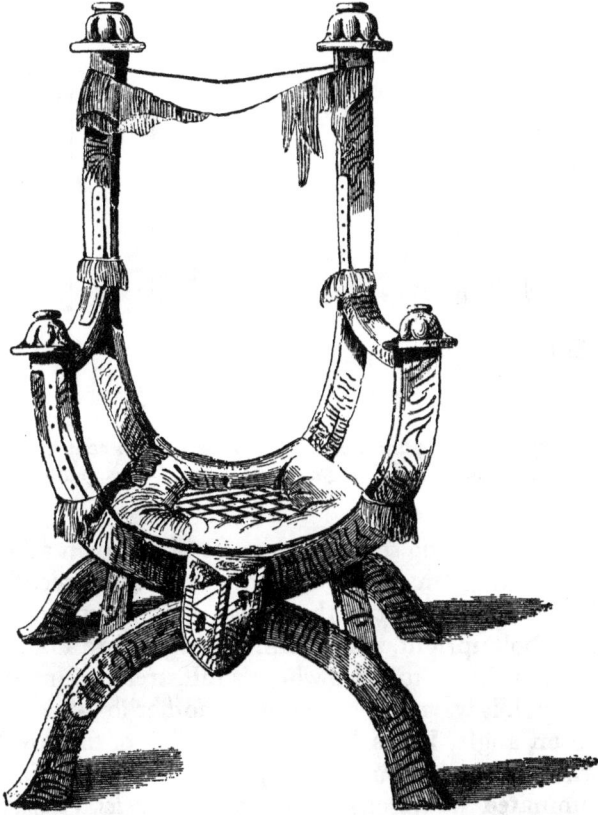

English coffer-makers' chairs were apparently copied from Flemish models, and a stout framework covered with leather or some fabric excluded grace of line in the interests of rich and brilliant covering material. This example, from the vestry of York Minster, is of late fifteenth or early sixteenth century origin, and is reproduced from plate VI of Shaw's *Specimens of Ancient Furniture*. Compare this with the X-framed chair in Winchester Cathedral on plate 22. Velvet was used for covering the framework of both these chairs, and probably for the chair depicted on plate 15, reproduced from *La Bible Historiale*, a high-backed design with ball finials, *circa* 1470.

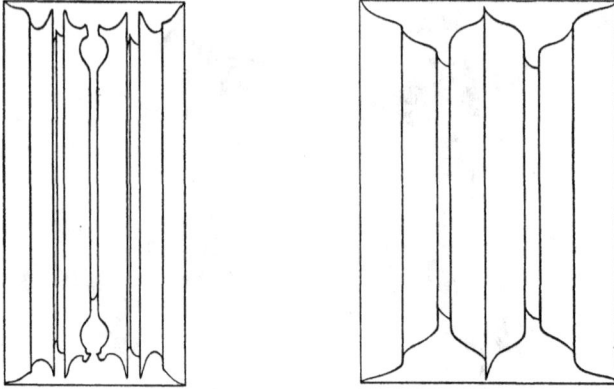

Detail of linenfold panels from the mid-sixteenth century chair on plate 16. *Left:* Back panel. *Right:* Base panel. *Drawn by Marcelle Barton.*

The free-standing settle on page 42 was known as a bank or bink. The drawing, made by Fairholt from the fifteenth century illuminated manuscript of the *Roman de la Violette*, portrays a couple seated bolt upright, as in a church pew, before a table "dormante", with their backs to a fire where a minstrel, presumably sitting on a low stool, is warming his hands. Another low-backed settle, fitting into an angle, like a bleak anticipation of the late Victorian cosy corner, is shown on page 43, also drawn by Fairholt from an illuminated manuscript, *Boccace des Nobles Femmes*, depicting a lady at work on a self-portrait, with a circular looking-glass at the right of her canvas. The finials on the uprights resemble those of the high-backed settle on plate 14.

When benches and chests stood against an unpanelled wall, a hanging called a dorcer or dorsal was used, allowing those seated to lean back, if not with comfort, at least with the thickness of a piece of fabric between them and the stone or plaster surface. Nobody in the Middle Ages had any idea of comfort as we understand it in the twentieth century: the dorcer was probably not intended to soften contact with a hard surface, or to diminish the chill exuded by stonework, but to protect the brilliantly-coloured clothes worn alike by men and women. Comfort has been defined by Mr Gordon Logie as "the absence of physical strain of any kind". He amplified this by adding: "We are only comfortable when our muscles, bones, nerves and blood vessels are relaxed and at ease." But relaxed attitudes, which were common enough in the Graeco-Roman world, have returned to Western civilization only since the end of the seventeenth century: mediaeval manners, clothes, and the limitations of furniture design excluded them.

The nearest approach to luxury in seating was the use of loose cushions, which were cases of leather or woven fabric, stuffed with feathers, down or hair. In the will of John Baret of Bury St Edmunds (1463), his niece inherited "a chayer, iij. footys-stolys, iij. cusshonges", from his parlour. The spelling varied: Chaucer uses quisshen, but quisshyn, qwishon and cusshyn were also used. A long cushion or a loose piece of cloth employed as a seat covering was sometimes called a banker, or banquer.

Craftsmen who used textiles and stuffing materials for seats and beds were called upholders—a term that persisted from the fifteenth century to the early nineteenth, when upholsterer finally replaced it: the Upholders' Guild has been traced back to 1489, but upholders were chiefly concerned with beds and pillows, hangings and cushions. Padded arms and stuffed fixed seats for chairs were unknown, and the only chairs that anticipated the yielding comfort of later times were those made by cofferers, who were primarily leather-workers, highly skilled in surfacing wood with that material when they made receptacles. Coffermakers' chairs, as they were called, had an X-shaped frame of wood, covered with leather, and an open frame seat with a platform of webbing and canvas on which a loose cushion rested. In construction they resembled a modern camp-stool, and the lighter types, like the camp-stool, could be folded up. Few early examples have survived, but like the chair from York Minster on page 45 they seem to have been narrow in width, with pommels or finials terminating the arms and the back uprights. There is a comparable type in Winchester Cathedral (on plate 22), dating from the mid-sixteenth century, with a seat restricted in width like the earlier specimen. The frame was originally covered in blue velvet, garnished with gilt nails. The York chair was covered in leather and fabric.

C

A turned chair with panels in the back and sides that appear to be of wicker work. The ancestor and descendants of such turned chairs appear on plates 10, 20 and 21. Drawn from a fourteenth century manuscript of the St Graal in the Royal Collection, British Museum, by F. W. Fairholt, and included in his *Costume in England* (1860).

The X-shaped folding frame was an ancient device, as attested by the Egyptian stool, *circa* 1300 BC on plate 3, and although it had reappeared in Europe in the faldestool during the twelfth century—perhaps earlier still—its structural significance and elegant potentialities were not fully appreciated until the early years of the Renaissance in Italy. The Italian variations of the form were light and graceful; quite unlike the English coffer-makers' chairs, which seem to have been based on Flemish models, and in Flanders and England, Italian grace was lost, the framework thickened, the air of civilized poise and the easy, flowing lines were muffled by an excessive dependence on rich fabrics, for in the fourteenth and fifteenth centuries luxury was identified with magnificence, with the richness and brilliancy of fabrics, never with soft, yielding surfaces: grandeur before ease was the rule, alike for clothes and chairs. (Two examples of the Italian type are illustrated on page 44.)

Chairs made by joiners were legless boxes with flat seats, sides vertically prolonged to form arms, and high, severely upright backs, rising above the level of the arms, like the mid-sixteenth century example on plate 16. Four panels of that chair are decorated with the linen-fold device, and the upper horizontal panel of the back is carved with Renaissance ornament—a concession to the "Italianate" fashions that were then invading England. The linen-fold pattern was invented late in the fifteenth century, probably by Flemish carvers, and as there was an international traffic in ideas among mediaeval craftsmen, the pattern soon appeared with regional variations in France, England and Germany. The device had no architectural prototype, and was a stylized representation of linen arranged in vertical folds, which may well have appeared originally on linen chests. It could be varied considerably without loss of its basic simplicity. The subtle differences between the panels in the base and back of the chair on plate 16 are shown on page 46. Although carvers worked with joiners, and were members of the London Joiners' Company, their identity as a separate craft was never disturbed: they were concerned with embellishment, joiners with structure.

The chief constructional forms used by joiners were the framed panel, and the mortice and tenon joint. The vertical members of the panel framework were called stiles, the horizontal members rails; and they held the panel securely, overcame the shrinkage of wood, and economized in material. Panelled construction is used for the chair on plate 16, which is a comparatively elaborate piece of joiner's work; but the stools and benches of the late fifteenth and early sixteenth centuries were far simpler, of trestle form, supported by two vertical boards with two horizontal members called apron pieces slotted into them, holding them securely, and on these members the flat wooden seat rested. The edges of the vertical boards were shaped like the stone buttresses of a late Gothic building; and the aprons were either pierced or left plain and shaped below, or more rarely decorated with carving, though not before the early sixteenth century. Very few English examples of these board-ended stools exist today, and R. W. Symonds has stated that not more than twenty-five to thirty have been recorded. (There is one in the Victoria and Albert Museum, which is shown on plate 16.) Joiners also made a dual-purpose chair, with a hinged back that swung over and rested on the arms to form a table, the table-chair or table-chairewise, both terms being used. Early specimens of these convertible chairs are rare; but they were made throughout the sixteenth and seventeenth centuries. (See page 65 and plate 27.) Stools with triangular seats and three turned legs appear in late mediaeval paintings, but no specimens have survived.

The antiquity of turning has been described in Chapter 2, and the use of turned members for chairs and stools gives a family likeness to such articles, whether they were made in ancient Egypt or Greece, the Roman Empire, mediaeval Europe or Tudor England. In the mid-fourteenth century school scene reproduced on the upper part of plate 12, the master is seated on a chair constructed from turned spindles, that anticipates the design of the ladder-back or slat-back types made three hundred years later in New England, and later still in the Georgian period, while the twelfth century bobbin-turned chair at Chartres Cathedral on plate 10 anticipates the form of the mid-seventeenth-century American "Carver" and "Brewster" chairs on plates 20 and 21. Records of turners appear early in the fourteenth century, but the use of the lathe was much older, and had been long-established in England. Turners were making chairs before joiners, producing their own characteristic types, and by the beginning of the six- teenth century they had advanced far beyond such elementary uses of spindles as the schoolmaster's chair on plate 12. They changed the basic shape of the chair, though not in the interests of comfort, for they used a triangular seat, with the angles socketed into three upright posts, the highest rising at the back to support a horizontal cross-piece that was not high enough to form a head-rest, and the other two supported the arms, which had bobbin turning. The legs were linked below with stretchers a few inches above floor level, and in front two vertical spindles joined the stretcher to the seat rail. This simple type is shown opposite: the decorative quality is indisputable, but the sitter was wedged into it, and when he rose, only the weight of the chair prevented it from rising with him. This was the forerunner of what was sometimes called a "turned-all-over" chair, when the turner, demonstrating his command of ornamental technique, produced something as ornate as the two examples on plate 19, which are in the Fitzwilliam Museum, Cambridge, and the Victoria and Albert Museum, London. The former is probably of East Anglian origin, *circa* 1600; the latter, in ash and oak, about the same date. Both have triangular seats and vigorous

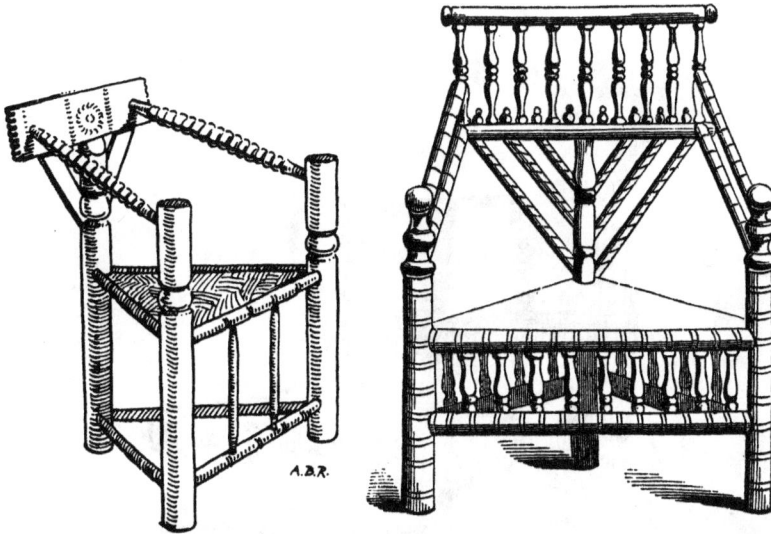

Left: Early sixteenth century turned chair with triangular seat; a relatively simple form, that developed into the elaborate "turned-all-over" type later in the century. *From a drawing by A. B. Read.* *Right:* The next stage in the development of the triangular-seated turned chair, with a lavish use of spindles. The final stage of elaboration is shown by the examples on plate 19. Drawn by F. W. Fairholt from the original in the Ashmolean Museum, Oxford, and included in *A History of Domestic Manners and Sentiments,* by Thomas Wright (1862).

bobbin turning, with vertical spindles connecting the front stretchers. The turner prolonged the life of the native English style, for his skill and ingenuity led to that ultimate triumph of stick-construction, the chair now known by the generic name of Windsor—the only traditional article of furniture that survived the transition from handicraft to mechanical production without loss of character.

Upholstered chair with X-shaped frame, at Knole, early seventeenth century. Compare this design with the chair on the lower part of plate 22, and with those on plate 23. With its greater width, it is far more comfortable than the earlier example on page 45. *From a drawing by Charles Lock Eastlake.* (This illustration and those on pages 57, 60 and 61 are reproduced from Eastlake's *Hints on Household Taste*, fourth edition, 1878.)

CHAPTER 4

THE TASTE OF THE NEW RICH
1550–1630

———

B Y the middle of the sixteenth century England had exchanged mediaeval civilization for something new and alien and a bit brash. The mercantile aristocracy that rose to power in Henry VIII's reign was arrogant, acquisitive and artistically adventurous. Like the new rich in all ages and countries, their taste was undisciplined and capricious, and they were enslaved by fashion. To be fashionable you had to be "Italianate". Manners improved, although contemporary critics, like William Harrison (1534–93), denied it and asserted that young noblemen and gentlemen who were sent by their parents to Italy returned with "nothing but meere atheisme, infidelite, vicious conversation, & ambitious and proud behaviour, whereby it commeth to passe that they returne far worsse men than they went out". Shakespeare was contemptuous of polished youths who imitated foreign ways or listened to:

"Report of fashions in proud Italy
Whose manners still our tardy apish nation
Limps after in base imitation."

Those modish youngsters, returning from the grand tour with a fine mixed bag of exciting ideas about building and furnishing, certainly encouraged the "base imitation" of classic architecture which they had observed without understanding, perhaps without even suspecting, the system of design that regulated the proportions of the five orders. Suitably impressed by the ornamental character of columns and capitals, moulded detail and carved enrichment, lumping them all together under that alluring label, "Italianate", they insisted that the superficial features of these fashions should be reproduced by English masons, carpenters, joiners and carvers; men bred and trained in the mediaeval tradition of design and obstinately suspicious of new-fangled foreign notions. But whether the new rich had acquired their taste direct from Italy or through the dubious medium of Flemish and German copybooks, they were confident of its decorative superiority to the native English style, which seemed by comparison both unenterprising and even dowdy. The new patrons were no longer satisfied by those serene Gothic stabilities and the common-sense use of materials. So, reluctantly, the craftsmen did what their customers told them to do, and their reluctance is apparent in the hybrid architecture and corpulent, overweight furniture of the first Elizabethan period. Even before Elizabeth I came to the throne the conflict between patron and craftsman was beginning to disrupt nearly every branch of design, and that conflict lasted far into the seventeenth century.

About the only articles of furniture that were improved in construction and design during the growing pains of the English Renaissance were chairs and stools. In the middle years of the century, luxury was still associated with the use of richly decorative fabrics. For example, the inventory of the household goods of Sir Henry Parkers, Knight of Norwich (1551–60), included the following:

"A chaier of Blacke velvett embrodeýd w.th twoo tres of gould withe A. & G. . . . xvjs," "A lytle stoole of Blacke velvett embroderyd withe a cypher of an H.A.R.P. . . . iijs. iiijd." "fformes yoined, foure. . . . vjs." "Stooles, yoigner's wo^rke, xij^{ve}. . . . viijs." "A Lytle stoole covered with Nedle worcke checkerid wth. white, blewe & tawnye cruell . . . xvjd." "A Redd chaier embroderid withe white and Redd Satten, xiijs. iiijd." "A lytle stoole embroderid with white and Redd satten, iijs.iiijd."

The chair in black velvet and the "redd" chair were most probably of the X-shaped type; the stools of "yoinger's" work would still be the trestle form described in the last chapter; and the "lytle" stool covered with needlework would be a footstool, for these had replaced the cushions formerly used. (The King in the fourteenth century illustration from "La Bible Historiale" on plate 15, is resting his feet on a cushion.) Footstools were generally made in pairs.

Despite Harrison's views and Shakespeare's censure, manners were far better at the end of the sixteenth century than at the beginning. The increased variety and convenience of furniture disclose new discoveries in the art of living that had taken place within Shakespeare's lifetime. The impact of Castiglione's treatise on manners, written in 1514, published at Venice by Aldus in 1528 and entitled *Il Cortigiano*, had been felt throughout Europe. The author, Count Baldassare Castiglione (1478–1529), was an Italian diplomatist, whose early experience in the service of Ludovico Sforza, Duke of Milan, was followed by his attachment to the most highly civilized court in Europe, that of Guidobaldo Malatesta, Duke of Urbino. In Italy his treatise was known as *Il Libro d'oro*, and it describes the attributes of the Italian gentleman of the Renaissance, the refinements of good breeding, and the virile nobility of the humanism that had given to Italy the intellectual and artistic leadership of the world. *Il Cortigiano* was translated into English in 1561 by Sir Thomas Hoby (1530–66), who called it *The Courtyer of Count Baldesar Castilio*, and by 1603 five editions had been printed. (Two centuries after the translation appeared, Dr Johnson called it "the best book that ever was written upon good breeding".)

Social habits were changing, and this led to greater privacy for individuals and, at gatherings like meals, to an easier and happier contiguity. The attractions of the private chamber and the chimney corner had seduced the master and mistress of the household from the communal life of the great hall; without abdicating patriarchal status, a nobleman or a wealthy landlord no longer felt obliged to symbolize that status by his presence at the table on the daïs; and this process of social segregation had begun in the late fourteenth century, when William Langland, deploring the desertion of the hall, had written: "There the lorde ne the lady liketh noute to sytte." The logical result of such exclusiveness was the private dining chamber, with the dining table in the middle of the room, the master and mistress in chairs at the head

c*

and foot, the guests and privileged members of the household ranged on both sides, and seated on joined stools. This made conversation and movement easier; you could address your *vis-à-vis* as well as your immediate neighbours, could rise without disturbing anybody, and your host and hostess were now brought into the party, which was far better than sitting back to a wall with host and hostess enthroned in the middle of a row, so to see them meant leaning forward and looking right or left, according to your place at the table. Now they were visible to all, sitting in their arm-chairs and leaning back when they wanted to, though nobody else could. Although the joined or joint stool of the late sixteenth century was an improvement on the trestle form, and had four turned legs, stretchers below, a flat, rectangular seat, with a carved frieze rail, in common with all other stools it had no back. To sit on a bench, hemmed in between the table and the wall, had disadvantages, but at least your back was supported. One of the first signs of an emergent sense of comfort was the invention of the back-stool, which as its name implies was simply a stool with a back. The front legs were turned, the back legs, square in section, were continuous with the uprights of the back, which were slightly inclined to increase comfort, and joined horizontally at first by a single rail, later by two, or more solidly by a panel. The back legs of chairs and back-stools were upright, parallel with the front legs, but in the second half of the seventeenth century they were splayed to give greater stability. The introduction of back-stools was no invasion of the privileges of those entitled to the dignity of chairs: lacking arms, they were not thought of as chairs, and though in time they were called side chairs or single chairs, the term back-stool survived for well over one hundred and fifty years. (As late as 1762 Ince and Mayhew described as back-stools two designs for single chairs with stuffed backs, in plates LV and LVI of *The Universal System of Household Furniture*.)

The joint stool was a sturdy piece of construction, held together by mortice and tenon joints, fixed by dowels or pegs without glue. (See plate 17.) A few were three-legged with a triangular seat; but those were exceptional; some were low-seated, under 1 foot 5 inches high, or as little as 1 foot 2 inches, the normal height being 1 foot 9 inches, and such low-seated types were almost

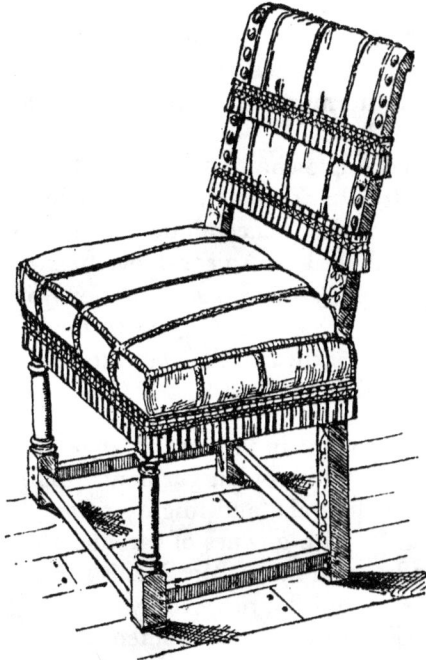

The so-called "farthingale" chair, an early seventeenth-century example at Knole. The turned front legs follow the proportions of a Roman Doric column, and should be compared with the profiles on page 18. Such chairs were a comfortable upholstered variety of back stool. (See page 66.) *From a drawing by Charles Lock Eastlake.*

certainly made for children. There is some contemporary evidence which suggests that ordinary joint stools were used as tables by children, sitting either on the low-seated types or on footstools. Sir Nicholas L'Estrange (1603–55) recorded a complaint that Privy Counsellors multiplied so fast the table would not hold them. " 'Why,' says another, 'then some must sitt by like children at joynt-stooles': for many in King James's time were very green and young." Some low stools had a well or compartment below the hinged seat, that was probably used for storing the child's tablecloth, bib, and utensils. The term coffin stool, wrongly used to describe a joint stool, possibly originated from an entry by Pepys' in his *Diary*: "My uncle's corps in a coffin standing upon joynt-stooles in the chimney in the hall. . . ." (July 6, 1661.) A contemporary term that frequently appears in late sixteenth and early seventeenth century inventories, is *buffet stool*. R. W. Symonds identifies this with the joined stool, because "no other type has survived in sufficient numbers, which would account for its so frequent mention".

The upholstered single chair, the so-called "farthingale chair", was a broad-seated back-stool, and the assumption that such chairs were first made to accommodate the hooped dress or farthingale is probably right. An early seventeenth century ballad, *The lamentable fall of Queen Eleanor*, mentions Spanish tailors as responsible for introducing fantastic innovations in dress. Although the ballad was about Edward I's wife, the clothes described are late Elizabethan and Jacobean.

> "They brought in fashions strange and new
>> with golden garments bright:
> The farthingale, and mighty ruffes,
>> with gownes of rare delight.
> Our London dames, in Spanish pride
>> did flourish everywhere,
> Our Englishmen, like women, then
>> did weare long locks of haire."

In another seventeenth century ballad of later date, called *The Lamentation of a new-married Man*, the husband complains of his wife's demands, after she has just become a mother:

> "Against that she is churched
>> A new gowne she must have;
> A daintie fine rebato
>> About her neck so brave;
> French bodies, with a farthingale,
>> She never linnes to crave."

A rebato was a falling collar, a form of ruff but without the stiffness or spread; linnes or lins meant ceases. Clothes and chair coverings, cushions, and curtains were rich in texture and colour. But all the same, Queen Elizabeth I and King James walked through the corridors and great rooms of their royal palaces, Nonsuch, Richmond or Hampton Court, on straw-covered boards; and though outwardly they and the ladies and gentlemen about the court appeared magnificently gowned and clad, their underclothing was as grubby as the straw underfoot, seldom changed or washed, however dazzlingly white and starched their ruffs might be. The farthingale was a Spanish fashion, and the whalebone hooped case on which the skirts were hung became enormously exaggerated in the reign of James I. Although, as Falstaff said to Mrs Ford, "the firm fixture of thy foot would give an excellent motion to thy gait in a semi-circled farthingale", it was a problem garment when the wearer sat down: an armchair was impossible: only a stool or a back-stool would do, so the great wheel of whalebone with its draperies could come to rest gracefully without being crushed. Such chairs, with seat and back covered by fabric, were made in Europe and England throughout the seventeenth century, and were then called *imbrauderers' chairs*—the term "farthingale chair" is probably of Victorian origin—and another description was *upholsterers' chair*. They were made and sold by the dozen, and could be hired from upholsterers when extra seating was needed. The plain underframe, with turned front legs, persisted, whether the seat and back were plainly covered, like the chair in the painting of The Housewife at Work by Nicolas Maes, dated 1656, on plate 25, or the richly upholstered chair in the portrait of the Countess of Derby, painted about 1635, probably by Gilbert Jackson, on plate 24. The gap between the seat and the bottom of the back varied, but the basic type, like that illustrated on page 57, remained constant. Only when back and seat were joined, so they became continuous, was the original character changed.

The X-shaped coffer-makers' chairs improved in design during the latter part of the sixteenth century; broader now in the seat and wider in the back, they were covered in brocade or coloured cloth embroidered with silk, or with an *appliqué* of cloth of gold or embroidery on velvet or satin. The example on the lower part of plate 22 is covered with crimson velvet, trimmed with galon and fringe, and garnished with gilt nails; a loose cushion rests on the deep padded seat, and the original matching foot-stool is shown. This early seventeenth century chair was formerly in the possession of William Juxon, Archbishop of Canterbury, who attended Charles I on the scaffold, and there is an unconfirmed

Early seventeenth century sofa at Knole, with adjustable sides. When the sides are lowered, the sofa is transformed into a day-bed. *From a drawing by Charles Lock Eastlake.*

tradition that the King used it during his trial at Westminster Hall. A contemporary portrait of the King at the trial certainly shows him sitting in a chair of almost identical design; but such richly upholstered X-shaped types would be found in palaces and great houses from the late Elizabethan period to the Commonwealth. There are some luxurious specimens of such chairs with stools to match at Knole Park in Kent, dating from the reign of James I, and a drawing of one appears on page 52. The painting by Marcus Gheeraedts on plate 23 of an interior in Old Somerset House, shows the eleven Commissioners, who had assembled there on August 18, 1604, to ratify a treaty of Peace and Commerce between the kings of England and Spain, and the archdukes of Austria, seated in such chairs on either side of a long table. The comfort of those upholstered chairs with their loose cushion had no effect on the upright, formal attitude of the Commissioners.

The upholsterer was extending his range; the apparatus for comfort by the turn of the sixteenth century included day-beds, couches and settees. Such specialized articles as day-beds for reclining were acceptable and their restful function recognized; but the settee, which was really a form of chair, broad enough to take two or three people, with the high-backed settle for an ancestor, did nothing to diminish the obligation to sit upright, although some settees had adjustable ends, which could be lowered on iron ratchets, converting them to day-beds. The day-bed, with a fixed, inclined head, more nearly a bed than a seat, was designed for the casual nap. In *Twelfth Night*, Malvolio speaks of "having come from a day-bed, where I left Olivia sleeping...."

Early seventeenth century upholstered settee at Knole, with rudimentary wings rising from the arms. The turned arm supports and front legs are squat versions of the Doric order. *From a drawing by Charles Lock Eastlake.*

Day-bed and couch were the terms used in the sixteenth and seventeenth centuries. John Evelyn, describing the "banquetting house of cedar" belonging to a Mr Tombs, mentions that "the couch and seats were carv'd *à l'antique*. . . ." (Diary, May 8, 1654.) The more exotic name *sofa*, of Arabic origin, was not current until the eighteenth century, and *settee* also came into use then, couch having been used previously.

The term armchair, or "arming chair" was first adopted to distinguish a chair with arms from a back-stool, but before that article was invented the word chair needed no qualification. The box-based joined chairs of the early sixteenth century gave place to the joined chair with turned front legs and arm supports, square-sectioned back legs and stretchers, a slightly raked back with a panel decorated either with inlaid patterns or by incised carving, and surmounted by carved cresting. The basic form of joined armchairs remained unaltered from the late sixteenth century until the reign of Charles II, and as a result of what we should now call a demarcation dispute about the relative functions and responsibilities of joiners, carpenters, turners and carvers, those joined chairs were responsible for the craft of chair-making acquiring and establishing a separate identity. Carpenters were involved, because they claimed with some justice to be the original controllers of every form of woodworking, while joinery and carving were only branches of carpentry. In 1632 the dispute was brought before the Court of Aldermen of London, and the respective responsibilities for furniture-making were defined. Joiners were not to undertake turned work, but must send such parts of their chair frames that required turning to a turner, but they were entitled to produce furniture made with mortice and tenon joints, dove-tailed, pinned or glued. In 1633 the Court of Aldermen laid down that turning and joining were two distinct trades which should not encroach upon each other, and although the dispute was never formally settled, after the 1630's the furniture industry developed specialized divisions which changed the structure of the trade during the next two centuries until the introduction of mechanical production changed it more drastically still. Meanwhile, carvers and turners secured their independence.

The two oak armchairs on plate 18 show how much variety could be given to their character by the form of decoration. The chair on the lower part, *circa* 1600, is inlaid with various woods; the influence of classic architecture is apparent in the scrolls and acanthus foliage of the cresting and brackets and in the fluted front legs and arm supports. Inlaying was done by forming slight sinkings, an eighth or a quarter of an inch deep, in a solid wood surface, and then filling them with woods of a different colour, ivory or mother-of-pearl, cut to fit the hollows exactly. Inlaid decoration in the sixteenth century was largely confined to the panelled fronts of chests and presses; but the back of the joined chair provided a perfect surface for such decorative work. The chair on the upper part of plate 18 is a simpler specimen, *circa* 1630, with incised carving on the back, in the form of an arch surrounding a diamond; the scrolls of the brackets and cresting are derived, like those on the earlier example, from architectural motifs; and very simple turning is used on the front legs and arm supports.

A modern name for these joined chairs is panel-back, and a contemporary term was wainscot chair, though this was equally applicable to any solidly-constructed chair, for the word denoted the material, not the design. An Essex inventory dated April 8, 1663, includes "one Wainsscott Chair". The two planks cut from the centre of an oak log supply the wainscot boards; and from the fourteenth to the early part of the seventeenth century, wainscot meant oak. Thereafter it became a generic term for any wood suitable for joinery work, furniture-making and wall panelling. Evelyn uses it in this sense in *Sylva*, saying of walnut that "it is of singular account with the *Joyner*, for the best grain'd, and colour'd *Wainscot*. . . ."

Folding chairs and stools, as mentioned in the last chapter, had long been known, and towards the end of the sixteenth century a new and improved design was introduced, probably derived from an Italian prototype. The drawing on page 64 shows how the rather unwieldy arms were hinged by a rod of wood, that passed through the side rails of the seat and the upper part of the legs in front. Such chairs are often found in the chancels of country churches, and since the Victorian period have been wrongly called "Glastonbury" chairs. This misleading term seems to have followed the publication in 1836 of the first English book on antique furniture, entitled *Specimens of Ancient Furniture*, which

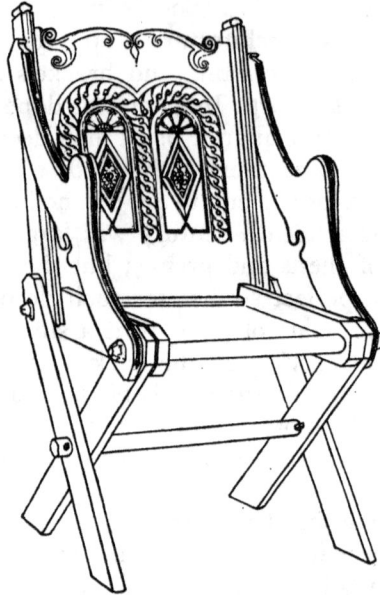

Folding chair, late sixteenth century. Since the Victorian period, chairs of this type have been called "Glastonbury", and specimens are often found in the chancels of country churches. *Drawn by Marcelle Barton.*

were drawn from "Existing Authorities" by Henry Shaw and described by Sir Samuel Rush Meyrick. One of these folding chairs, illustrated on plate IX of that work, was described as "The Abbot's Chair, Glastonbury", on the assumption that the words *Monachus Glastonie* carved on the top rail of the back and the character of the ornament proved an early Tudor origin; Meyrick suggested Henry VIII's reign—half a century too early; but the romantic link with the plundered Abbey was very appealing, so the name persists.

During the early part of the seventeenth century the chair-table became a familiar item of furnishing; ponderous but convenient. When the top was rectangular it made a good table but an unwieldy chair, for the needs of the table gave inordinate height and additional breadth to the hinged back; when circular it was an equally convenient table, but a very odd-looking chair. There is an example with a rectangular back, *circa* 1630, in Southwark Cathedral; another, *circa* 1650–60, in the Victoria and Albert Museum, which is shown both as a chair and a table on plate 27. They were common enough in the countryside, and a "table-chaire" valued at 2s. is included in the inventory of Alexander Reynoldson of Writtle, Essex, dated February 28, 1671. Monk's seat or monk's bench are modern terms.

The wicker chair continued in use, providing comfort for those unable to afford the more finished work of joiners, turners and upholsterers. An early reference to it as a basket chair occurs in

Chair table or table chairewise, mid-seventeenth century. This is the circular type: compare with the example that has a rectangular table top on plate 27. *Drawn by Ronald Escott.*

Elegie I, on Jealosie, composed by John Donne in the last decade of the sixteenth century:

> "Nor when he swolne, and pamper'd with great fare
> Sits downe, and snorts, cag'd in his basket chaire. . . ."

John Aubrey mentions that Ben Jonson had a studying chair of straw, like those used by old women. "One wicker chayer" is an item of an inventory of the goods of William Carding of Roxwell, Essex, dated November 27, 1637. Over a century later Henry Fielding mentions "a great chair made with rushes", in *Tom Jones*. Another contemporary name was twiggen chair. Evelyn uses the word twiggie in *Sylva* when discussing oziers, which he recommended "for all *Wicker*, and *Twiggie* works", and gave a list that included cradles and chairs. Such unpretentious seats, immune from changes in fashion, were unaffected by Puritan restraints on luxurious furnishing which followed the practical application of Oliver Cromwell's belief that people should have "not what they want but what is good for them."

Back stool with an arched, open back rest, slightly inclined. The seat is flat, and the front legs, seat rails and stretchers resemble those of a joint stool. See plate 17.
  Drawn by Marcelle Barton.

CHAPTER 5

PURITAN INTERLUDE
1630–60

———————

WOODWORKERS, especially those in the countryside, were faithful trustees of the native English style, continuing and developing a mediaeval tradition of design with more than mediaeval skill, for during the sixteenth and seventeenth centuries the tools and methods used by joiners and turners had improved. Carvers, by the middle years of the seventeenth century, were feeling more at home with classic ornament; scrolls and sprays of acanthus no longer looked as if they had been hacked out unsympathetically; instead their lines flowed, firm and crisp, robust rather than delicate, but indicating the confidence of a craftsman working creatively instead of copying resentfully. "Italianate" had lost its alien flavour. Inigo Jones, the first great English architect to interpret classic architecture, whose inspired use of the orders gave new life to architectural design, brought enlightenment to his fellow architects, to all the crafts that served architecture, and to patrons. Sir Henry Wotton's paraphrase of Vitruvius, an essay in two parts entitled *The Elements of Architecture*, published in 1624, gave to the next generation of travellers a far better understanding of what they saw in Italy than their Tudor grandfathers: more important still, the book helped to establish critical standards for design. As time passed, those who carved wood and stone became as familiar with the proportions and decoration of the orders as their predecessors had been with the characteristic forms and decoration of Perpendicular Gothic.

For furniture-makers the range of materials was progressively enlarged. Oak was still the chief furniture wood, though the English variety, which had been used almost exclusively in the Middle Ages was supplemented by imports from Scandinavia during and after the Elizabethan period. Spanish walnut was also imported for joiners' work, and had so many commendable properties that chair-makers continued to use it long after mahogany was introduced. There has never been "an age" of any particular wood: those alluring but misleading labels, "The Age of Oak", Walnut, Mahogany and Satinwood, invented by Percy Macquoid and used as titles for the four volumes of his *History of English Furniture*, in 1904–8, were related to periods of design when those woods were used: but no wood has been used exclusively in any period. Apart from oak and walnut, the Elizabethan and Jacobean chair makers had ash, elm and beech—the latter being employed chiefly for the X-shaped frames which coffer-makers covered with leather or fabric. Yew was occasionally used, also such fruit woods as apple and cherry, with pearwood and lime for carved ornament.

Even if no written records of the Commonwealth had survived, the character of the chairs alone would have disclosed the bleak austerity of mid-seventeenth century England. Long before the Puritans attained power, Francis Bacon had written: "Let them take heed that it is not true which one of their adversaries said, *that they have but two small wants, knowledge and love.*" They certainly lacked knowledge of human nature and had no love for life on earth, which they regarded as a period of trial and preparation for Heaven. Pleasures were banned; William Prynne declared in his attack on the theatre, published in 1633 under the title of *Histrio-mastix*, that they were "no part, no particle of a Christian's comfort; he can live a most happy joyful life without them; yea, he can hardly live happily or safely with them". In this frigid spiritual climate, any hint of gaiety in form, colour or conduct was condemned. When the Puritans at last ruled the country, civilized people who could afford to, went abroad and stayed there. Those who remained at home lived cautiously, prudently avoiding conspicuous clothes and furniture. The portrait of the Countess of Derby, reproduced on plate 24, shows her wearing a costume and standing by an upholstered chair that would have been in dangerous taste within ten years of the date it was painted. She and her husband, James Stanley the seventh earl, were royalists, and in 1651 he was tried and executed.

As the Puritan gloom thickened, artistic amenities disappeared. Even an agreeable expression was suspect. A sanctimonious air was safer. Aubrey reported that when Wenceslaus Hollar, the engraver, had first visited England, he remarked on the prevailing cheerfulness of the people; but when he returned about 1649 he found that nobody smiled and faces everywhere looked miserable or spiteful. Even the chairs, with their leather seats and backs, had a sober, severe air, and, apart from the gleaming brass-headed nails which fastened the leather to the framework, were as innocent of ornament as Puritan maids and matrons of frills, lace and jewellery. The nails being functional were permissible: the fact that they were incidentally decorative might have been deplored by a sensitive conscience; but love of ornament is too deep-seated in humanity to be legislated out of existence; and, fanatical though the Puritans were, their prohibitive measures were softened by inconsistencies which suggested that even under spiritual totalitarianism the English genius for compromise still had a flicker of life. Maypoles went, so did plum pudding and mince pies and other Christmas jollifications; but gin and tobacco were officially free from sin. So, apparently, were the tentative flirtations with decoration that turners and carvers indulged in: at least they were not stopped: no godly fanatic took to visiting their workshops to insist on austerity or to check a gay inventiveness that visibly challenged glum tyranny. Reel, bobbin and ball turning gave sparkling vivacity to chair legs and stretchers, and to the rails and uprights of backs.

The ingenuity of turners was even more sprightly in the New England colonies, where Puritan rule was savagely repressive. In Massachusetts and Connecticut, the spontaneous gaiety and variety of the turned spindles used in chair-making, forecast the competent and varied design of American Windsor chairs during the eighteenth and nineteenth centuries. Notable among New England turned work was the Carver chair, so-called because the prototype is alleged to have been owned by John Carver, an Englishman born in Nottinghamshire about 1575, one of the "Pilgrim Fathers" who founded and became the first governor of

Plymouth Colony in 1620. The Carver chair is an elaboration of the twelfth century type reproduced from the sculpture at Chartres Cathedral on plate 10, and the fourteenth century example on page 48. The Carver and Brewster chairs on plates 20 and 21 from the Metropolitan Museum of Art, New York, are made of hickory and ash. The Carver chair is generally rush-seated, with turned legs that rise above the seat to form framing posts for the back, and front legs rising to support the arm spindles. The back usually consists of two horizontal rails joined by three vertical spindles, with a turned top rail. The back posts are surmounted by turned finials, the arm supports by balls, and in the Brewster type the front legs have two stretchers joined by three vertical spindles. Many of these chairs were made between 1640 and 1660.

Professor Ronald Syme, discussing the number of labourers and artisans who emigrated to New England, has stated that "the local extraction of the emigrants can be established from various types of historical record, not to omit the appellation of villages in New England or the names that a man can read today when he contemplates the gravestones in their cemeteries". Estimating that the population of the Colony in the mid-1640's could hardly have exceeded 25,000, he observed that "the emigration as a whole exhibits strong local characteristics—Cambridge rather than Oxford, East Anglia rather than Southern and Central England". This is significant, for East Anglia was well-known for skilled turned work, as exemplified by the chair from the Fitzwilliam Museum on plate 19.

Ball, bobbin and ring turning had been known and practised for centuries, but throughout the Puritan period this form of ornamental work was lavishly used on chair legs and stretchers, back rails and uprights; and at some time the refinement of the twist was introduced, hand-carved at first, though after the restoration in 1660, spiral turning became common, and the technique was probably developed and perfected during the middle years of the century. The twist was known and used on chair and table legs in Spain and Flanders before it appeared in England; and, like other ornamental devices, had an architectural prototype. The grand exemplar was Bernini's baldacchino at St Peter's, Rome, with four gigantic twisted columns supporting

This type marked the transition from the back stool to the side or single chair. The use of hooped back rails, scroll finials and split-balusters ornamenting the back uprights was regionally associated with Yorkshire and Derbyshire. Such chairs were made during the late 1650s and after the Restoration. Compare with the back stool on page 66. *Drawn by Ronald Escott.*

the bronze canopy. In England such columns had been used with indifferent success on some Jacobean monuments, and the most conspicuous examples were those on the south porch of St Mary the Virgin, the University Church of Oxford, built in 1637. Nothing executed by masons in stone could approach the easy grace of spiral turning in wood; the scale was different, the material more suitable, and the ancient skill of the turner newly enlarged by adventurous experiments in elaboration. Although the double rope or double twist was not introduced till Charles

II was back in London, experimental work must have begun during the last years of the Commonwealth. The vigour of the twist on the stretchers of the walnut single chair, *circa* 1660, shown on plate 26, reveals how accomplished turners had become by that date: the double twist was an inevitable development, and was used not only on the legs and stretchers of chairs, settees and day-beds, but for the underframing of tables, cabinet stands and the hoods of long-case clocks. The frequently used term, "barley-sugar" twist, is not contemporary. Although barley-sugar was probably made early in the eighteenth century, one of the first traceable references is a recipe for making and twisting it, in a work published by F. Nutt in 1789, entitled *The Complete Confectioner* by "a Person, late an Apprentice, to the well-known Messrs Negri and Witten, Berkeley Square".

The transition from the back stool to the single or side chair was accomplished during the Puritan period; thereafter the terms arming chair and armchair were used, as *chair* had now become the accepted name for any seat with a back that accommodated one person. The term elbow chair appears in inventories in the second half of the seventeenth century, and was no doubt current earlier. Items in the inventory of goods owned by William Eree, of Writtle, Essex, dated May 28, 1677, include "one elbow chair, & one little chair, 15s." The line, "He nodded in his elbow chair", occurs in "Hans Carvel", a poem by Matthew Prior (1664–1721). At some time, probably in the mid-nineteenth century, the term "carver" was introduced to distinguish the elbow chair in a dining room set used by the carver at the head of the table, a salesman's tag unknown when sets of single chairs with one or two slightly broader-seated matching elbow chairs were produced. (The Victorian "carver" should not be confused with the New England turned chairs mentioned earlier.) Sets of upholstered chairs, similar in design, had existed in Elizabeth I's reign; the eleven chairs on which the Commissioners are seated in the room at Somerset House on plate 23 appear to be a set, though there is some variation in the shape of the finials; but the suite which included single and armchairs, stools and couches, became fashionable later in the seventeenth century, and in France—where it sometimes numbered as many as twenty-four chairs and stools and two or four couches—the design was related

SCROLL
FINIAL

BACK
RAILS

BACK
UPRIGHT

SEAT
RAIL

STRETCHERS

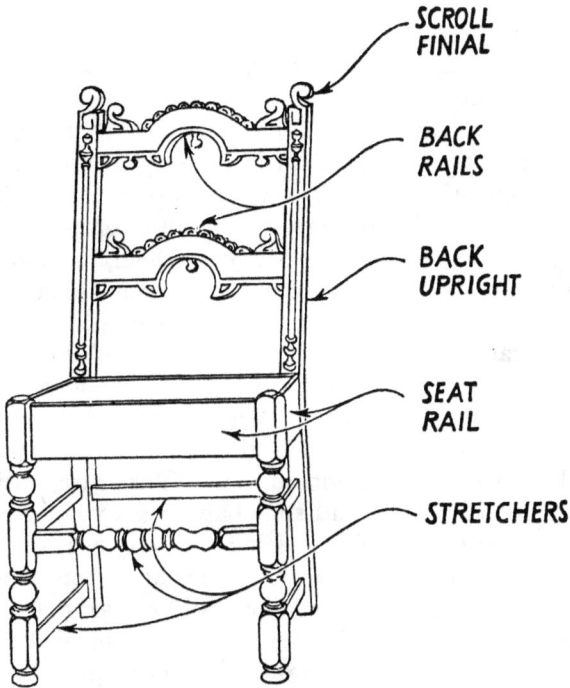

Diagram of structural members of a single chair, *circa* 1660. See page 71 for details of the ornament, and page 93 for descriptive diagram of an early eighteenth century bended-back elbow chair. *Drawn by Marcelle Barton.*

to the interior treatment of the salon, bringing walls and furniture into a coherent decorative relationship. In England upholstered suites were used only in the galleries and withdrawing rooms of the wealthy upper classes, until the early eighteenth century.

The flat-seated wooden stool persisted as the basic form of seat, unaltered by the ornamental turning of legs and stretcher, and the addition of back uprights and cross rails. The seat rails and upper part of the legs on the turned and joined walnut chair, *circa* 1650, on plate 26, top left, are structurally identical with the joint stool on plate 17. The early back stools, narrower than the "farthingale" chairs, had flat seats, not shaped or dipped, though sometimes the seat frame would be half an inch or so higher than the seat itself, convenient enough for keeping a loose cushion in place, but thrusting a hard ridge into the under side of the thighs when no cushion was used. Some of those early examples were open backed, with uprights and rear legs continuous, the posts above seat level slightly raked and joined by an arch with carved spandrels below the top rail, giving support for the shoulders only, like the example on page 66; later the uprights—the back posts—had a carved panel between them, surmounted by decorative cresting, with a six to nine-inch space separating panel and seat. Another development was the open arcaded back, with two horizontal members linking the uprights, the upper consisting of three arches, joined by spindles to the lower, with split spindles on the inner side of the back posts to enhance the suggestion of a miniature arcade. Regional variations of such forms appeared in Derbyshire, Lancashire and Yorkshire, with hooped and scalloped back rails, and split balusters applied to the back posts. (See page 71.) A risky expression of loyalty has been identified with Derbyshire and Yorkshire, for some chairs from those regions bore on the centre of the arched back rail a carved mask, supposed to portray the head of Charles 1. These have been called "mortuary" chairs, but the name does not appear to be contemporary. They were made during the third quarter of the century, and most probably originated in the decade following the King's execution, when the risk to owner and chair-maker was considerable, which explains why they appeared only in districts far distant from London.

When single or elbow chairs had seats and backs upholstered in leather, decoration was confined to the under-framing; and presently the carver invented the arched stretcher to join the front legs, a far more daring piece of ornamental gaiety than anything the turner had ventured to produce, wickedly close to luxurious display when flaunting supple, sinuous scrollwork, like that on the single chair shown on plate 26, top right, one of a set of twenty-four, made about 1660, perhaps a little earlier. The front stretcher, carved with classical scrolls of an almost Gothic vigour, is as incompatible with the staid leather upholstery as a cavalier's plumed hat would have been with the sombre garments of a roundhead. Chair-makers, upholsterers, embroiderers and other craftsmen, especially those who had catered for the taste of the vanished Court, may have shared the optimism of Martin Parker who wrote, in the darkest days of the Civil War, this cheerful prediction of the Restoration:

> "Though for a time we see Whitehall
> With cobwebs hanging on the wall,
> Instead of silk and silver brave
> Which formerly it used to have,
> With rich perfumes in every room,
> Delightful to that princely train,
> Which again you shall see when the time it shall be
> When the King enjoys his own again."

Carved ornament on chairs, confined largely to back rails, or to panels and cresting, was generally in low relief. The simplest form of incised carving, consisting of single lines scratched on the surface of woodwork and known as scratch carving, often decorated chairs and stools made in the countryside. Applied ornament had been used since the late sixteenth century, and, concurrently with split balusters and spindles, the strapwork, diamonds and lozenges, copied originally from the plates of German and Flemish books on architectural details, were still popular in the 1650s. They appear on the hinged back and seat rail of the oak chair-table on plate 27.

The repressions of the Puritan period, and the consequent decline of the luxury trades, temporarily liberated craftsmen from the tyranny of foreign modes, and as velvet and brocade and costly embroidery were no longer used on chairs, the woodwork of the frame acquired a decorative significance that remained for two hundred years. The respite from foreign influences gave such confidence to chair-makers that, in common with other furniture craftsmen, they were able to absorb and Anglicize foreign ideas gracefully, when French, Dutch and oriental fashions invaded England after the Restoration.

CHAPTER 6

THE RESTORATION OF LUXURY,
1660–1690

THE King came back. It was safe to smile. Maypoles, forbidden as sinful "in the hypocriticall times", as Aubrey called them, "now were sett up in every crosse way". It was also safe to wear extravagant and beautiful clothes, to order carved and gilded furniture, to indulge a taste for delightful inutilities, and to flout every Puritan sentiment by behaving exactly as the moralizing author of "The Praise of Brotherhood" expected modish men and women to behave when he wrote:

> "He that will have the world to his minde,
> Must search well his wits new fashions to finde,
> And study new fangles to pleasure fond fooles,
> For wantons are willing to follow bad rules."

But the rules for design were excellent, and so widely understood by craftsmen that "new fangles" could be gracefully accommodated. Architecture followed a "good Roman manner", as Wren called it; the proportions of the classic orders affected the form and decoration of furniture, and the discipline they imposed affected the anatomy of chairs. In the thirty years between 1660 and 1690 the mediaeval stiffness that had survived from the early sixteenth century was replaced by a new flexibility of line; back rests, arms, seat and underframing had a new relationship; and early in Charles II's reign the seats and backs of chairs acquired a new and comfortable resiliency from cane-work, formed by a mesh of split canes, an idea that came from the Far East, and provided an agreeable alternative to upholstery. Chair frames were resplendent with carved decoration, and the fluid lines of scrolls were often an integral part of the framework, as in the walnut elbow chair at the top of plate 28, *circa* 1670, which shows a new and productive collaboration between carver and turner. The frame was assembled by the joiner, but no upholsterer had a hand in this chair as the seat and the divided back panel are of canework. Before the end of the seventeenth century the cane chair-maker was established as a specialized, independent craftsman.

Chair-making had become a distinct craft, named as such, and uniting the skills of joiner, turner, carver and upholsterer; and after 1660 the leadership of the joiner, who had hitherto employed and co-ordinated the skills of the other partners in the team, was exchanged for that of the cabinet-maker, when cabinet-making, which depended on the technique of veneering, was introduced from France and Holland. The dispute between joiners and turners which the Court of Aldermen of London had attempted to settle in 1633 was, as we saw in Chapter 4, the beginning of specialization in the furniture industry; so when cane chair-makers set up their own shops, and began to manufacture light, cheap and popular chairs by something very like mass-production, nobody regarded their enterprise as unusual, though some branches of the industry were perturbed by the results. The seats and back rests of upholstered chairs were usually covered either with leather, cloth or Turkey Work, sometimes known as "set-work", a knotting process similar to that used in the making of Turkish pile carpets. With the advent of a new and highly competitive material, that was not only cheap and comfortable but soon became fashionable, the demand for cloth-covered chairs declined, and upholsterers and woollen manufacturers saw their market shrinking. Bradford, faced with a rapidly decreasing woollen trade, petitioned unsuccessfully for the suppression of cane chair-making. (Towards the end of the seventeenth century worsted manufacture restored the town's prosperity.)

Canework never replaced the silk and velvet and needlework used on costly and elaborate furniture; but the cane chair-makers satisfied a new demand, that was suddenly and dramatically expanded by the Great Fire of London in 1666, which destroyed hundreds of homes, and left thousands of people and families without furniture of any kind. Sets of six, eight or twelve single and two armchairs of canework could provide comfort for the dining room, particularly when squab cushions were used; and they introduced to any room an air of lightness and elegance, strikingly different from the sombre solidities of leather-covered Cromwellian chairs and the squat back-stools of an earlier age. The high, slender, cane-filled backs had dignity, while the rake of the back and the springiness of the canework promised ease. When made for fashionable interiors, a dextrous use of ornament conferred a richness which was never overbearing or clumsy like that of Elizabethan and Jacobean furniture, a richness, moreover, that owed nothing to the texture or pattern of fabrics, but was achieved by the shape, proportions and embellishment of the chair frame. Upholsterers had good reasons for worrying; chair carvers had none.

The chair frame was never distorted to create a decorative effect; legs, stretchers and back retained structural integrity; and carved ornament was used with the sureness of touch that comes not only from skill but from trained imagination. The immature years of the English Renaissance were over: the great golden age of good design was beginning: and the confidence and competence with which classical motifs were handled by chair carvers are illustrated by the walnut day-bed on plate 29. The acanthus scrolls, the paw feet, the restrained but apposite use of turning on legs, centre stretchers and back posts, the three shallow concave upright members of the back flanked by foliated scrolls, and the long, plain canework seat give evidence of a fresh approach to design, unhampered by obligations to honour a traditional form or imitate a foreign model. The single chair of walnut, on plate 28, shows how well a balance was struck between turned and carved work, with less dependence on classical motifs and greater prominence for the spiral twist. The armchair on plate 28, described earlier, and the stool of carved beech on plate 30, both exhibit a mastery of the scroll as a decorative and structural form.

The ornamental possibilities of underframing had been tentatively explored before the Restoration, and the leather covered single chair mentioned in the previous chapter and illustrated on

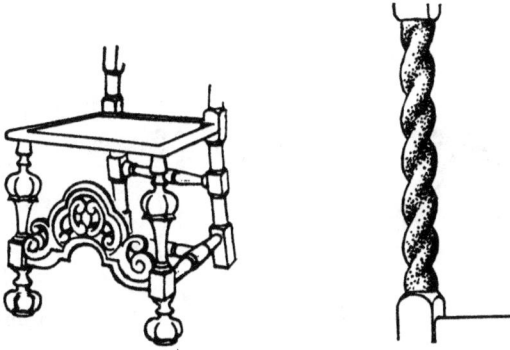

Left: The arched stretcher, which developed after the Restoration from the rudimentary type on the chair on plate 26 to the more elaborate example shown here and on plate 30. *Right:* The "barley-sugar" or double twist.

plate 26 is an early example of the chair carver's handling of the front stretcher, a feature that was progressively elaborated, not in isolation, but as a contributory part of the decorative character of a chair. The scrolls, crown and rose on the front stretcher of the armchair on the upper part of plate 28 are repeated on a smaller scale by the cresting; and this repetition of the scrolls and crown motif appears also on the carved and turned single chair on the same plate, decorating front stretcher, cresting, and lower rail of the back rest. The arched, or upward-curving hooped stretcher became an emphatic feature, like that on the beech stool on plate 30. Spirited renderings of fruit, flowers, foliage, heraldic emblems and sportive cupids adorned front stretchers and cresting and the framework of back rests. Towards the end of the century diagonal stretchers linked the four legs, just above the feet, formed by a double spur, a saltire or St Andrew's Cross, or serpentine with four S-shaped curves, and there were also rising stretchers with the members curving upwards to the point of intersection, which was surmounted by a turned finial.

Chair-makers had discovered the explicit beauty of curves when used in three dimensions: hitherto the arms of joined chairs, like those on plate 18, had formed two-dimensional curves, but Carolean chair arms were curved in length, depth and width. The

D

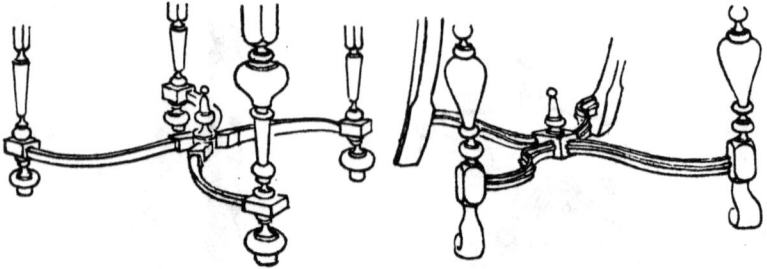

Two examples of diagonal stretchers. *Left:* A double spur, forming a saltire or St Andrew's Cross. *Right:* The serpentine type, with four S-shaped curves.
Drawn by Marcelle Barton.

scroll leg, with a slight concave line, like the front legs of the arm-chair at the top of plate 28, or the broken scroll legs of the stool on plate 30, were already foreshadowing the interplay of curves that characterized the cabriole leg, which came into use in the reign of William and Mary. Such discoveries and the lessons learnt from Holland and France led to a curvilinear conception of chair design, that melted away the last traces of mediaeval and Puritan stiffness in the early years of the eighteenth century.

Luxury after the Restoration meant far more than the use of such materials as damask, brocade, brocatelle, exquisite needle-work, embroidery, cut velvet, and trimmings of braid, threaded with gold, and thick silk fringes, tasselled and scalloped: in addition to such magnificent upholstery, the visible framework of chairs was carved with the copious invention and fluency of unrepressed skill. When walnut was used, the wood was polished; if the frame was of beech, then legs, stretchers and arms would be painted in cream or some other colour, with the ornament picked out in gold, or else the complete framework would be gilded or, more rarely, silvered. The art of gilding was known in Ancient Egypt, and in Europe, during and after the Middle Ages, two methods of using gold leaf on wood surfaces were used: water gilding, that was a combination of burnished and matt finishes, and oil gilding, which could not be burnished, though it could be applied to wood and iron and was weather-resisting. Nearly all the gilding used for interior decoration and furniture was burnished, and this was the most expensive of the two processes because the surface of the wood had to be prepared with considerable care. (See Appendix II.) The processes used for silvering were much the same as those employed for gilding; but silvering was cheaper, tarnished more easily, and was occasionally protected by the application of a transparent varnish.

Japanning was introduced, a process that imitated Japanese lacquerwork, which was imported to meet part of a growing taste for oriental things. After the publication in 1688 of *A Treatise of Japanning and Varnishing*, by John Stalker and George Parker, japanning was established as a craft, and soon in a flourishing condition, because as practised in England it met a popular demand, with a range of gay colours—green, yellow, scarlet and blue, far more exciting than the rich black of the original oriental product. Such exotic finishes were seldom used on chair frames until the early eighteenth century, though there is a set of japanned chairs, *circa* 1682, at Ham House, Surrey.

Until the Restoration, chair backs were low and rectangular, but during the 1660s high-backed chairs were introduced, and were called "French" chairs, for like many other Carolean fashions they originated in France. The high backs allowed the head to be rested, and marked another stage in the evolution of

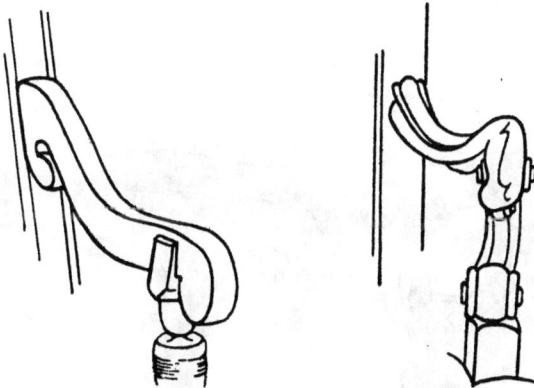

Left: The arm of a joined chair, forming a two-dimensional curve. *Right:* The arm of a Carolean chair, curved in length, depth and width. *Drawn by Marcelle Barton.*

chair design, so that the person seated could enjoy complete relaxation which follows (to repeat Gordon Logie's definition), "the absence of physical strain of any kind". Sometimes the elbows of French chairs were covered and fringed, and within ten years of the Restoration, the high-backed winged armchair became a national symbol of ease and comfort, thereafter called an easy chair. (The sentimental name of "Grandfather Chair" was invented about 1880.) The wings, also known as lugs or cheeks, varied in shape and size. The arms were either open, with padded elbows, or continuous with the seat, and scrolled outwards, with the scroll often repeated at the top of the wings. Seat, arms, back and wings glowed with rich needlework. The frontispiece illustrates an example, *circa* 1700, upholstered in gros-point and petit-point embroidery, worked from plates engraved by Wenceslaus Hollar and Pierre Lambort, showing eleven scenes from the *Aeneid*. Such convenient refinements as the "sleeping chayre" were invented, with iron ratchets fitted to the winged back, so that it could be lowered. Two of these chairs, with carved and gilded frames, *circa* 1675, in the Queen's Closet at Ham House, Surrey, are shown on plate 29. The front feet are in the form of recumbent sea-horses, the back feet are splayed.

All kinds of ingenious dualities had long existed in Europe: Evelyn described two examples he saw at Rome in 1644: "a conceited chair to sleep in with legs stretched out, with hooks,

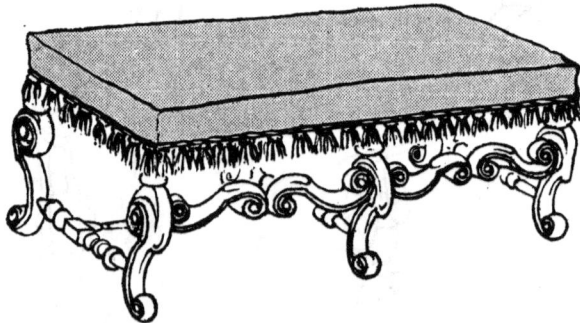

Long stool with scroll legs and stretchers. The opposing curves of the cabriole form are suggested by the broken scrolls. *Drawn by Marcelle Barton.*

and pieces of wood to draw out longer or shorter" (*Diary*, November 10th), and "a whimsical chair, which folded into so many varieties, as to turn into a bed, a bolster, a table, or a couch" (November 29th). Many years later he mentioned a "wheel-chair for ease and motion", in Lord Aubigny's lodging (January 11, 1661–62). There were trick chairs, such as that shown to Pepys by Sir William Batten, "a chair, which he calls King Harry's chaire, where he that sits down is catched by two irons, that come round about him, which makes good sport". (*Diary*, November 1, 1660.)

Wide chairs, on which two people could sit very closely side by side, were introduced; they have since been called "love-seats", or "courting chairs", which are not contemporary terms; and settees to accommodate two or three people were made to match the chairs in a set, often with a double or triple chair back. Single and double stools were made, also stools with circular seats, and low, caned footstools contributed to fireside comfort.

Design in this easy-going age was liberated from cramping precedents. The conflict between patron and craftsman had been resolved: both accepted the architect as the master-designer, and the architect's work was already influencing, directly or indirectly, every art and craft, while patrons, architects and craftsmen were informed by an alert and subtle sense of style. The graces of the Georgian period were generated in Charles II's reign. The world of fashion, though potent, was small: the taste of the Court that controlled the furnishing of Royal and other apartments in Whitehall and, to some extent, determined what went into the great town and country houses of noblemen and wealthy merchants, was far in advance of the rest of the country. A rising ambitious civil servant like Pepys could afford to pay nearly forty pounds "for a set of chairs and couch", and as he was congratulating himself on being worth £5,200 when he made that entry in his *Diary* on April 30, 1666, he had probably invested in something well abreast of fashion. But new ideas travelled very slowly to the provinces; in some remote rural districts few changes in the form of furniture had occurred since the early sixteenth century. Furniture was intended to last beyond a lifetime, and it did: the sturdy joined chairs and stools made by country craftsmen endured for generations. In inventories of the second half of the seventeenth century, the survival of traditional types of chairs and stools is recorded, so that joined armchairs and leather-covered single chairs made at the turn of the century differed little from those made fifty years earlier. Wicker chairs are frequently mentioned, also "chairs bottom'd with rushes". The latter probably had turned legs and ladder-backs of spindles, resembling the mid-fourteenth-century chair described in Chapter 3 and shown on plate 12. At some time during the second half of the seventeenth century, stick construction was improved, so that the method of inserting turned wooden spindles into solid wooden seats led to the production of the Windsor chair. This became a generic name for chairs of stick construction, with the solid seat as the stabilizing structural unit, that united legs and back. (The development of stick furniture is the subject of Chapter 9.)

Even in the towns traditional types remained, though the low, wide "farthingale" chairs must have been dwarfed by the slender elegance of the types that became fashionable in the William and Mary period. The farthingale was still worn in Charles II's reign. Evelyn describes the arrival of the Queen, "with a train of Portuguese ladies in their monstrous fardingales, or guard-infantes, their complexions olivander and sufficiently unagreeable. Her Majesty in the same habit, her fore-top long and turned aside very strangely". (*Diary*, May 30, 1661.) The ladder-back was occasionally used for cane-seated chairs, with rails in the form of scrolls; and in the last decade of the seventeenth century the back splat became emphatically decorative, carved, pierced, often dividing two caned panels, and making the high back look even higher. The cabriole leg had already appeared, rudimentary and a little stiff, but unmistakable. Design was now so distinctive, that it became possible to place a chair within a decade or so of its origin, and although dating by design is not infallible, the shape and decoration and finish of chairs usually disclose the prevailing fashions of a particular period, even when pieces have been hotted-up with additional carved ornament in the present century by some dishonest dealer.

Knowledge of design can destroy legends and historical illusions. For example, the chair illustrated opposite was believed throughout the nineteenth century, and far into the twentieth, to have been the subject of a picture called "Sedes Busbiana", the

"Sedes Busbiana", alleged to be the work of Sir Peter Lely (1617–80); but actually an early nineteenth century hoax that was taken seriously for well over a hundred years.

alleged work of Sir Peter Lely, presented by the artist to Charles II, as Dr Busby, the headmaster of Westminster School was a favourite of the king's. The portrait at the top is that of Dr South, who succeeded Dr Busby. Now if Lely had really depicted this ill-proportioned jumble, his use of cabriole legs with grotesque masks on the knees was prophetic—some decades ahead of his time. Many prints of this supposed work of Lely's were in circulation after 1800, but nobody tested its authenticity by critically examining the design. The truth about its origin was published by William Hone in *The Every-Day Book*, as early as 1826–27. It was, the editor revealed, "a mere *bagatelle* performance of a young man some five-and-twenty years ago. It was engraved and published for Messrs Laurie and Whittle, in Fleet Street, took greatly with the public, and had 'a considerable run'." The picture had never existed outside the fancy of a sprightly leg-puller, who would have been diverted by the serious attention his joke received from writers about old furniture for more than a century.

Thomas Sheraton, in *The Cabinet Dictionary*, published in 1803, described the organization of the chair-making industry, and what he said then was already applicable over a hundred years earlier. "Chair-making is a branch generally confined to itself", he wrote; "as those who professedly work at it, seldom engage to make cabinet furniture. In the country manufactories it is otherwise; yet even these pay some regard to keeping their workmen constantly at the chair, or to the cabinet work. The two branches seem evidently to require different talents in workmen, in order to become proficients. In the chair branch it requires a particular turn in the handling of shapes, to make them agreeable and easy: and the only branch of drawing adapted to assist such, is that of ornaments in general. It is very remarkable, the difference of some chairs of precisely the same pattern, when executed by different makers, arising chiefly in the want of taste concerning the beauty of an outline, of which we judge by the eye, more than the rigid rules of geometry."

No want of taste or faulty judgment marred the design of chairs of the late seventeenth and early eighteenth centuries. English makers had absorbed French and Dutch ideas and vastly improved their own technique.

CHAPTER 7

CURVILINEAR DESIGN AND THE END
OF RIGIDITY, 1690–1730

———

EARLY in Queen Anne's reign a new, curvilinear conception
of design gave fresh graces and greater structural stability
to chairs, which became as different from the Tudor and
Cromwellian turned and joined types as the Greek *klismos*
of the fifth century BC was from its archaic predecessors. Chair-
makers had rediscovered a natural and graceful form, comparable
with that invented by the Greeks. They used the well-defined
curves of the cabriole leg in three dimensions, which gave them
far more freedom than Greek makers, who had confined within
two dimensions the sweeping concave curves of their chair legs.
When the Greeks introduced the cabriole profile for the privileged
seats of a theatre, like those shown on plate 6, the nature of the
material they used, which was marble, and the fact that such seats
were components of an architectural concept, still imposed a two-
dimensional limitation. The cabriole leg, that subtle unity of
opposing curves, convex above and concave below, was originally
suggested by the limbs of some four-footed animal. The lion's legs
of the Roman seat from Pompeii on page 25 show how such
natural forms were stylised. In England the first tentative approach
to the cabriole profile followed the development of scroll legs,
through the Carolean period to the reign of William and Mary.
The carved stool, *circa* 1685, on plate 30, and the long stool on
page 82 both have scroll legs, but the cabriole form is struggling
to emerge; those convex knees, and the abrupt transition to a
concave line below, foreshadow the cabriole legs with broken

D*   87

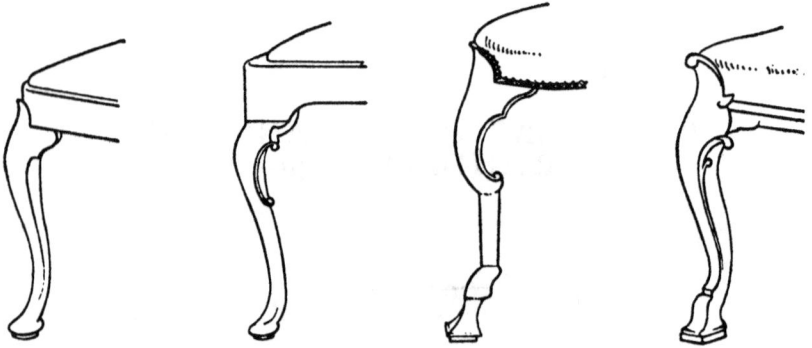

Variations of the cabriole leg from early eighteenth century chairs. Those on the left are simple types, with the gently curved leg ending in a flat toe, like the single chair on plate 32; those on the right are more elaborate, with formalized hoof feet, broken curves—the centre right example has the type of break, just below and inside the knee, that is sometimes called a hock leg—and both are hipped, the legs rising through the seat rail, the example on the extreme right extending to seat level. The leg on the extreme left is also hipped.
Drawn by Marcelle Barton.

curves—sometimes known as hock legs—that were introduced fifteen to twenty years later.

The term *cabriole* for a leg with a double curve was not contemporary; during the late eighteenth and early nineteenth centuries the name was used for an "arm-chair stuffed all over", according to Sheraton in *The Cabinet Dictionary* (1803), who also described a cabriole as "a French easy chair—from the name of the person who invented or introduced them". This last suggestion is typical of Sheraton's capacity for misleading conjecture. Certainly the word cabriole was of French origin, but it was a term used in dancing, spelt *capriole*, derived apparently from the Italian *capriola*, a goat's leap, originally from *capra*, the Latin name for she-goat. The association of the word cabriole with double curved legs dates from the close of the Victorian period and the opening years of the present century; until then such legs were known as bowed or bandy. When cabriole was used by Arthur Hayden in the first edition of his *Chats on Old Furniture* (1905) it had become an accepted and familiar term; R. S. Clouston referred to "the heavy

Dutch cabriole leg" in *English Furniture and Furniture Makers of the Eighteenth Century* (1906); and some writers have since described the first forty years of the eighteenth century as "the Cabriole Period". Picturesque names for periods and individual pieces of furniture have multiplied during the last century and a half; the "Glastonbury" chair mentioned in chapter 4 is a typical example; and more recently the terms "Lion mahogany" and "Lion Period" have been coined to describe a phase of early Georgian furniture design, when lions' masks were carved on the knees of cabriole legs and the arms of chairs. Those "Lion" classifications arose from an article by Haldane Macfall, published in *The Connoisseur* in 1909, who wrote of "The Lion Years of Mahogany", and headed one of his paragraphs: "Lion Mahogany, 1720 to 1730". Such descriptive labels, referring specifically to some feature of design or decoration are less confusing than amorphous generalizations about "The Age of" this, that, or the other wood,

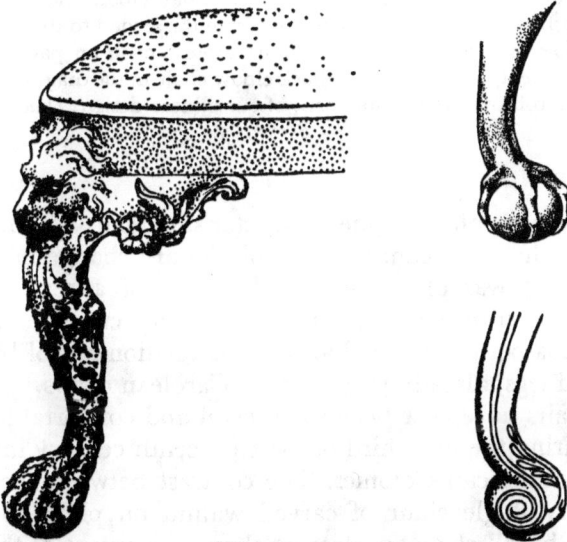

Left: Cabriole leg with lion's mask carved on the knee, and claw-and-ball foot. *Right, above:* Claw-and-ball or talon-and-ball foot. *Right, below:* Knurl foot, a form of scroll foot with the scroll formed on the inner side of the leg, unlike the whorl foot where the scroll is visible and curls up in front, as on the settee, page 108, and the foot of the Chippendale design, page 124.

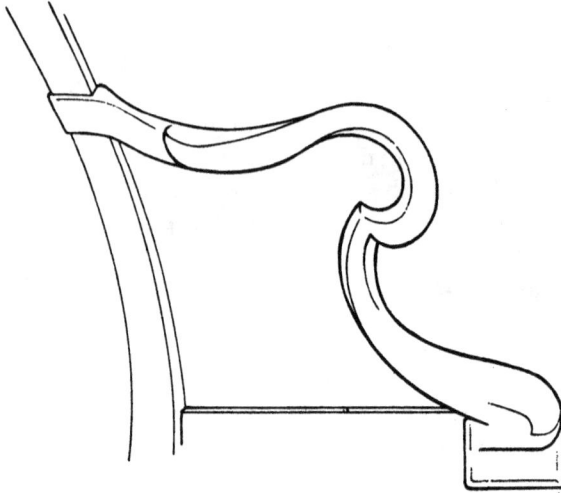

Side view of scroll over arm on an early Georgian elbow chair. This form of
arm was fashionable among chair-makers from the second to the fourth decade
of the eighteenth century. The arm of the Carolean chair on page 81 forecasts
this development, and the bended-back elbow chair in the diagram on page 93
shows the scroll over as a component of curvilinear design. *Drawn by Marcelle
Barton.*

although pin-pointing one characteristic tends to obscure, or
minimize the significance of a revolutionary change in style. The
cabriole leg was only one manifestation of a revolution that
relaxed the framework of chairs, allowing curve to flow into
curve, thus perfecting the harmonious relationship of back, seat,
arms and legs, already predicted by Carolean chairs.

No chairs have ever been so graceful and comfortable as those
made during the first third of the eighteenth century in England
and the American Colonies. The contrast between the William
and Mary single chair of carved walnut on plate 30 and the
"bended back" chair on plate 32 shows the extent of the change
that had taken place in a couple of decades; the first example is an
assembly of parts, the second a unity of complementary curves.
The earlier chair is distinguished by a contrived and conscious
elegance; the scroll legs, arched front stretcher and double-looped

central stretcher linking the turned side stretchers, a tall narrow back filled by canework, with twin arches in the lower rail, repeated in a simpler form in the top rail below the pierced cresting, every carved and moulded detail emphasizing height and slenderness, from the finial on the central stretcher to the elongated back uprights. In such a chair you sat erect, with the austere formality of a mediaeval king; but the bended-back chair invited you to sit at ease without loss of dignity. The vase-shaped splat and the back uprights were curved to accommodate human contours; in such a chair you didn't sit *up*—you sat *back*. The example on plate 32 is a country-made type, with a loose seat that was dropped into place, instead of upholstery being permanently fixed to the seat rails; in this case woven rushes are used instead of a stuffed cushion. In such country-made chairs the stretchers were retained long after fashionable town chair-makers had discarded them. One theory which attempts to account for the prolonged life of stretchers in the countryside is their secondary use as foot rests. Straw was still used to cover the stone flagged or wooden floors of rooms in farms and the smaller manor houses long after that insanitary habit had been abandoned in town houses; nobody could have tucked up their feet on the decorative arched front stretchers of Carolean and late-seventeenth-century chairs, but the simpler country types were more accommodating. This may have been a subsidiary and perhaps unconscious reason for retaining stretchers on chairs and tables, though a time-lag of ten to twenty years between the work of town and country makers favoured the survival of traditional ideas in rural areas.

The development of curvilinear design led to a new understanding of stability, and when chairs were released from structural dependence upon underframing, fresh aspects of elegance were disclosed by such examples as the walnut chair with scroll-over arms, *circa* 1710, in the Fitzwilliam Museum, Cambridge, shown on plate 33, and the more elaborate early Georgian armchair on plate 37. Although curvilinear design had been foreshadowed as the cabriole leg gradually acquired its shapely profile, perfection was suddenly reached early in the eighteenth century when the bended-back chair was first made. That abrupt change from modified rigidity to curves which united comfort with matchless grace was on a small scale as striking as the structural discoveries in mediaeval architecture, when the thrust-absorbing flying buttress was invented and the weight of vaults and towers redistributed so that buildings attained an unwonted slenderness and delicacy of form. The Gothic cathedral was the result of a structural revolution: so was the bended-back chair.

Improvements in the cabriole leg could not alone have stimulated such sudden enlightenment, and R. W. Symonds has attributed an oriental origin to the bended-back chair. In an article entitled "A Chair from China", published in *Country Life* in 1953, he said: "A chair with a splat bent to accommodate the curve of one's back and with a cresting rail like a milkmaid's yoke, supported on uprights of a round section, suddenly made its appearance in England during the reign of Queen Anne. This was a design of almost startling originality: apart from the small seat and the tall and narrow proportions of the back, it was quite unlike any other English chair, for no transitional stages were to be observed." Similar chairs from China had been imported into England by the East India Company; and in the anglicized version the yoke rail was either modified, as in the example on plate 32, or replaced by an arched rail that followed a continuous curve with the uprights. The side view of the chair on plate 32 shows how the bend of the uprights corresponded with that of the splat. That broad back splat (or splad as it was sometimes called) was shaped like a vase or a baluster. Scroll-over arms added complementary curves to those of the back and legs, and in the more elaborate work of town chair-makers, the splat, back uprights and seat rails were veneered with figured walnut. When the back uprights had a concave curve near the seat, producing a waisted effect, the chair was called a fiddle back, a contemporary term aptly descriptive of a shape resembling that of a violin, while the spaces between the uprights and the splat suggested the sound holes. (The term was later applied to a type of ladder-back chair with pierced back slats, as those openings were also like the sound holes of a violin.) In settees two splats were often used, though the outline of an upholstered back would resemble an elongated splat, as on the walnut settee on plate 36, while writing chairs had two splats linking the fan-shaped seat with the semi-circular top rail, like the example on plate 33. The addition of a high head-rest,

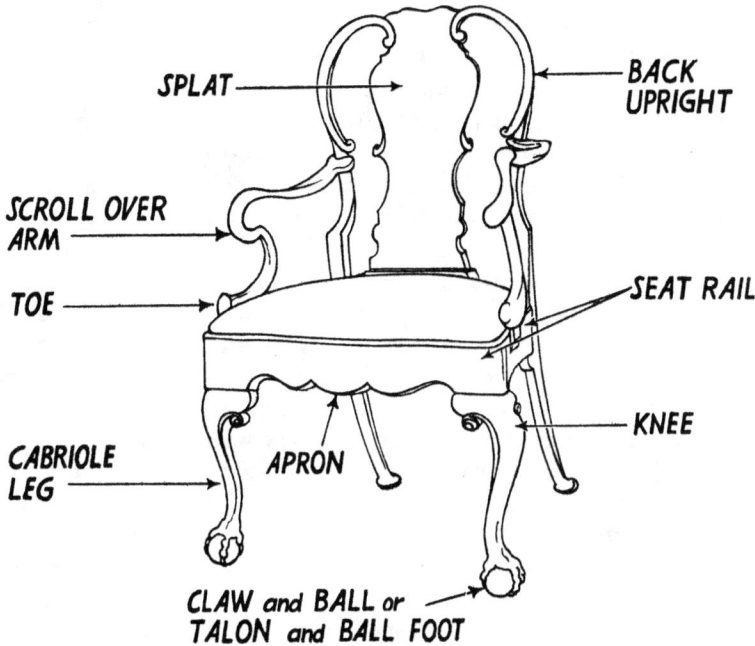

SPLAT

BACK UPRIGHT

SCROLL OVER ARM

TOE

SEAT RAIL

KNEE

CABRIOLE LEG

APRON

CLAW and BALL or TALON and BALL FOOT

Chair-makers and upholsterers had special trade terms for the various parts of the things they produced; obviously descriptive, like most of those in this diagram of the anatomy of a bended-back walnut elbow chair. The upper member of the back frame was called the top or cresting rail, sometimes the yoke rail, from its resemblance to a milkmaid's yoke. The front view of the bended back single chair on plate 32 clearly shows how this term originated. In the mid-eighteenth century some top rails were shaped like a cupid's bow, and were known by that name; later in the century, a rectangular panel, painted or carved, broke the line of the yoke rail and was called a tablet. A horizontal yoke back in the form of a continuous arm rail appears on the early Georgian writing chair on plate 33 and on the much later design by Thomas Sheraton on page 107. This type was described by Sheraton as the "top yoke". The terms yoke or yoke-back were also used for a plain type of cheap chair.

Drawn by Marcelle Barton.

rising from the centre of the top rail, transformed the three-cornered writing chair into a shaving chair. Both types are illustrated by the drawings on page 97. The alternative but not contemporary names for writing chairs are angle and corner, and in America the term *roundabout* is current, though that is more generally applied to a type of circular-seated chair with a low, concave back following the curve of the cane-work seat, supported on eight cabriole legs, linked by front stretchers just below the knees with a complex underframing of stretchers lower down. Sometimes known as burgomaster chairs—probably a modern name—they were made by the Dutch in the East Indies and exported to Holland, other parts of Europe and England, in the late seventeenth and early eighteenth centuries. Such emphatic foreign types were never anglicized; and by the end of Queen Anne's reign, English makers with the confidence conferred by their own inventive powers would reject anything as basically clumsy or as coarsely ornamented as the burgomaster chair. They drew on classical sources chiefly for their carved decoration, and the function of ornament had changed, for it was no longer used to soften hard lines but to accentuate the subtle beauty of curves.

On the knees of cabriole legs shells were carved, also female masks and those of lions or satyrs; sometimes the legs would be furred, to terminate in lion's claws, grasping and almost concealing a ball, like those on the mahogany armchair in Sir John Soane's Museum illustrated on plate 39. The club foot resting on a circular base was replaced by the claw-and-ball or talon-and-ball foot. When this old device was reintroduced, it may have come from the far East, for a dragon's claw grasping a pearl is of Chinese origin. It was known in Carolean times and still earlier in sixteenth-century England, but was not widely adopted until the early eighteenth century. (A contemporary painting of Edward VI shows an X-shaped chair with a carved frame and claw-and-ball feet.) Another short type of foot used with cabriole legs was formed like a cloven hoof, or *pied de biche*, introduced from France and originally derived from Roman furniture. (See the folding stool on page 25.) Scaly legs and claws are used for the front feet of the armchair on plate 37. Arms were often terminated by the heads of eagles or lions.

Chairs of this type were made by the Dutch in the East Indies and exported to Holland, other parts of Europe, and England in the late seventeenth and early eighteenth centuries. They were known as roundabout or Burgomaster chairs, though the latter term is probably modern. Reproduced from Shaw's *Specimens of Ancient Furniture.*

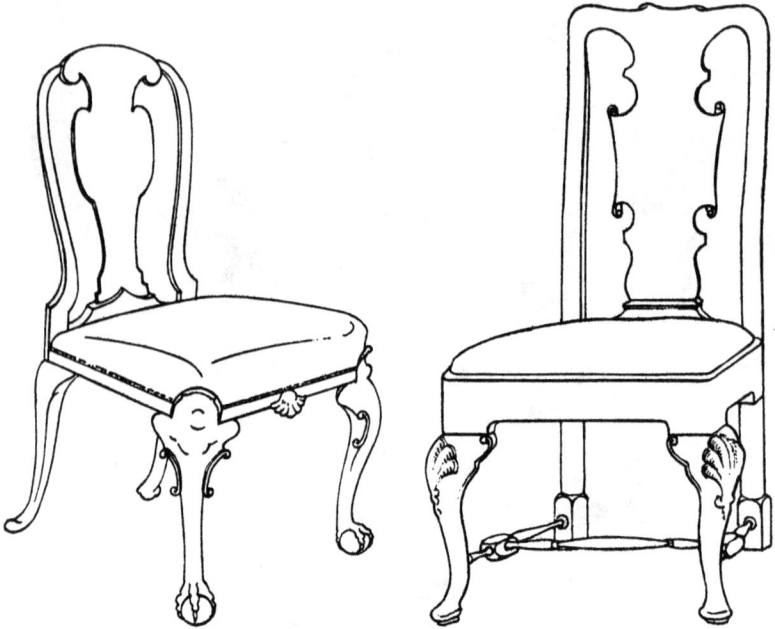

Two early eighteenth-century chairs, showing variations of the splat and back uprights. *Right:* The back still has some rigidity of line, and cabriole legs are used in front only. The stretcher has not yet been discarded. (See plate 32.) *Left:* A later type, with the back uprights bowed, the front legs hipped, breaking upwards into the seat rail. By the second decade of the eighteenth century stretchers were seldom used, and chairs had a new structural independence.

Below, right: Example of the fiddle back. This was a contemporary term used when the back uprights curved inwards, giving a waisted effect, so that the open spaces between them and the sides of the splat resembled the sound holes of a violin, and the general shape suggested the outline of the instrument.

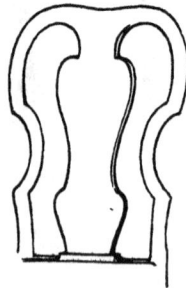

Left: Writing chair, with fan-shaped seat, early eighteenth century. (See plate 33.) Such chairs were sometimes called corner or angle chairs. *Right:* A shaving chair, similar in design to a writing chair, with a high head-rest rising from the yoke rail.

The shape of the bended-back chair persisted until the 1730s, when mahogany began to be used more extensively by makers. At some time, probably during the mid-nineteenth century, Hogarth's name became identified with the bended-back chair, which was habitually described as a "Hogarth Chair", possibly because the artist frequently introduced both single and arm-chairs of this type in his paintings. His self-portrait, reproduced on plate 34, shows him seated in a rather stunted example, with heavy scroll-over arms, and a few of these chairs may have furnished his studio, though he was not always faithful to the type. Chairs with tall upholstered backs, joined to the seats, appear in the painting, "Shortly After Marriage", one of the *Marriage à la*

Mode series in the National Gallery, and his portrait of Benjamin
Hoadly in the Fitzwilliam Museum at Cambridge, reproduced on
plate 35, shows that divine inflexibly vertical in an upholstered
chair which has a high, inclined back, with frame and cresting
lightly carved, clumsy arms, cabriole legs in front ending in club
feet, and thick, square-sectioned back legs that continue the line
of the back; a conspicuously inelegant design. In his famous
caricature of John Wilkes, shown on page 100, he used a bended-
back single chair, for although he is supposed to have made the
sketch in Westminster Hall with a porte-crayon he finished it off
at his house later with pen and ink. The caricature was published
in 1763, but the chair in it was over thirty years out of date, for
fashions changed with the introduction of mahogany, frames
became lighter, splats were pierced, and carved decoration replaced veneer. An example of this transition is the broad mahogany
armchair in Sir John Soane's Museum shown on plate 39, which
retains all the graces of the bended-back chair, but asserts a fresh,
vigorous conception of design. The carved decoration is crisp and
flexible, with satyr's masks on the knees of the cabriole legs and
the arm scrolls ending in eagle's heads. The lambrequin or
valance with a suspended tassel on the cresting rail is a device
used occasionally on chairs made between 1720–30. According
to R. W. Symonds, "The seat rail with its rounded corners—
its contemporary name was a compass seat—points to a date
somewhere between 1715 and 1730". The canework probably
replaced an original drop-in upholstered seat. The date of 1730
disposes of the often-repeated story that this particular chair is
directly attributable to Chippendale (who was only thirteen in
1730), because of his receipt for payment, alleged to have been
formerly in the possession of the Museum, though no record of
such a receipt has ever existed. (This legend started life apparently
in the 1890s, and has since appeared in several books on furniture.)

Mahogany was known in England in the second half of the
seventeenth century, perhaps earlier, though it was not used for
furniture-making until the early Georgian period. A London
cabinet-maker named Wollaston of Long Acre is reputed to have
been the first to use Jamaica wood as it was then called, because
that island was the chief source of supply. As well as exporting
the indigenous product, Jamaican merchants bought Spanish

The second of Hogarth's paintings in the series, *Marriage à la Mode*, shows the bored young couple in a room furnished with high-backed upholstered single chairs. The original paintings are in the National Gallery, and Hogarth printed and published plates of the series. This illustration, which gives a close-up view of one of the chairs, is reproduced from a section of an engraving made by B. Baron, April 1, 1745. The chair has a shaped seat, cabriole legs, and the upholstered seat and back are continuous.

Hogarth's caricature of John Wilkes, published on May 16, 1763, showing a bended-back chair of a type that had then been out of date for some thirty years. Compare this with the chair in the portrait shown opposite.

Another portrait of John Wilkes, published in *The Universal Museum*, May
1763. He is shown seated on a contemporary chair, with a simple vase splat
and upholstered seat. Chairs of this type are shown displayed for sale outside
the shop of Bailey, the chair and cabinet makers in St John Street, in the
engraving on page 278.

mahogany from Cuba and Honduras and shipped it to England. At some time early in the 1720s Wollaston was commissioned to make a candle-box and subsequently a bureau by Dr William Gibbons (1649–1728) from some mahogany planks which had been brought to England as ballast by his brother, a sea captain engaged in the West Indian trade, though the material had been specially imported for joinery and cabinet work from about 1720, perhaps even earlier. *The Dictionary of English Furniture* records its use in 1722 at Cannons House, Middlesex, which had been rebuilt for the Duke of Chandos by James Gibbs and completed in 1720–21 by John Price, the Duke's own surveyor, and the fourth architect employed on the work. The Duke, though a difficult client, was enterprising enough to import mahogany for the decoration of the saloon at Cannons. By the mid-1720s mahogany was employed for chair-making, and although it was used concurrently with walnut throughout the second quarter of the eighteenth century, it became the accepted material for town makers, and remained in favour throughout the Georgian and Victorian periods. Thomas Sheraton in *The Cabinet Dictionary* (1803) stated that: "The kinds of mahogany employed in chair making, ought to be Spanish or Cuba, of a clean straight grain. Wood of this quality will rub bright, and keep cleaner than any Honduras wood. Yet there is wood of the last quality, if properly selected for chair making, to which there can be no material objection; and where lightness is preferred, as is sometimes the case, it will demand the preference." He described Cuba wood as: "A kind of mahogany somewhat harder than Honduras wood, but of no figure in the grain. It is inferior to Spanish wood, though probably the Cuba and Spanish mahogany are the same, as the island of Cuba is a Spanish colony. . . . That, however, which is generally distinguished by Spanish mahogany is finer than what is called Cuba, which is pale, straight grained, and some of it only a bastard kind of mahogany. It is generally used for chair wood, for which some of it will do very well."

Chair-makers continued to use walnut long after mahogany had become fashionable. Elizabeth Purefoy, the mistress of Shalstone Manor House, in a letter dated July 14, 1736, addressed to a local chair frame maker named King at "the King & Queen", Bicester said: "As I understand you make chairs of wallnut tree frames with 4 legs without any Barrs for Mr Vaux of Caversfeild, if you do such I desire you will come over here in a week's time any morning but Wensday. I shall want about 20 chairs." This attests not only the continued popularity of walnut, but the increased competence of country craftsmen, who now made chairs without "barrs" or stretchers.

John Wood, the elder, in *An Essay Towards a Description of Bath*, published in 1742, described the cheap and indifferent furnishing of houses in that city about 1727, before he and his son had begun rebuilding it, and recorded that "With Cane or Rush bottomed Chairs the principal Rooms were Furnished, and each Chair seldom exceeded three half crowns in Value. . . ." That is quoted from the second edition, issued in 1749, when the author said: "To make a just Comparison between the publick Accommodations of *Bath* at this time, and one and twenty Years back, the best Chambers for Gentlemen were then just what the Garrets for Servants now are." Walnut was still acceptable for high class furnishing at that date, for he wrote: "Walnut Tree Chairs, some with Leather, and some with Damask or Worked Bottoms supplied the Place of such as were seated with Cane or Rushes. . . ." The social status of canework had clearly declined; it was rejected by contemporary taste in the mid-eighteenth century, though its use was revived some thirty years later and it remained popular throughout the following century.

Country makers used oak, beech, ash, elm, yew and fruit woods like apple and cherry, and for the ornately carved and gilded furniture, such as that designed by William Kent (?1685–1748), pine wood had, since the Restoration, provided carvers and gilders with an admirably tractable material. The properties of fir and pine were described by John Evelyn in *Sylva*, which was first published in 1664. "*Fir* is exceeding smooth to *polish* on," he wrote, "and therefore does well under *Gilding* work, and takes *black* equal with the *Pear-tree*: Both *Fir*, and especially *Pine*, succeed well in *Carving*, as for *Capitels*, *Festoons*, nay *Statues*, especially being *Gilded*, because of the easiness of the *Grain*, to work, and take the *Tool* every way. . . ."

Kent's designs for chairs were lavishly decorative, but the motifs he used with such florid vitality were always under control; acanthus scrolls and foliations, shells, and masks were so skilfully

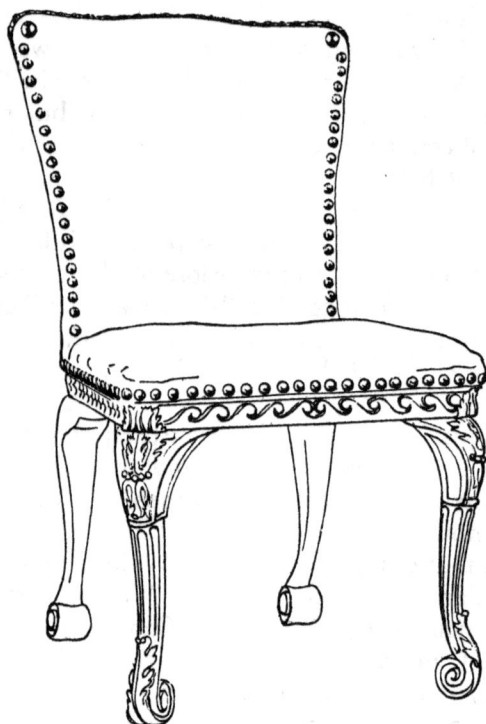

One of a set of chairs in mahogany, designed by William Kent. Back and seat are upholstered and trimmed with brass nails; the seat rail is ornamented with a wave device, the knees of the cabriole legs are lightly carved, and knurl feet are used. *Drawn by Marcelle Barton.*

chosen and disposed that they seldom disturbed good proportion, as the armchairs opposite and on plate 38 demonstrate. Horace Walpole, while admitting that Kent "had an excellent taste for ornaments" qualified the admission by adding: "Yet chaste as these ornaments were, they were often unmeasurably ponderous." An architect, painter, and designer of gardens, Kent created an impressive individual style in furnishing and interior decoration, which had baroque affinities, and was a comfortably corpulent anticipation of the gay rococo forms that came to England from

Front and side views of an armchair designed by William Kent. Elaborate carved and gilded chairs like this and the example on plate 38 are really components of some large, decorative scheme, designed by the architect. Reproduced from *Some Designs of Mr. Inigo Jones and Mr. Wm. Kent*, published by John Vardy (1744).

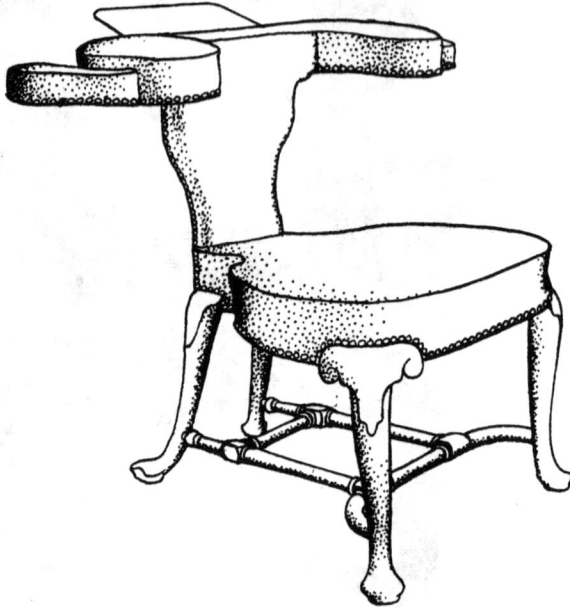

An early eighteenth century reading or library chair. See plate 41, also
Sheraton's design opposite. *Drawn by Ronald Escott.*

France in the middle years of the century. His style, said Walpole,
"predominated authoritatively during his life; and his oracle was
so much consulted by all who affected taste, that nothing was
thought complete without his assistance. He was not only consulted for furniture, as frames of pictures, glasses, tables, chairs,
&c. but for plate, for a barge, for a cradle." Like other architects
of his time, he was recognized as a master-designer, working in the
universally accepted classic idiom; so his tables, cabinets, bookcases and chairs were nearly always conceived as parts of a classic
composition, for which he had devised the decorative background
as well as the furniture. The elaborate carved and gilded chairs
illustrated on page 105 and plate 38 cannot really be judged as
individual designs; like much of Kent's furniture they belong to a
larger decorative conception. His thorough understanding of
chair design is declared by the relatively simple example on page

A reading chair designed by Thomas Sheraton, reproduced from plate 5 of *The Cabinet Dictionary* (1803). This is a development of the library chair on plate 41, and, like the early eighteenth century reading chair shown opposite retained the basic form. It was intended, said Sheraton, "to make the exercise easy, and for the convenience of taking down a note or quotation from any subject. The reader places himself with his back to the front of the chair, and rests his arms on the top yoke. The desk is moveable to any point in the circumference of the yoke or top rail, by means of a grove cut in the wood, and plates of iron screwed on. Before these plates are screwed all round the top yoke, there must be tee headed iron plates screwed to the underside of the piece of mahogany, about $1\frac{3}{4}$ wide, which is made hollow at one edge to fit the top, to which the desk is hinged". The total height of the chair "may be 31 or 32 inches, over the seat 19, from the inside of back to front 21, the height of seat 16. . . ." The reading flap was "12 by 16 inches long". Entry ARM, pages 17–18.

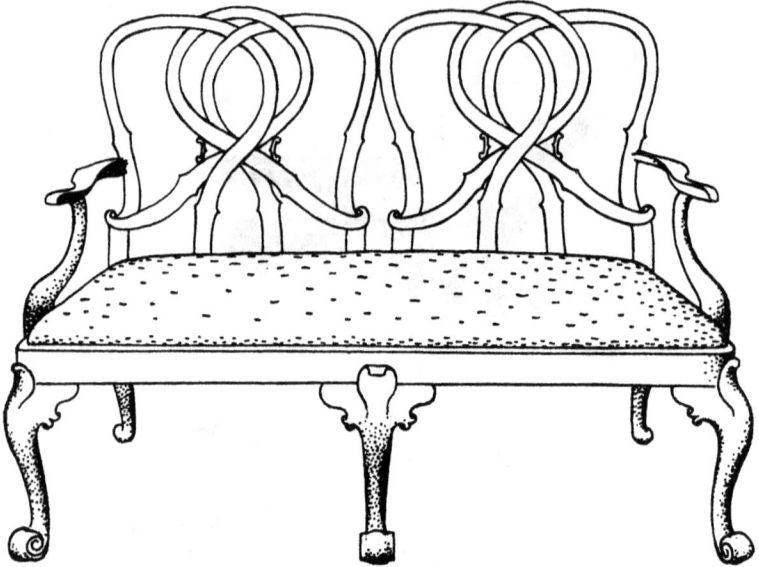

An early Georgian double chair back settee, with whorl feet.

104, one of a set, made in mahogany with cabriole legs, knurl feet, and a restrained use of carved ornament. Architects could command the skill of expert craftsmen for executing their designs, and fashionable chair-makers and cabinet-makers regulated their work by a close knowledge of the proportions of the classic orders of architecture.

Broad-seated armchairs became more popular in the Queen Anne and early Georgian periods, and although they could just accommodate two people, the clothes worn by men and women discouraged such cosy proximity. Men's coats were long and full at the sides; women's voluminous skirts had long trains, and were gathered in loops to disclose a silk petticoat with a row of flounces, while the hoops that supported and expanded the skirts, were comparable in size with those used for the farthingale. Although improved upholstery invited relaxed attitudes, fashionable people continued to sit upright; the men to avoid disarraying their wigs or their dignity, the women because their corsets were in control, and tight-lacing was obligatory unless pregnancy was almost imminent. In *The Way of the World*, Mirabell denounced "all strait lacing, squeezing for a shape", when Millamant was breeding; but only then were fine ladies excused the excessive compression of the waist that determined their attitude when seated. Those modern names, "love-seat" and "courting chair", mentioned in the last chapter, were invented on the assumption that affection would overcome the discomfort of loving couples being immovably wedged into a space about three feet wide. Another term for a wide-seated chair, almost certainly of Victorian origin, was drunkard's chair; established, accepted and explained early this century by furniture historians. Constance Simon, writing in 1905, asserted that such seats "were known as drunkard's chairs, probably because their large size enabled our forefathers to repose comfortably therein after an evening's carouse". Another fancy name for a far broader seat, capable of holding up to four persons, was Darby and Joan chair, a name derived from a song called "The Joys of Love Never Forgot", published in the "Poetical Essays" section of *The Gentleman's Magazine*, for March 1735. The long devotion of a physically repulsive couple was the theme; their names for over two centuries have signified enduring affection, as a result of these lines:

> "Old Darby with Joan by his side,
> You've often regarded with wonder,
> He's dropsical, she is sore-eyed,
> Yet they're ever uneasy asunder. . . ."

The wide-seated chair was really a half-settee, and settees were in appearance often elongated chairs, with double or triple chair-backs, as described in the last chapter. The chair-back settee, which had first appeared after the Restoration, was re-introduced in Queen Anne's reign, and throughout the eighteenth century was as popular as the upholstered type. There were variously specialized chairs; some combined the functions of armchair and library steps, with an ingeniously hinged framework; others could be extended to form a long seat. In the will of Celia Fiennes, dated November 6, 1738, an easy chair on wheels is mentioned, and two "square stools that have hooks and staples to hang on to

Armchair with stuffed seat and back. The arms are padded and the back is inclined for greater comfort. (See Chippendale's design for a "French" chair on page 134, also plate 45.)

the chair as a couch". Writing chairs and shaving chairs have been mentioned earlier, and there was a type of reading chair, with a desk and broad arm rests, so that the reader could sit facing the back with a book open on the desk and his elbows supported. They were also known as library chairs, and an example, *circa* 1735, in the Fitzwilliam Museum at Cambridge, is reproduced on plate 41, and another earlier type shown on page 106. These have sometimes been called cock-fighting chairs, which is not a contemporary term, though they may have been used occasionally by spectators at a cock-match.

The technique of upholstery was improved, as more attention was given to making surfaces soft and yielding: wool, hair, and odds and ends of waste fabric were used for padding the seats, back and arms of chairs, so comfort was no longer partly dependent on supplementary cushions. Materials were richly varied, and those used for covering high-backed chairs were often protected by a silk flap that hung down behind the chair back, ready to be pulled over the top so it came between the covering material and the powdered wigs worn by men and the greasy make-up of women—a discreetly functional Georgian anticipation of the Victorian anti-macassar.

An early Georgian armchair, with stuffed and padded back and seat, that retains all the grace of the bended back type.

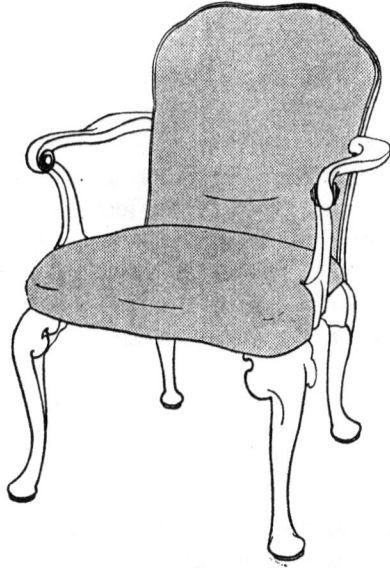

The sumptuous effect of needlework and rich fabrics is described by Celia Fiennes, when she visited the house of Mr Rooth at New Inn Lane, Epsom, at some time between 1701 and 1703. "You enter one room hung with crosstitch in silks," she wrote, "the bed the same lined with yellow and white strip'd satin, window curtains white silk damaske with furbellows of callicoe printed flowers, the chaires crosstitch, and two stooles of yellow mohaire with crostitch true lover knotts in straps along and a cross, an elbow chaire tentstitch. . . ." Cross-stitch was the term for two stitches crossing each other at right angles; tent-stitch was nearly always used in petit-point, a form of fine embroidery worked upon fine-meshed canvas, that was usually held in a frame during the work. Tent-stitch is the finest of all canvas embroidery stitches, and gives a closely and evenly filled hard-wearing surface, very suitable for chair seats and backs. The fineness of tent-stitch allowed highly detailed pictorial designs to be used, and as the stitch was worked diagonally over single vertical and horizontal threads of the canvas, and was always the same on

E

both sides of the work, a smooth and even effect was obtained. Gros-point was a form of cross-stitch embroidery in wool on canvas, giving an effect similar to petit-point, but coarser and more rigid. (Both are used in the embroidery of the chair shown in the frontispiece.) Fine woollen yarns were used, sometimes combined with silk in a single piece of embroidery, the silk emphasizing the high lights. Dark grounds were generally favoured for chair backs and seats and for loose, separate cushions.

Mohair, or mohaire, a fabric made from the hair of the Angora goat, was used for upholstery in the late seventeenth and early eighteenth centuries. The word is derived from the Arabic *muhayyar*. Pope refers to the material in this couplet:

"And when she sees her friend in deep despair,
    Observes how much a chintz exceeds mohair."

In her detailed account of the furnishing of Mr Rooth's house, Celia Fiennes noted two chairs, "one red damaske the other crostitch and tentstitch very rich", also "green damaske chaires", and she observed that "the windows in all the roomes has cusheons", for the tall, double-hung sash windows of Queen Anne and Georgian houses usually had wide window seats, far more conducive to intimate conversation and tender passages between courting couples than the so-called courting chairs and love seats. In *Evelina*, Fanny Burney mentioned this attraction with prudish distaste when she wrote: "Upstairs, therefore, I went; and seated on a window, with Mr Brown at her side, sat Miss Polly. I felt a little awkward at disturbing them, and much more so at their behaviour afterwards; for, as soon as the common enquiries were over, Mr Brown grew so fond, and so foolish, that I was extremely disgusted."

Fixed seats, fitted into bay windows, often with a receptacle below, had been in use since the early sixteenth century; but the Georgian window seat was part of the interior design of a room. The relation of windows to the furnishing of rooms was set forth in detail by Isaac Ware in *A Complete Body of Architecture* when he described "houses of the common size for moderate families in town", and observed that in many houses of that size "the builder now puts but two windows in front, and, where the extent is not too great, it is very proper. The pier between these is large, and gives great strength to the building, and it is capable of receiving better and nobler furniture, without more expence: one glass and one table does in this dining-room, in the place of two, and the effect is much finer. . . ." Also: "The windows, in this case, are to be made larger than they would otherwise have been, and the breadth of the pier between very well suits with this." Ware's book first appeared in 1756, and he recorded what had been common practice for at least twenty years. As windows broadened, and the lower sash was often carried down to floor level, the window stool or French stool was introduced, a small, independent upholstered seat, with four or six legs and scrolled ends, sometimes with a low back, like a dwarf settee, designed for a deep recess. (Examples are shown on page 145.)

At the close of the early Georgian period, the variety of seats of all kinds was far greater than at the beginning of the century. Chair-makers had proved that ease need never be unmannerly; the sprawling, lounging attitudes invited by Victorian armchairs were still a hundred years ahead; meanwhile, dignity was maintained without discomfort.

LANDALL & GORDON.
*Joyners, Cabinet, & Chair-Makers
At y⁰ Griffin & Chair in Little Argyle Street
by Swallow Street,
Makes all sorts of Tables, Chairs, Setee-Beds,
Looking-Glasses, Picture-frames, Window-
Blinds, & all sorts of Cabinet Work*

D. 2   1273

1806

The trade card of Landall and Gordon, joiners, cabinet and chair-makers, whose sign was "Ye Griffin and Chair". *Circa* 1750. The chair depicted, with furred cabriole legs, paw feet, and shaped, ornamented splat, was out of date in the mid-eighteenth century, but may have been retained to suggest that the firm was long-established, though it also suggested that their knowledge of good proportions was limited. *Reproduced by courtesy of the Trustees of the British Museum.*

114

CHAPTER 8

THE GREAT CHAIR-MAKERS, 1730–1810

CHAIRS figured prominently on the signs and trade cards of many makers, even though they were engaged in producing every description of household furniture, like Thomas Chippendale, whose "Cabinet and Upholstery Warehouse" was at *The Chair*, in St Martin's Lane. There were others, less well-known to posterity, whose names appear in the selected list of cabinet-makers, upholsterers, carvers and gilders established between 1660 and 1840, which Sir Ambrose Heal gives in his book, *The London Furniture Makers*. For example, Pierce Hall, cabinet and chair maker, also worked at the sign of *The Chair*, in St John's Street, near Hicks Hall, *circa* 1760; so did a turner, Joseph Warwick of Upper Shadwell nearly forty years earlier; James Pitt, cabinet-maker and upholder, *circa* 1760, had his address at *The Easy Chair*, near Bethlem Walk, between New Broad Street and Old Bethlem, No. 7, Old Moor Fields; Richard Roberts, "Joiner", *circa* 1723, at *The Royal Chair*, Marylebone Street; and there were specialist makers, like William Gardner, *circa* 1709, whose sign was *The Cane Chair*, on the south side of St Paul's Church. An advertisement of his wares, quoted in *The London Furniture Makers*, ran thus: "Maketh and selleth cane chairs, couches and cane sashes at reasonable rates of Dry Wood."

Another chair-maker, Samuel Spencer of Aldermanbury, used *The Golden Chair*; William Chesson, upholsterer, *The Three Chairs*; William Cauty, cabinet-maker and upholsterer, *The Chair and Curtains*; William Jellicoe, upholsterer, *The Chair and Anchor*; while Landall and Gordon, joiners, cabinet-makers and chair-makers, whose trade card is reproduced on page 114, worked "at *Ye*

Griffin & Chair in Little Argyle Street by Swallow Street". The names of such makers have been recovered by chance or by the researches of furniture historians; they are not identified with a style, but the illustrations of chairs on some of their trade cards suggest that they were well abreast of contemporary design, though occasionally lagging behind, like Landall and Gordon, whose card dates from about 1750, and includes a chair with cabriole legs and a back splat of a type that was by then old-fashioned.

The three outstanding names that we have come to associate with the second half of the eighteenth century are those of Thomas Chippendale, George Hepplewhite, and Thomas Sheraton. They have been linked with the furniture of that age ever since late Victorian times, when antique furniture generally became an emotional study and a commercial pursuit. The popularity of their names as labels for styles would doubtless have astonished their owners; so too would the confident, and of course convenient, attributions to their personal skill that have been made by collectors and dealers during the last seventy or eighty years. We know that Chippendale had a flourishing chair and cabinet-making business at 60, St Martin's Lane, and was, according to John Thomas Smith, who wrote in 1828, "the most famous Upholsterer and Cabinet-maker of his day, to whose folio work on household-furniture the trade formerly made constant reference". All we know about Hepplewhite is that he was apprenticed to Gillow of Lancaster, came to London at some unknown date, opened a shop at St Giles's, Cripplegate, and died in 1786. No pieces of furniture have ever been identified with his firm. Thomas Sheraton, who was born in 1751 at Stockton-on-Tees, worked as a journeyman cabinet-maker, came to London about 1790, and established himself as a drawing master, making designs for cabinet-makers. No pieces of furniture have ever been traced to him either. All three owe their posthumous fame to the illustrated catalogues they published of their work, copy books that were useful to the furniture trade during and after their lifetime.

The names of some designers are rightly identified with a specific style; such an association is indisputable when concerned with the ornate and emphatically individual furniture designed by an architect like William Kent, or the much later and far more

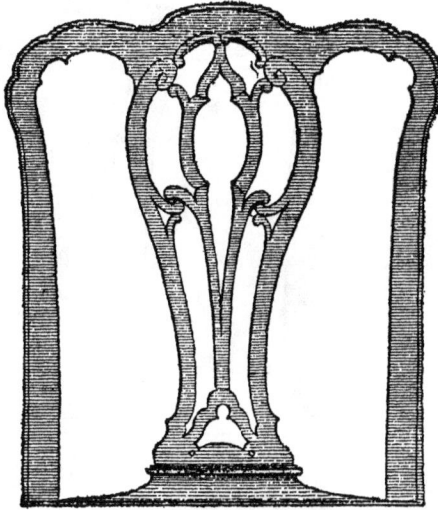

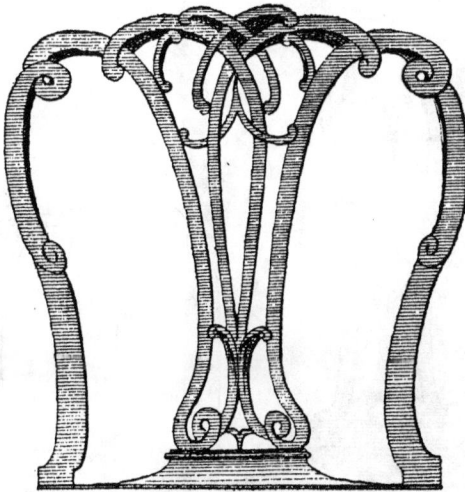

Two of the six chair-back designs given on plate XVI of Chippendale's
Director (third edition). The other four are reproduced on the next two pages.
(See also plate 42.)

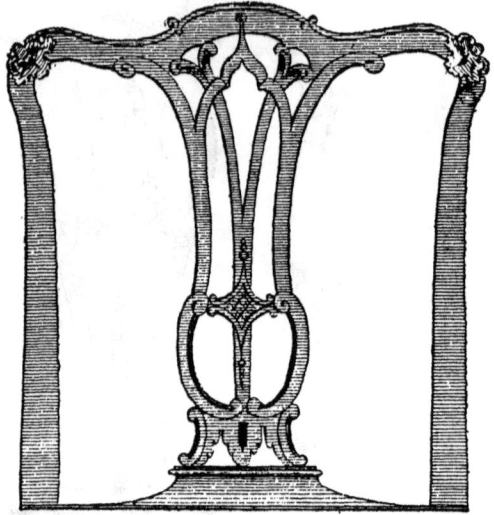

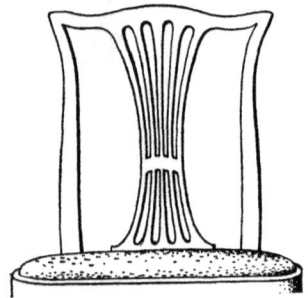

Above and left: Two designs for chair backs, reproduced from plate XVI of Chippendale's *Director* (third edition). *Right:* A simplified version of the splat, pierced and waisted but owing something to the prototype on the left. These "wheatsheaf" backs were often used by provincial chair-makers.

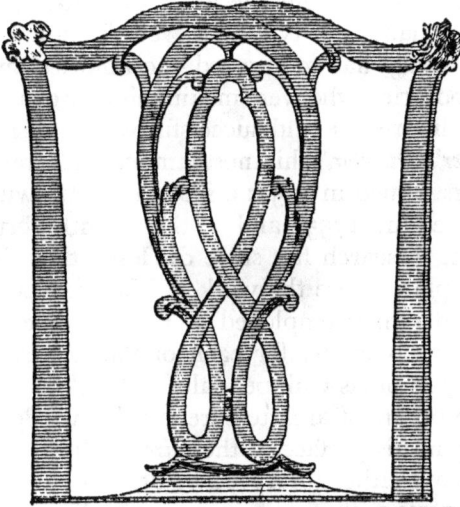

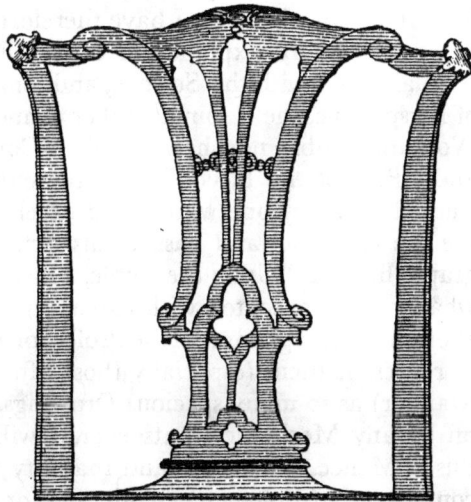

Above and right: Two designs for chair backs, reproduced from plate XVI of Chippendale's *Director* (third edition). *Left:* The lancet back of a country-made Gothic type. The pierced openings in the splat resemble the more elaborate piercing in the chair-back on the right. Two views of this elbow chair are given on plate 43.

E*

delicate creations of Robert Adam; but the fortuitous linking of Chippendale's name with chairs of a type that were fashionable in the mid-eighteenth century has minimized the abilities and importance of his contemporaries, who were making similar chairs, but did not publish such impressive and successful works as *The Gentleman and Cabinet-Maker's Director*. This most famous of all trade books on furniture was first issued in 1754; a second edition with the same contents followed in 1755, and a third, with forty additional plates, in 1762. Research has since disclosed that the original drawings for the plates were the work of Matthias Lock and Henry Copland, two designers employed by Chippendale, to whom no acknowledgement is made, for each of the engraved plates bears the signature, Thomas Chippendale, *invt et del*.

The respect due to the orders of architecture is acknowledged by Chippendale, who begins his preface to the *Director* thus:

"Of all the Arts which are either improved or ornamented by Architecture, that of CABINET-MAKING is not only the most useful and ornamental, but capable of receiving as great Assistance from it as any whatever. I have therefore prefixed to the following Designs a Short Explanation of the Five Orders. Without an Acquaintance with this Science, and some Knowledge of the Rules of Perspective, the Cabinet-Maker cannot make the Designs of his Work intelligible, nor shew, in a little Compass, the whole Conduct and Effect of the Piece. These, therefore, ought to be carefully studied by every one who would excel in this Branch, since they are the very Soul and Basis of his Art." In the concluding paragraph, he said: "Upon the whole, I have here given no Design but what may be executed with Advantage by the Hands of a skilful Workman, though some of the Profession have been diligent enough to represent them (especially those after the Gothic and Chinese Manner) as so many specious Drawings, impossible to be worked off by any Mechanic whatsoever. I will not scruple to attribute this to Malice, Ignorance, and Inability; and I am confident I can convince all Noblemen, Gentlemen, or others, who will honour me with their Commands, that every Design in the Book can be improved, both as to Beauty and Enrichment, in the Execution of it, by Their Most Obedient Servant, Thomas Chippendale."

The first eight plates were devoted to the Tuscan, Doric, Ionic, Corinthian, and Composite orders, with their details, followed by

The ribband-back chair, admittedly a piece of rococo extravagance, is a variation of the basic form shown on pages 118 and 119. Few sets were made, and few have survived; such delicately interwoven splats were too fragile, and the attempt to simulate a silk ribbon in wood, with the grain running in all directions, was a misuse of material — even the finest mahogany could not resist any strain when carved into those wafer-thin convolutions. Reproduced from the *Director* (first edition, 1754).

twenty-five plates of chairs and other seats. The French, Gothic, and Chinese styles were all represented. Chippendale used certain basic shapes for his open chair backs, a framework that permitted many variations of the piercing and interlacing of the splat, and the curves and ornamentation of the yoke rail. To a large extent, the character of the chair was determined by the back; for the legs, whether cabriole or tapered, were carved to match the type of decoration used on the splat, the back uprights, and the yoke rail. The six designs for chair backs reproduced on pages 117, 118 and 119, exhibit this characteristic framework; and the ribband-back chair on page 121 is a rococo version of the basic form. Of this intricate, but perfectly-controlled design, Chippendale said that "Several Sets have been made, which have given entire Satisfaction. If any of the small Ornaments should be thought superfluous, they may be left out, without spoiling the Design. If the seats are covered with red Morocco, they will have a fine Effect."

Five chairs from plates IX, XII, XIII and XIV of the *Director* appear on pages 123 to 127, which are described as "various Designs of Chairs for Patterns. The front Feet are mostly different, for the greater Choice. Care must be taken in drawing them at large. The Seats look best when stuffed over the Rails, and have a Brass Border neatly chased; but are most commonly done with Brass Nails, in one or two Rows; and sometimes the Nails are done to imitate Fretwork. They are usually covered with the same Stuff as the Window-Curtains. The Height of the Back seldom exceeds twenty-two Inches above the Seats."

The chair shown on plate 42, one of a set of six in the Fitzwilliam Museum, Cambridge, has the seat stuffed over the rails and finished with brass-headed nails. The back has the characteristic treatment of the specimen designs from the *Director*, reproduced on pages 117 to 119, but is much simpler; the legs are of square section, those in front fluted, those behind left plain and slightly splayed; and although there is no apparent structural need for them, stretchers have been used. The practical directions Chippendale gave when describing the plates, and his remark in the Preface about the execution of his designs by a skilful workman, indicate that he regarded the *Director* as far more than a catalogue of his own works; he foresaw and welcomed its use as a copy-book,

[*continued on page* 128

A simpler form of the interlaced splat, and alternative treatments for the back uprights. From plate IX of Chippendale's *Director* (third edition).

Like the designs on pages 121 and 123, and those that follow, this chair from
plate XIII of Chippendale's *Director* (third edition) shows the immense range
of decorative variations made possible by the basic shapes of the back. All
these models ring the changes on the six types shown on pages 117, 118 and 119.

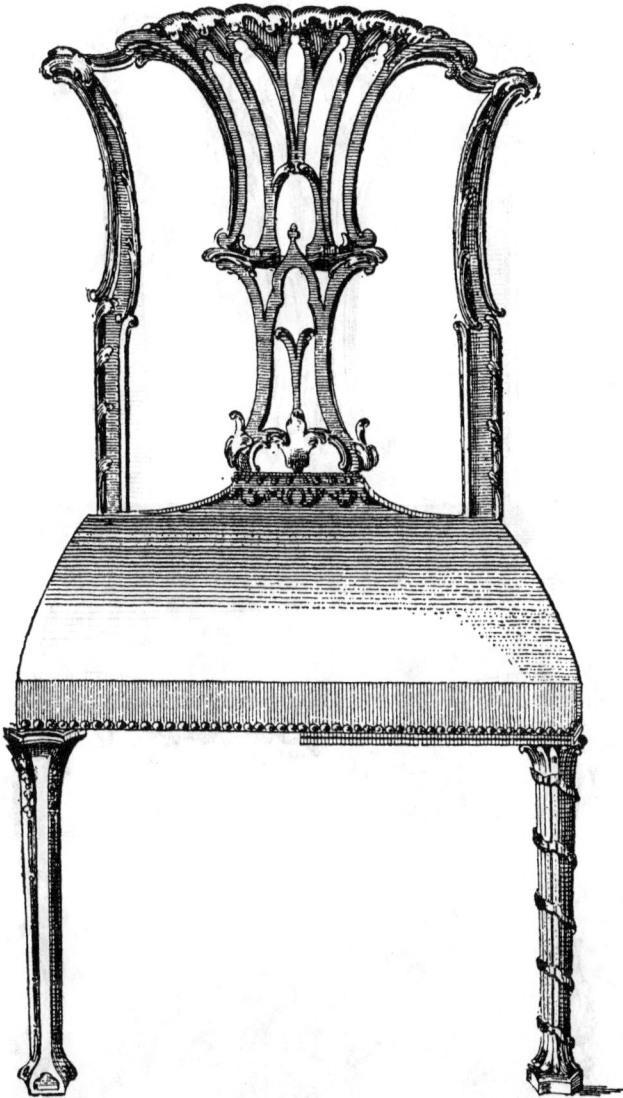

Alternative suggestions for legs are shown in this model, from plate XII of Chippendale's *Director* (third edition); and the cabriole form has been replaced by the tapered leg. This also appears on the French chair on page 134.

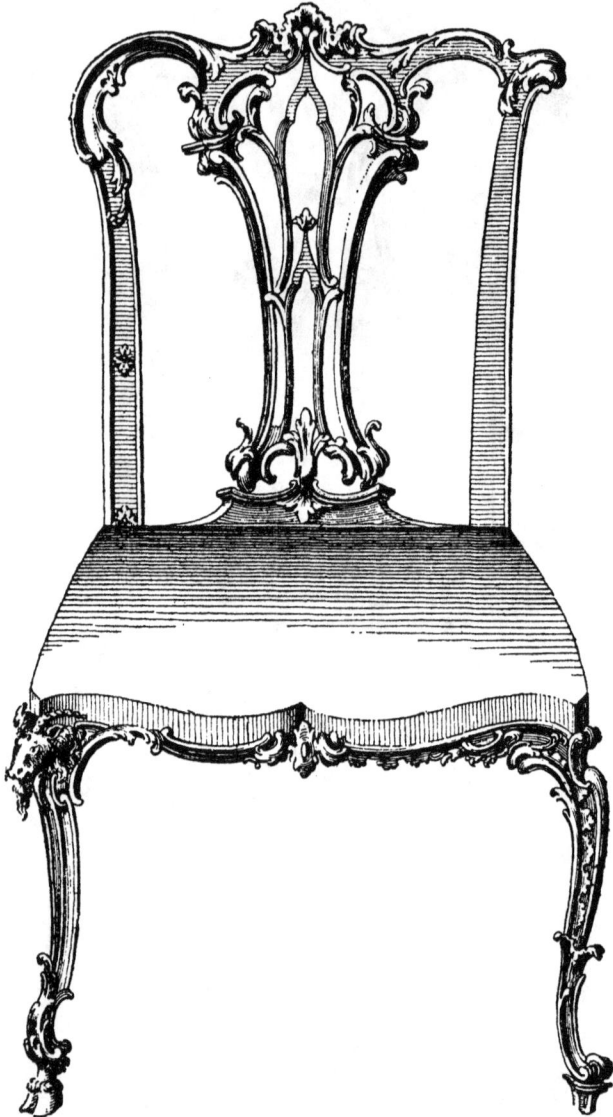

This chair is an English interpretation of the rococo style; fanciful, but not too fragile, with the light froth of ornament on the splat and yoke rail well under control. The gay frenzy of French rococo always sobered down when the style crossed the Channel. From plate XIV of Chippendale's *Director* (third edition).

The splat of this chair has lancet piercing, which is shown in a less elaborate form by the chair-back design on the lower part of page 119, and with simple directness by the country-made elbow chair on plate 43. This is "accidental" rather than conscious Gothic; for the chairs that Chippendale described as Gothic were an amalgam of rococo and Chinese motifs, like the example on page 129. Reproduced from plate XVI of Chippendale's *Director* (third edition).

127

and it *was* used extensively as such by other makers, especially in provincial towns and the countryside. The modern term, "Country Chippendale", describes the simplified, and often greatly improved, versions of designs from the *Director* produced by rural craftsmen, who were content to take the chair-back only as a model, and to provide drop-in or solid wooden seats, with plain, square-sectioned legs and stretchers. They invented what are now called the wheatsheaf and the lancet back. The former had a pierced, waisted splat, like that shown on page 118 side by side with its obvious prototype from the *Director*. The lancet back was a graceful acknowledgement of the Gothic taste, and the example on plate 43 of a country-made elbow chair is not only simpler but has greater subtlety than Chippendale's own complex mixture of Gothic and rococo motifs; and although lancet piercing is used in the splats of some chairs in the *Director*, notably those reproduced on pages 123, 126, and 127, they appear to have been formed unintentionally, and those particular models are not classified as Gothic. (The example on page 119 may have suggested the simplified and far more elegant version on plate 43.) Only three of Chippendale's designs are specifically labelled Gothic, and they are barely distinguishable from the Chinese types. (See pages 129 and 131.)

Three examples of Chinese chairs are illustrated on pages 130, 132 and 133, on two of them the characteristic Chippendale back is used to frame the frets that have replaced the splats. (See also plate 41, the subject below at the left.) These chairs, "after the Chinese manner", were described as "very proper for a Lady's Dressing-Room: especially if it is hung with India Paper. They will likewise suit Chinese Temples. They have commonly Cane-Bottoms, with loose cushions; but, if required, may have stuffed seats, and Brass Nails".

A French elbow chair, with a plain upholstered back joined to the seat, is shown on page 134 and in the portrait of Robert Adam on plate 44, and two of the more elaborate types, described by Chippendale as "open below at the Back; which make them very light, without having a bad Effect", appear on pages 136 and 137. The dimensions of such chairs were varied "according to the Bigness of the Rooms they are intended for". Chippendale gave eight designs, and said that "A skilful Workman may also lessen

[*continued on page* 135

One of Chippendale's "Gothic" chairs; an untidy medley of rococo and Chinese odds and ends of ornament, with alternative suggestions for the front legs, one cabriole, the other with a pierced fret. This badly muddled design would hardly have been acceptable to sensitive supporters of the Gothic Taste. Reproduced from plate XXV of the *Director* (third edition), but not described in the notes. There is another plate numbered XXV in that edition, with three chairs on it, one of them described as suitable for a library, the other two also called Gothic, with even less reason than the example shown above.

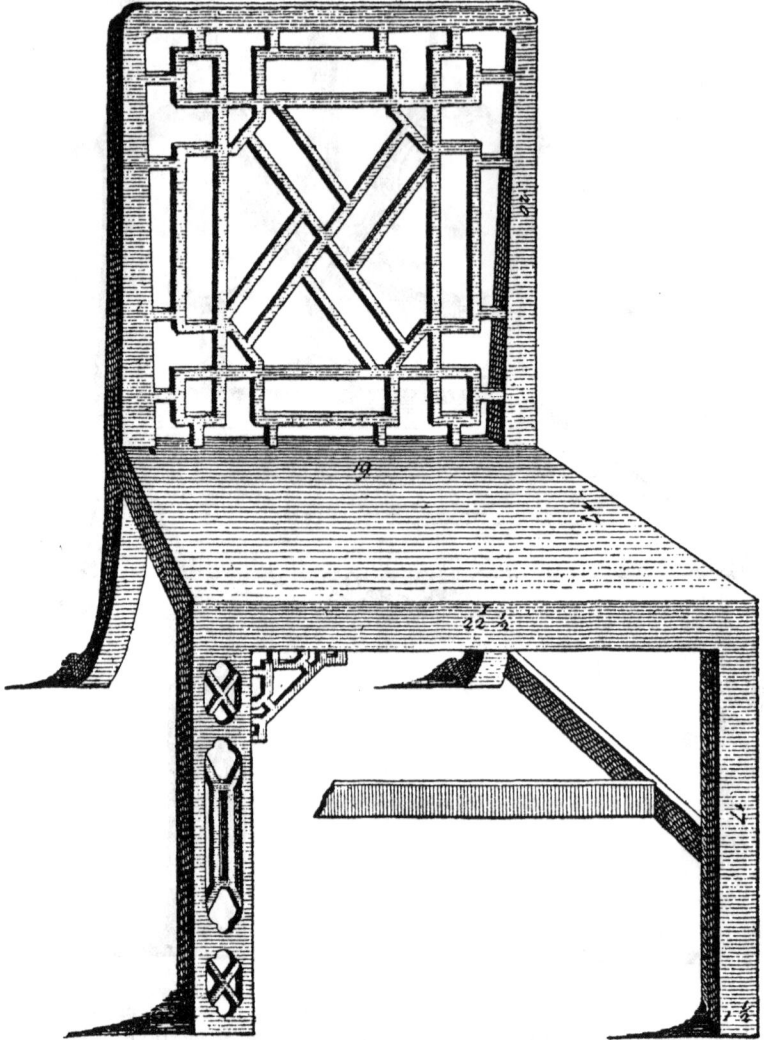

A simple type of Chinese single chair, with plain back uprights and yoke rail framing a geometrical fret pattern. From plate XXVI of Chippendale's *Director* (third edition).

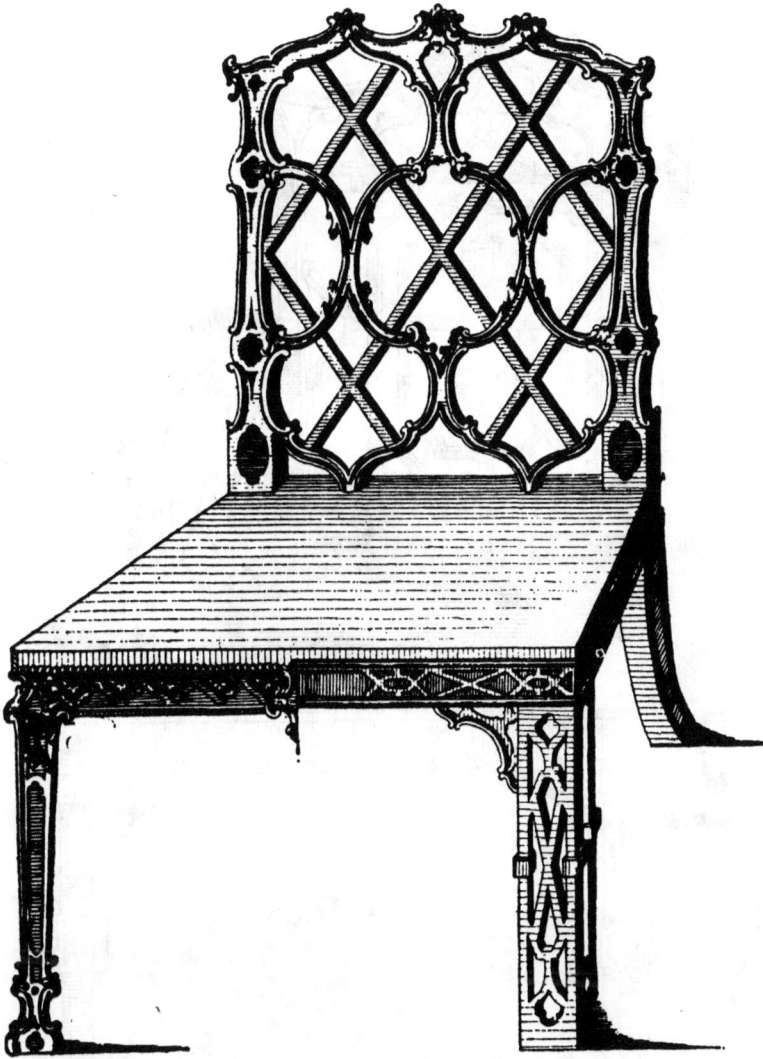

Another of Chippendale's "Gothic" designs, with a vague suggestion of pointed arches in the upper part of the back, comparable shapes inverted below, and a diagonal fret disrupting the flow of the curves, quite unrelated to the back uprights and top rail. Compare this with the chair on page 129, and the Chinese examples opposite and on page 133. Reproduced from plate XXV of the *Director* (third edition).

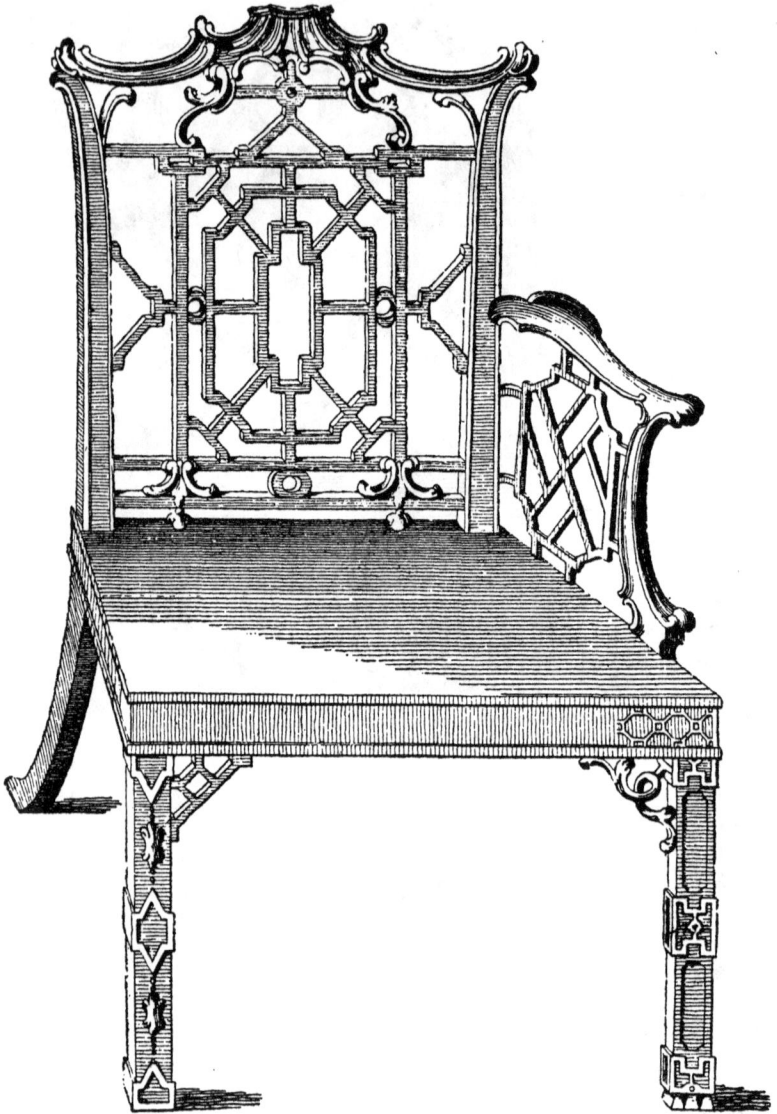

Chinese elbow chair, with the typical uprights and yoke rail of Chippendale designs, and an arm that is grafted from a French chair with the opening filled by a fret. From plate XXVII of Chippendale's *Director* (third edition.)

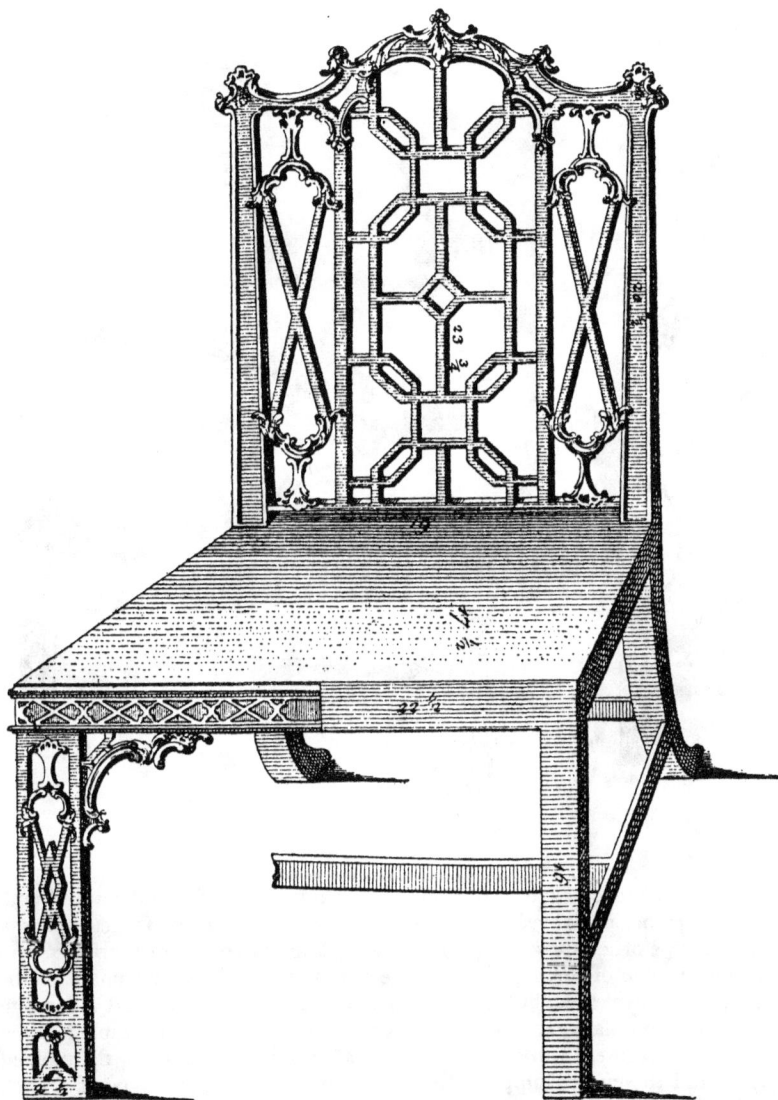

A single Chinese chair, with the characteristic uprights and yoke rail framing the fret in the back. From plate XXVIII of Chippendale's *Director* (third edition).

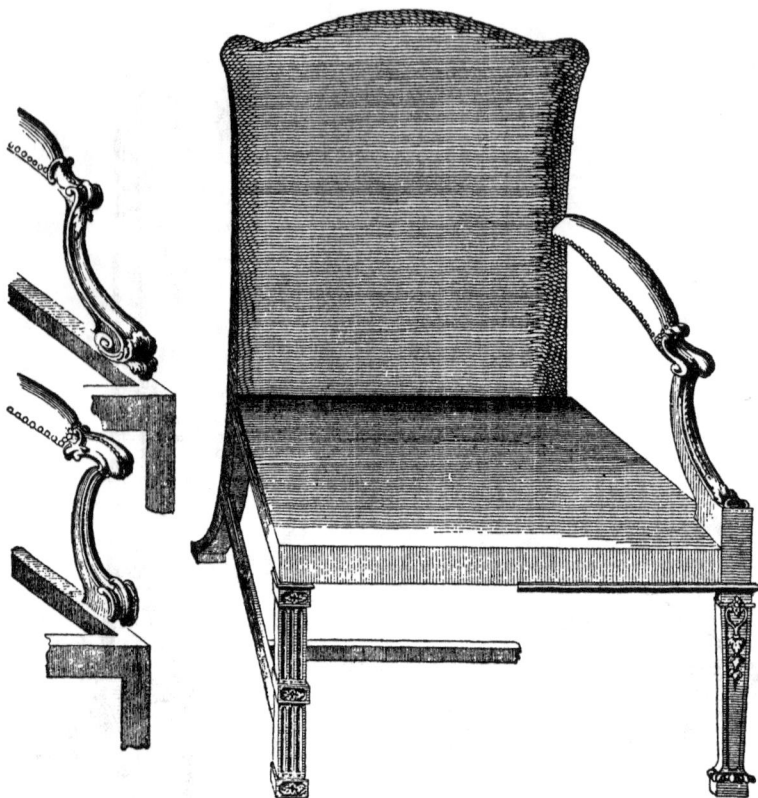

Design for a French chair with elbows, back and seat stuffed and covered with Spanish leather or damask. One of the alternative suggestions for legs shows a tapered type of square section; the back legs are splayed. Three forms of arm are shown, one of them (below on the left) is an obvious descendant of the earlier scroll-over type, but far less graceful. (See page 90.) Robert Adam, in the portrait on plate 44, is seated in such a chair, but in that example a much simpler arm is used, without carved decoration at the junction of the padded elbow and the curved support. Compare this relatively plain type of French chair with the design on page 136, which has an opening between the seat and the back. From plate XIX of Chippendale's *Director* (third edition).

the Carving, without any Prejudice to the Design. Both the Backs and Seats must be covered with Tapestry, or other sort of Needlework."

After the mid-eighteenth century chairs became wholly different in character from the graceful Queen Anne and early Georgian types, with their easy, flowing curves. In many of Chippendale's designs the cabriole leg survived in an attenuated form, with the curves modified, the bold knee abandoned, and delicate carved decoration lightly accentuating an elegant slenderness of line. Fashionable makers had discarded the claw-and-ball and the crisply carved paw foot, using instead a variety of scrolled shapes, like the whorls or upturned scrolls on the chair on page 124, which were sometimes called French scroll feet, while the cloven hoof also reappears or, more fancifully, a dolphin forms the complete leg and foot of a French style chair. (See pages 126 and 137.) In the provinces and the American Colonies, makers still retained the claw-and-ball foot and the cabriole leg; and at Philadelphia a type of chair was made that united the vigour of curvilinear design with the refinements introduced by Chippendale and his contemporaries. This American regional variation has been called "Philadelphia Chippendale", and in that city, the richest in the colony of Pennsylvania, the most accomplished makers had established thriving businesses. (See plate 41.)

When cabriole legs were supplanted by the classical tapered type, those members became less important as components of chair design; the harmonious partnership with the back, so marked in the chair on plate 32, was partly dissolved, though the side view of the country-made elbow chair on plate 43 suggests that it was not altogether lost, merely in abeyance, ready to be resumed, as it was when the swept or sabre leg was introduced with the Greek Revival, later in the century.

Chippendale's *Director* was the first book on furniture produced by a cabinet-maker, and it was soon followed by other collections of designs published by men in the furniture trade. In 1759, William Ince and John Mayhew began to issue in separate parts, sold at a shilling each, *The Universal System of Household Furniture;* this appeared later in book form, apparently in 1763, though no date is given on the title page or elsewhere, and it was anticipated by an anonymous collection that was advertised in *The Whitehall*

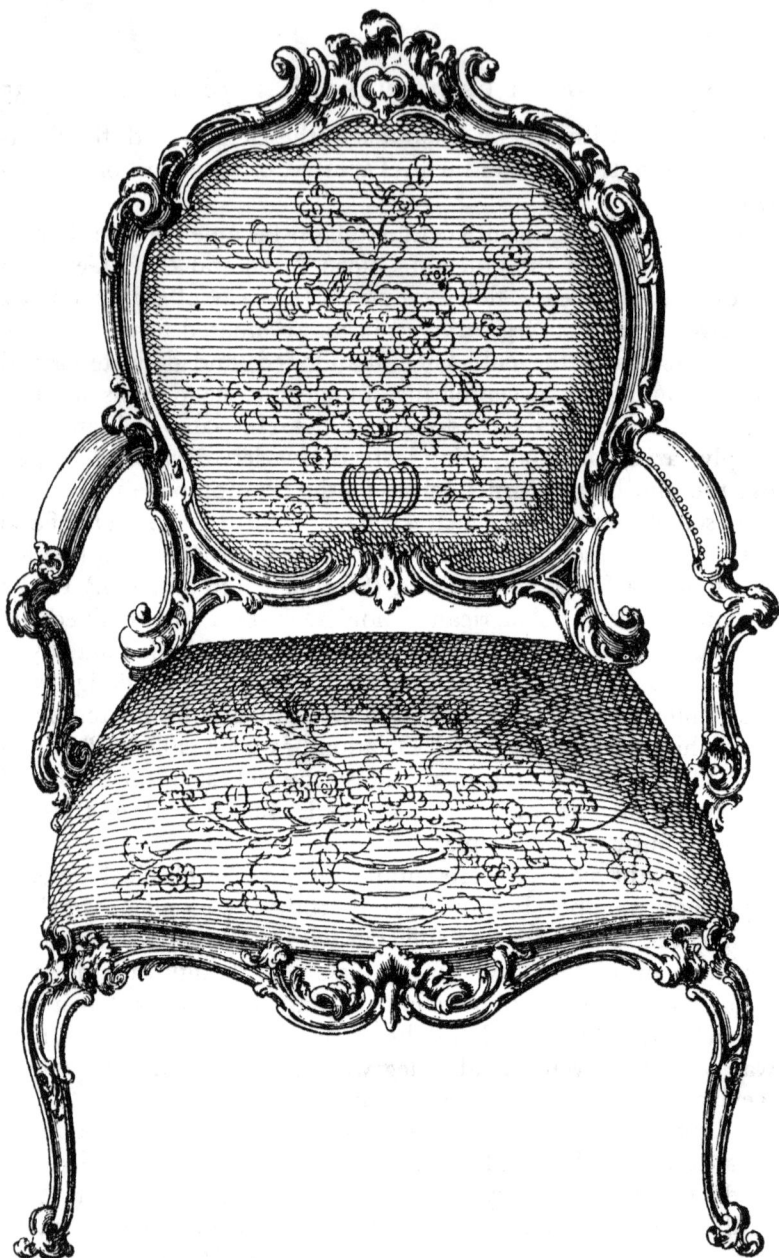

A French chair, "open below at the back", but without the central link
between the back frame and the seat in the example opposite. From plate
XXII of Chippendale's *Director* (third edition).

Another of Chippendale's designs for a French chair, also described as
"open below at the Back: which makes them very light, without having a bad
Effect". A variation of this type is shown opposite. Both strongly resemble
the carved and gilded chairs that French makers were producing in the mid-
eighteenth century. From plate XXI of the *Director* (third edition).

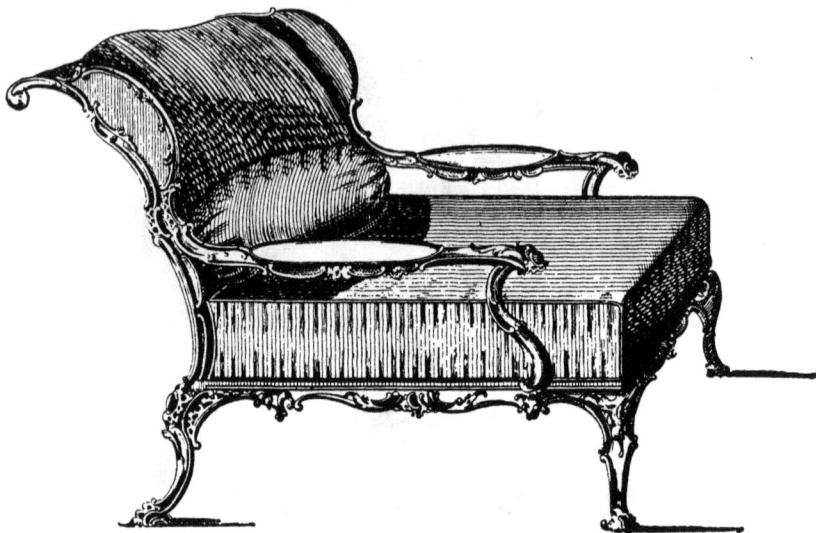

A burjair, or half-couch, illustrated on plate LX of *The Universal System of Household Furniture*, by Ince and Mayhew. An alternative design is shown opposite.

Evening-Post; or, London Intelligencer, for June· 26–28, 1760, as follows:—

"This Day was publish'd, in One Neat Volume, Octavo, (price 6s. sew'd, bound 7s) HOUSEHOLD FURNITURE in genteel Taste, for the Year 1760. By a Society of Upholsterers, Cabinet-Makers, &c. Containing upwards of One Hundred and Eighty Designs on Sixty Copper-Plates. Beautifully Engraved by M. Darly. Consisting of China, Breakfast, Side-Board, Dressing, Toilet, Card, Writing, Claw, Library, Slab, and Night Tables; Chairs, Couches, French Stools, Cabinets, Commodes, China Shelves and Cases, Trays, Chests, Stands for Candles, Tea Kettles, Pedestals, Stair-Case Lights, Bureaus, Beds, Ornamental Bed-Posts, Corniches, Brackets, Fire-Screens, Desk, Book and Clock-Cases, Frames for Glasses, Sconce and Chimney-Pieces, Girandoles, Lanthorns, Chandalears, &c &c with Scales. Printed for Robert Sayer, Map and Printseller, at the Golden Buck in Fleet-Street."

Mathias Darly, mentioned in that advertisement, was an engraver, publisher and designer, who had issued a work entitled *A New Book of Chinese, Gothic and Modern Chairs* in 1750–51; an undistinguished performance, for he was a good engraver but an indifferent designer. Chippendale, who was one of his friends, employed him for engraving the plates of the *Director*, and his signature appears also on all but the last six plates of Ince and Mayhew's book. *The Universal System of Household Furniture* included eight designs for parlour chairs, resembling types illustrated in the *Director*, dressing chairs in the Chinese taste, and dressing stools, single chairs with upholstered seats and backs (still described as "back stools"), French chairs, stools and corner chairs, and two half-couches, or Birjairs (as they are spelt in the notes, though on plate LX, they are called burjairs), one of them having an adjustable back that "is made to fall down at pleasure", as the authors said. Bergère was the French name for upholstered arm-chairs, and the Ince and Mayhew designs, which are reproduced

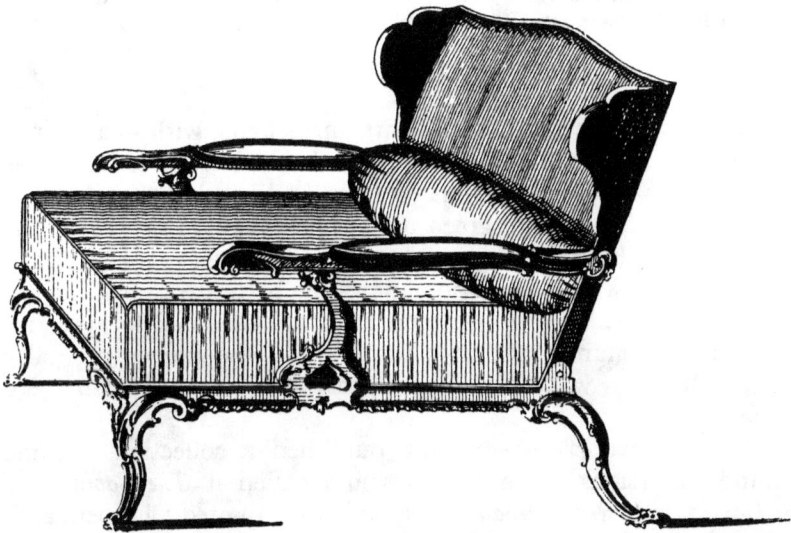

A burjair with an adjustable back, "made to fall down at pleasure, by that and the Elbows going in a Centre, and a Pin to go through the Elbow in the Holes marked", according to the note on plate LX, page 8, of *The Universal System of Household Furniture*, by Ince and Mayhew. See opposite page.

The two designs for couches, shown above and opposite, are from plate XXXII of Chippendale's *Director* (third edition, 1762). Compare them with the duchesse on page 147. (Both examples are reduced in size from the original.)

on pages 138 and 139, are elongated armchairs, with small wings or side-pieces on the upper part of the back. Gillows of Lancaster made what they described as "a large and handsome mahogany bergier, stuffed back in green morocco". Sheraton in *The Cabinet Dictionary* included a bergère among the armchairs as a type with "a caned back and arms. Sometimes the seats are caned, having loose cushions. The top rail and arms are moulded to agree all round. The stumps and legs turned, and the frames generally painted." This was clearly the prototype of the modern bergère chair.

In 1765 Robert Manwaring published a collection of some hundred designs on forty plates and called it *The Cabinet and Chair-Maker's Real Friend and Companion*. He quoted Chippendale's advice about the study of architecture and illustrated the classic orders. "The Art of Chair-Making," he said in his preface, "as well as that of Cabinet-Making, hath of late Years been brought to great Perfection, notwithstanding which, it will be ever capable of

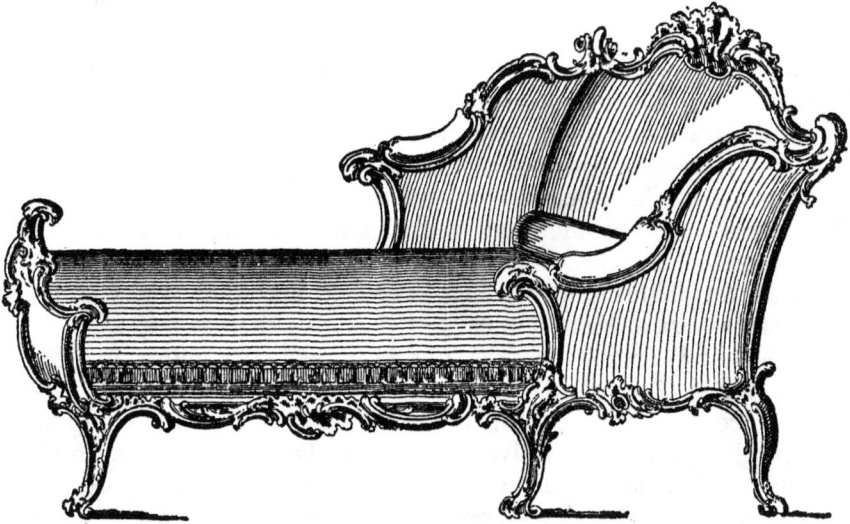

The second example from plate XXXII of Chippendale's *Director* (third edition, 1762). The alternative design is shown on the opposite page. Chippendale referred to the French name, Péché Mortel.

Improvement; and although there have appeared of late several Treatises and Designs for Household Furniture, some of which must be allowed by all Artists, to be of the greatest Utility in assisting their Ideas for composing various Designs; yet upon the whole, the practical Workman has not been much instructed in the Execution of those Designs, which appear before him so very rich and beautiful. The Intent therefore of the following Pages, are to convey to him full and plain Instructions, how he is to begin and finish with Strength and Beauty, all the Designs that are advanced in this Work, by which Circumstances the Author thinks himself sufficiently justified for intitling it, *The Cabinet and Chair-maker's real Friend and Companion*."

Many of the chair backs shown in Manwaring's plates could have been adapted from Chippendale's *Director*, although he claimed that they were "actually Originals and not pirated or copied from the Designs and Inventions of others, which of late hath been too much practised". He included Hall, Gothic and

Chinese chairs, saying that "though they appear so very elegant and superb, are upon a simple Construction, and may be very easily executed. . . ." There was no uncommercial modesty about his descriptions, and he mentioned that "many of the other Designs are finely and beautifully enriched with Carvings and Ornaments: the Author has the Boldness to assert, that should the ornamental Parts be left out, there will still remain Grandeur and Magnificence behind, and the Design will appear open and genteel". Like Ince and Mayhew, he used the old term, back stool, for single chairs. Like Chippendale, his Gothic and Chinese designs were almost identical.

Although great concessions had been made to comfort since the beginning of the eighteenth century, chairs were always designed to encourage an erect posture; but men and women could sit upright with comparative ease, certainly on the French style chairs which had well-stuffed seats and backs, and if they desired to relax, then such designs as the burjair, the truncated settee that Ince and Mayhew called a French corner chair, and a variety of long, cushioned seats—couches, sofas, and composite seats like the duchesse—were available. That untidy collapse of body and limbs into a deep upholstered pit, which a later age called lounging, was not practised by Georgian ladies and gentlemen: in private they might loll, and to loll, as a mid-eighteenth century dictionary put it, is "to lean or lie upon". Horace Walpole, writing to Sir Horace Mann from an inn at Newmarket, criticized the furnishing, though admitted that he would have thought it "a paradise" compared with an Italian inn. The letter was dated October 3, 1743, and he said: "Now I am relapsed into all the dissatisfied repinement of a true English grumbling voluptuary. I could find it in my heart to write a *Craftsman* against the Government, because I am not so much at ease as on my own sofa. I could persuade myself that it is my Lord Carteret's fault that I am sitting in a common arm-chair, when I would be lolling in a *péché-mortel*." A *péché-mortel* was a couch, of the type described by Ince and Mayhew as "single-headed". One is illustrated on plate LXIV of *The Universal System of Household Furniture*; Chippendale includes two on plate XXXII of the *Director*, which he described, referring to their French name, as follows: "They are sometimes made to take asunder in the Middle; one Part makes a large Easy-Chair, and the other a stool,

A lady's dressing stool, with an X-shaped underframe formed by elongated scroll supports. Reproduced from plate XXXIV of *The Universal System of Household Furniture*, by Ince and Mayhew.

and the Feet join in the Middle, which looks badly." Just how badly this severance would look, may be judged from the reproduction of Chippendale's two designs on pages 140 and 141. This type of seat was graciously luxurious, as Thomas Gray implies in his letter from Cambridge to Edward Bedingfield, dated December 29, 1756, when he wrote: "*Frere Thomas* is not so devoted to his books or orisons as to forget the promise you have made him; & whenever any occasion calls you this way, his *other* Great-Chair holds open its arms to receive you, if not with all the grace, yet with as much good-will, as any Dutchesses quilted Péché-Mortel, or Sofa with triple gold-fringe."

Although the single-headed couch could be made "to take asunder in the Middle," so you were left with a half-couch or burjair and a long stool, a far more gracefully divisible long seat was the duchesse, which consisted of two tub-backed easy chairs with a stool between them. This was a well-designed version of

F

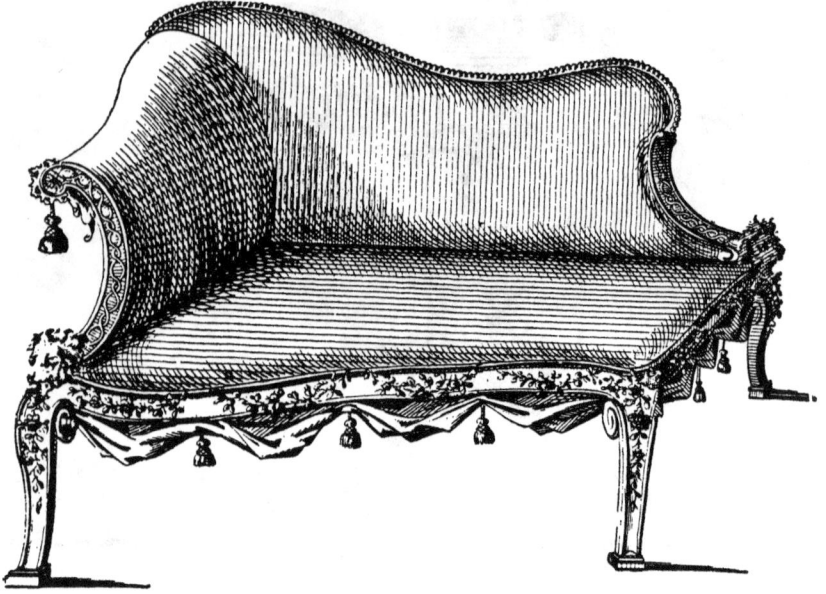

Ince and Mayhew gave two designs for French corner chairs or settees, and this example shows that such seats suffered no loss of elegance from being asymmetrical. Reproduced from plate LVII of *The Universal System of Household Furniture.*

that rather clumsy easy chair with square stools hooked on to it to form a couch, mentioned in the will of Celia Fiennes and referred to in the last chapter. The reproduction on page 147 from Hepplewhite's *Guide* shows how compact and comfortable a duchesse appeared. Sheraton in *The Cabinet Dictionary* illustrates a complicated transformation of this triple seat into a bed, made by erecting a canopy over it, supported by four posts inserted into sockets at the backs of the two armchairs, which then form the head and foot of the bed, while curtains hang from the elaborately draped canopy. The duchesse was long enough to be a comfortable bed even without the canopy, but in the eighteenth century and throughout a great part of the nineteenth, a bed without curtains would hardly have been accepted as a bed at all.

Seats for use outdoors were often made to match natural sur-

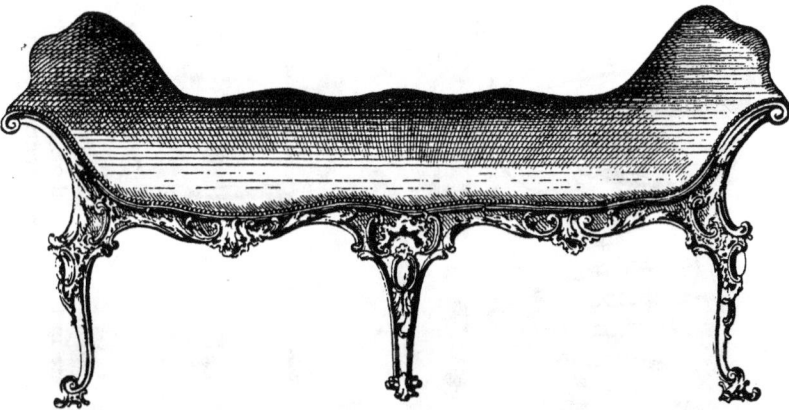

Two French stools, a term used by Ince and Mayhew for seats with curved ends and six or four legs, with or without backs. These examples, reproduced from plate LXI of *The Universal System of Household Furniture*, are described as "Designs of stools for recesses of Windows". The supporting figures at the ends of the upper seat are similar (except for their sex) to those used by Robert Adam on the sofa at the top of plate 48.

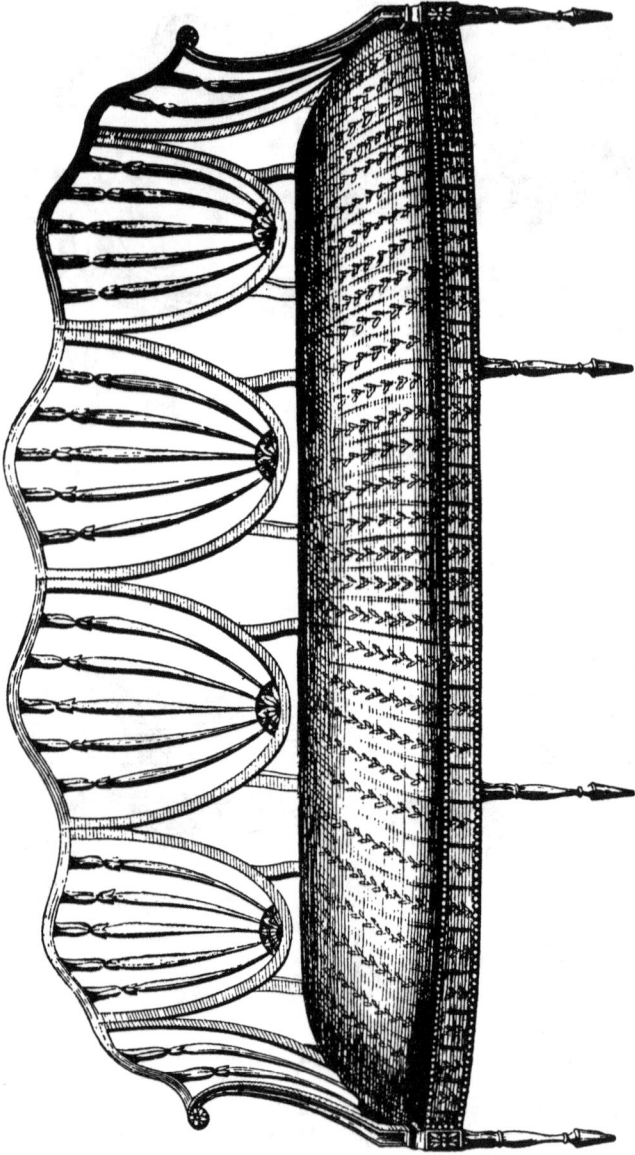

A bar-back settee, reproduced from Hepplewhite's *Guide* (1788). Unlike earlier settees with conjoined chair-backs, the shield-shaped backs are in two pairs; those in the centre being larger than the flanking pair, while the serpentine top rail is continuous with the elbows. (See page 108.)

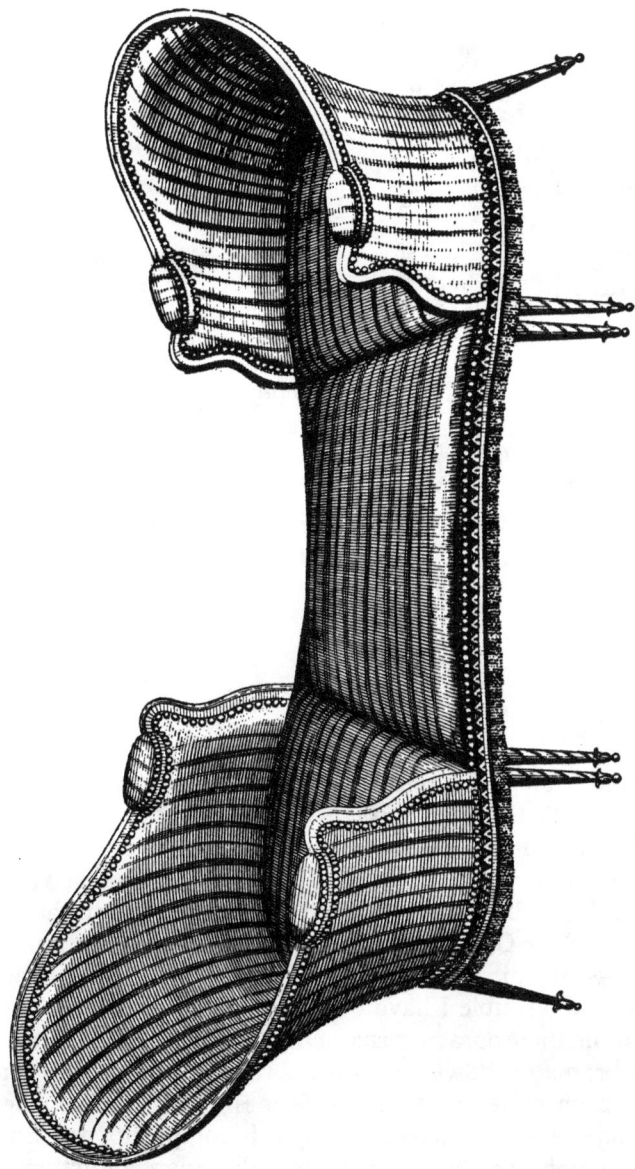

A duchesse, reproduced from Hepplewhite's *Guide* (1788). When taken apart, the duchesse was transformed into two tub-backed easy chairs and a stool. In the illustration the engraver has shown an unbroken line of braid and fringe; but this would have stopped at the junction of the chairs and stool and continued on the sides of the stool and fronts of the chairs.

A rural chair, designed for a summer house, by Robert Manwaring. *Drawn by Marcelle Barton*, from plate 27 of *The Cabinet and Chair-Maker's Real Friend and Companion* (1765).

roundings, and Manwaring included ten designs for "rural chairs" in *The Cabinet and Chair-Maker's Real Friend and Companion*, intended, as he said, for "Summer-Houses, Gardens and Parks". He claimed that they were "entirely new, and are the only ones that ever were published. . . ." He hoped they would "give general Satisfaction with respect to their Grandeur, Variety, Novelty and Usefulness; and if I succeed in this Point, I shall think myself amply satisfied for the Time and Trouble I have been at in composing them". In some of them he incorporated ornamental representations of tree-trunks and branches, flowering shrubs, rockeries, even pastoral scenes painted on panels with rococo frames. Chair-backs loaded with such subjects were remarkable for their complexity and little else, but although they anticipated the Victorian addiction to involved and overwrought naturalistic carved decoration, as seats

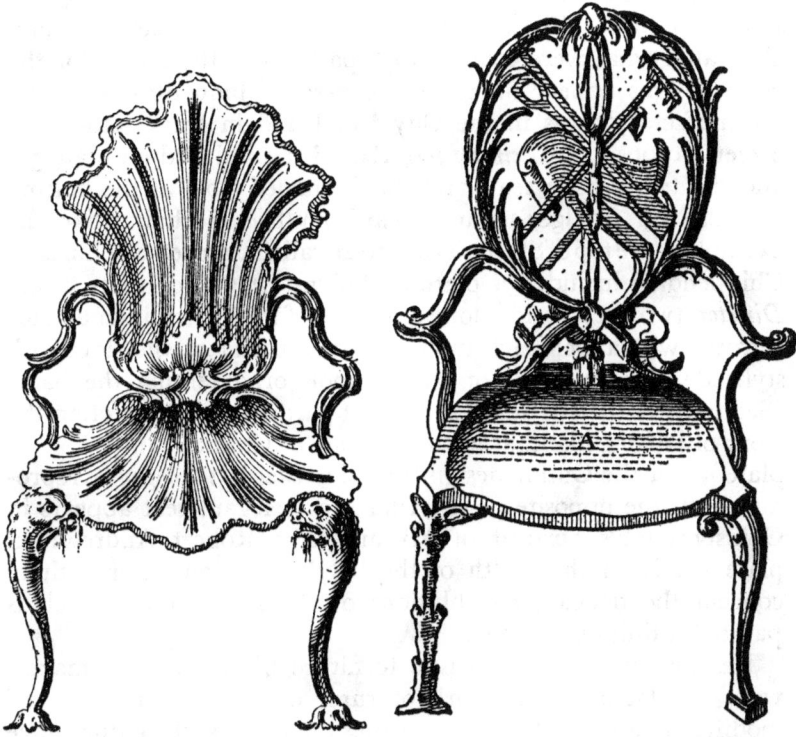

Two designs for garden chairs from plate XXIV of Chippendale's *Director*
(third edition). The decorative motifs are handled in an orderly manner, and
in the right hand example alternative suggestions are given for the legs.
Chippendale described such seats as "proper for arbours, or summer houses".
They are less complex than the "Rural Chair" on the opposite page, and far
more graceful than the examples of seats on page 151.

they retained basic good proportions. Sometimes the term "Forest
chair" was used, and it occurs in an advertisement published in
Jackson's Oxford Journal, July 13, 1754, when William Partridge, a
cabinet-maker, included among his wares, "Garden Seats,
Windsor and Forrest Chairs and Stools, in the modern Gothic, and
Chinese Taste. . . ." The "rural" seats retained their popularity
for a long time, especially those that looked as if they were constructed from logs and branches. Lock^n Foulger, chair-maker "at

Wallam Green" issued a trade card, *circa* 1773, advertising "all sorts of Windsor Chairs, Garden seats, Rural Settees &c" and illustrated what were clearly stock patterns of the latter, for the same designs appear on the trade card of John Stubbs, whose "Manufactory" was in the City Road and in Brick Lane, Old Street. Stubbs's card, *circa* 1790–1803, is reproduced on plate 51, and the two garden seats and the X-shaped stool at the bottom are also on Foulger's earlier card. (Wheeled chairs, like the example at the top of Stubbs's card were called "garden machines".) Chippendale included a plate of designs for garden seats in the *Director*, two chairs and a long seat; one of the chairs, intended for a grotto, with a shell back and seat and dolphin legs, the other with stylized representations of garden tools ornamenting the back. (See page 149.) The simpler types of garden seats were often the work of joiners, like that in the portrait of Charles James Fox on plate 51, or the Gothic design from *The Builder's Companion* reproduced on the opposite page. A far more elegant seat appears in Gainsborough's portrait of Mr and Mrs Robert Andrews on plate 50. Even the width of the lady's dress does not entirely conceal the delicate convolutions of the iron frame, which is painted a dull olive green.

Designs for rural and rustic furniture by fashionable makers were unrelated to the work of rural craftsmen, whose adroit modifications of modish styles during the eighteenth century gave fresh direction to the native English style. Back-stools with horizontal members linking the uprights had been introduced early in the seventeenth century, and the slat-back chair with three, four, five and sometimes six cut and shaped slats, was elaborated later, though it was known in an elementary form in the mid-fourteenth century, as mentioned in chapter 3 and illustrated by the school scene on plate 12. These ladder-back chairs, originally developed in the countryside, were adopted by town makers, who gave them such refinements as dipped seats, back slats shaped like a cupid's bow, and pierced with openings resembling the sound holes of a violin, from which, as mentioned in the previous chapter, the contemporary name of fiddle-back arose. A rush-seated ladder-back chair is illustrated on the right of the trade card of Stubbs's Manufactory on plate 51. Two examples of the town-made types are shown on page 153.

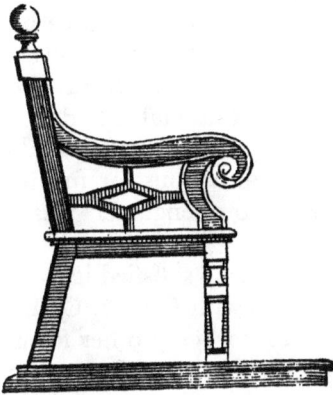

Above: Many garden seats were made by joiners, like this example, which is drawn from the portrait of Charles James Fox on plate 51. *Left and below:* The back and profile of a garden seat in the "Gothick taste". The pattern of the back, like that of the seat above, might equally well be labelled "Chinese". The bowed top rail curls into scrolls in the centre, and a split baluster is applied to the side of the front leg. Reproduced from plate 89 of *The Builder's Companion, and Workman's General Assistant,* by William Pain. (London: printed for Robert Sayer. Third edition, 1769.) The author described himself on the title page as "Architect and Joiner".

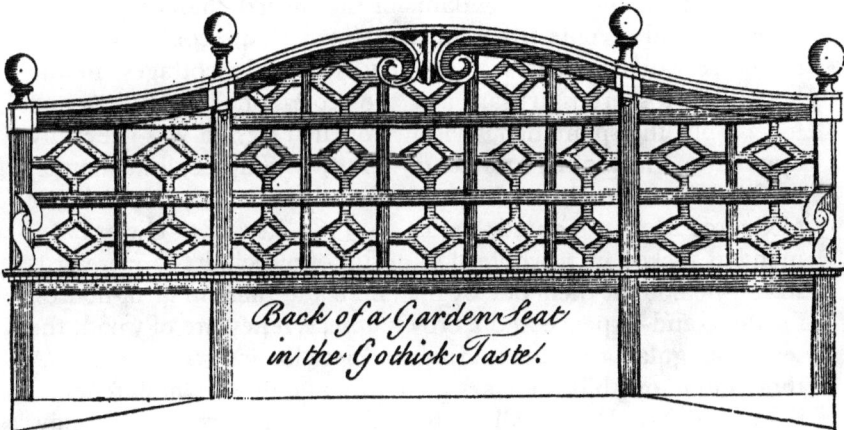

Back of a Garden Seat in the Gothick Taste.

Occasionally fashionable makers executed orders for the simple kind of work that was usually entrusted to country craftsmen. R. W. Symonds has recorded "the retail price of five shillings and sixpence that Chippendale charged for a plain but completed yolk-back chair when he sold a set of eight to Sir Rowland Winn". The original creative powers of the country maker were recognized by his fellow tradesmen in the towns; but after the end of the century, when the professional, scholarly designer, with a head full of Greek and Roman ornamental motifs, began to control taste, the work of the man at the bench was contemptuously played down. Thomas Hope's references to the "mere plodding artisan" and Richard Brown's to "mere plodding mechanics" have been quoted in chapter 2, and they typified the detachment of early nineteenth century furniture designers from the structural problems, the skills, and the materials that the actual maker had to live with, understand and master. The result of that separation between designer and craftsman was as disastrous for furniture design as the separation of architect from engineer was for architecture.

While the modish world and the makers who satisfied its whims and graceful extravagances were occupied with Gothic, Chinese, rococo, even Indian variations of chairs and every other form of seat, and presently with the classical revival inspired by the work of Robert Adam, the country makers, as richly inventive as their mediaeval forerunners, were producing ranges of chairs with graces of their own—descendants of the turned chairs of the late sixteenth and seventeenth centuries. Such chairs could be found in the servants' quarters of country houses, in cottages, in the houses of prosperous artisans and the professional classes in small towns; but the spontaneous vitality of their design was generally ignored by the nobility and gentry. Horace Walpole, for example, preferred to collect their more primitive predecessors. In a letter to George Montagu dated August 20, 1761, he said: "Dicky Bateman has picked up a whole cloister full of old chairs in Herefordshire—he bought them one by one, here and there in farm-houses, for three-and-sixpence and a crown apiece. They are of wood, the seats triangular, the backs, arms, and legs loaded with turnery. A thousand to one but there are plenty up and down Cheshire too—if Mr and Mrs Wetenhall, as they ride or drive out, would now

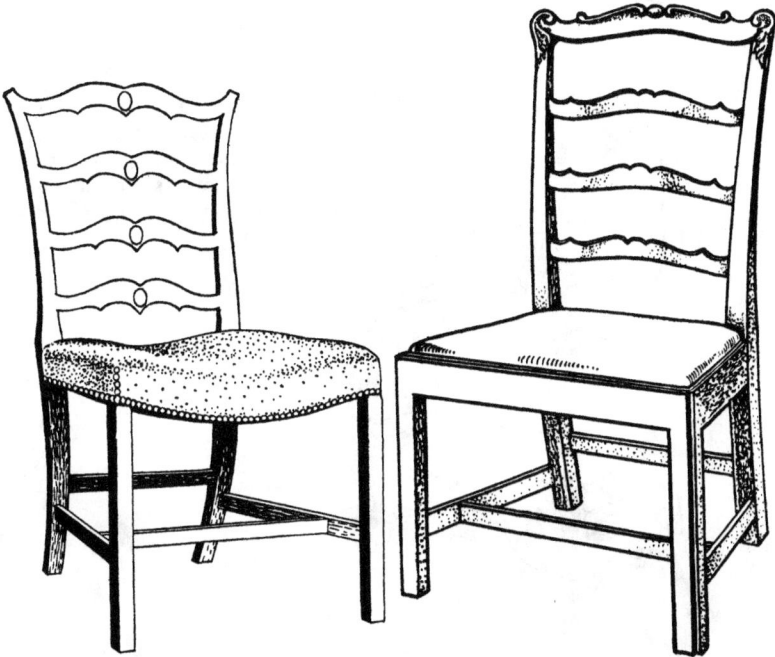

Ladder-back is a modern term for a chair with horizontal slats or rails linking the back uprights; a structural form used by mediaeval craftsmen, as the mid-fourteenth century example on plate 12 testifies, and persisting in the countryside, until its decorative possibilities were recognized by town makers. Late in the seventeenth century, tall ladder-back chairs were occasionally made, with rails in the form of double scrolls; but these were rare, and the more familiar type with four rails, like those shown above, was developed during the second half of the eighteenth century. A very simple rush-seated ladder-back chair appears on the right of the trade card reproduced on plate 51.

and then put up such a chair, it would oblige me greatly. Take notice, no two need be of the same pattern."

The operative word in that letter is *cloister:* in the eyes of the master of Strawberry Hill, such chairs had an authentic "Gothic" air, and as they had been made by men working in a mediaeval tradition he was not deceiving himself, although apparently

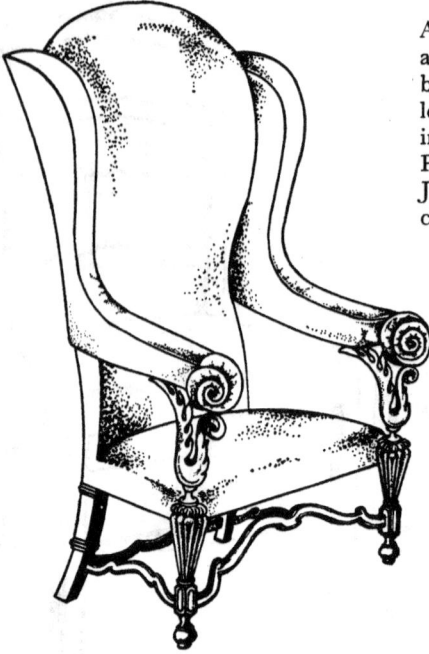

A high-backed winged chair, open at the sides, with arms supported by scrolls, tapering fluted front legs, splayed back legs, and a rising arched stretcher. Alexander Pope, in the portrait painted by Jervas, is shown seated in such a chair. *Drawn by Marcelle Barton.*

unaware that the tradition was still alive in his own day in the form of the Windsor chair. Stick construction and the origin of the Windsor chair have been touched on briefly in chapter 6, and the evolution of that chair and the work of country makers, are described in the next chapter.

During the second half of the eighteenth century, the technique of buttoning gave fresh decorative character to upholstered furniture, and also increased comfort when leather was used as a covering. The French stool reproduced at the top of page 145, from *The Universal System of Household Furniture*, appears to be finished by this method, as the fuzzy, star-shaped marks spotted over the seat, back and ends were probably the best the draughtsman and engraver could do to represent the depressions made by the buttons in the covering material. The inclusion of an example of buttoning by Ince and Mayhew suggests a date between 1759 and 1762, though the method was almost certainly known earlier.

The winged easy chair, introduced in the late seventeenth century, and made with minor variations of the basic form for over two hundred and fifty years. This plain, country-made example with a mahogany underframe, is closely related to Hepplewhite's "Saddle check" on page 157. The sleeping chairs on plate 29 are winged, so is the example on the frontispiece and the mid-twentieth-century settee on plate 64. *Drawn by Ronald Escott.*

By the 1780s it was used to give a bold, quilted effect, like that displayed by the buttoned leather settee from Hatfield House illustrated on plate 49. Although primarily a decorative device, the method produced a hard-wearing and resilient surface. The back and seat of the chair or sofa were well padded, covered with light canvas, while the material was stretched into place more loosely than for ordinary upholstered work before it was attached to the outer frame. Strong thread was then stitched through the padding and outer cover to the back, the stitches pulled in tightly to draw the padding and covering into a form of quilting, and hidden by a button, usually of the same material as the cover. The

chair or settee back was then covered to conceal the stitching that
had been taken through from the front. The buttons were disposed
in a regular pattern, generally in the form of elongated diamonds
and half-diamonds, though squares were used occasionally.
Coach-builders, who used this technique extensively for the interior
lining of all kinds of vehicles, described it as quilting; and from the
early days of rail travel, to the 1930s, buttoning was used in first
class compartments, with three upholstered seats a side, divided
by arm-rests and winged side-pieces, so their resemblance to high-
backed easy chairs justified Harriet Beecher Stowe's remark that in
England "every arrangement in travelling is designed to maintain
that privacy and reserve which is the dearest and most sacred part
of an Englishman's nature". When he travelled by train, the
Englishman's easy chair went along too, if he could afford the
fare. Mrs Stowe also observed that the "first-class cars are beyond
all praise, but also beyond all price"; while second class "are
comfortless, cushionless, and uninviting". She wrote that in 1853;
Abraham Solomon's painting, "The Return", reproduced on
plate 49, was executed in 1855; the first-class compartment he
depicted has buttoned upholstery similar to that used on the settee,
circa 1785, which is shown on the same plate, and the seat divisions are identical with the wings of the chair illustrated on page
155, and in some types of compartment they closely resembled the
Hepplewhite "saddle check" chair shown opposite. The railway
carriage inherited buttoned upholstery and winged divisions from
the interior of the passenger coach, which had in turn inherited
them from the high-backed easy chair.

Chippendale, Ince and Mayhew, Manwaring and other makers
who designed chairs during the third quarter of the eighteenth
century, were affected by two streams of taste, Gothic and Chinese,
the latter mingling with the rococo style, which came from France,
frothing with gaiety and occasionally exhibiting structural irres-
ponsibility. Such engaging eccentricities of shape and ornament
were more or less soberly anglicized but were not uncritically
accepted, for English society was not fashion-ridden like French
society, nor was luxury the governing motive of design among
English craftsmen, whose work was never divorced from reality
like that of their French contemporaries. The fragile ribbon-back
chairs designed by Chippendale are a rare instance of material

This winged chair, reproduced from plate 15 of Hepplewhite's *Guide* (1788), is described as "a design for a Saddle Check, or easy chair; the construction and use of which is very apparent; they may be covered with leather, horsehair; or have a linen case to fit over the canvas stuffing". The shape of the wings has some resemblance to that of a saddle, which may account for the name. (See page 155.)

Shield-back chair with a vase splat. Reproduced from Hepplewhite's *Guide* (1788). Compare this treatment of the shield shape with the settee on page 146. The turned, tapering legs are fluted.

misused in the interests of ornament, for the attempt to simulate a silk ribbon in wood with the grain running in all directions was structurally unsound, even when such a fine, tractable wood as mahogany was employed.

William Whitehead, writing in *The World*, in March 1753, deplored the popularity of exotic oriental fashions. "According to the present prevailing whim," he wrote, "everything is Chinese, or in the Chinese taste; or as it is sometimes more modestly expressed, *partly after the Chinese manner*. Chairs, tables, chimney-pieces, frames for looking-glasses, and even our most vulgar utensils, are all reduced to this new-fangled standard...." Sir William Chambers, who had travelled in the East and had first-hand knowledge of Chinese architecture and decoration, published an authoritative treatise in 1757 entitled *Designs of Chinese Buildings, Furniture, Dresses, Machines, and Utensils*, which begot fresh enthusiasm for the Chinese taste. But neither Chinese nor Gothic furniture fashions diminished the universal respect for the classic idiom; they were as ephemeral as fashions in hats, walking canes, snuffboxes or coach painting, and their popularity declined when Robert Adam created a new, delicate style that became identified with national taste during the last three decades of the eighteenth century, and profoundly affected the work of all cabinet and chair makers. That style was based on a fresh interpretation of classical architecture and ornament, following Adam's prolonged and exacting study of antique remains in Italy; but the public responded to the gay femininity of his designs rather than to the authenticity of their classical derivation. Not that there was anything flimsy or fragile about Adam furniture; no Adam chair could ever be described, in the words of Marryat's Mr Turnbull in *Jacob Faithful*, as "one of those spider-like French things".

Perhaps the most comprehensive record of Robert Adam's contribution to furniture design is the large collection of his original drawings, preserved in Sir John Soane's Museum. Subjects reproduced from that collection appear on plates 46 to 48, and they illustrate his masterly use of classical motifs. The controlled sprightliness of ornament on Adam chairs and furniture, while very different from the wanton frivolity of French rococo, had affinities with contemporary French design: for example, the oval-backed armchair, made for the bed chamber at Osterly House (which Adam remodelled for Robert Child, 1761–80), is a lighter version of a comparable Louis XVI chair: both are shown on plate 47. Like Kent, he designed complete buildings, with interior decoration and furniture; such individual articles as chairs and seats being elements in a grand conception, which included every-thing—fireplaces, grates, door knockers, carpets, curtains, chande-liers: all related in style, all expressing, individually and collec-tively, a neo-classical revival. The authority of the Adam style remained undisturbed until the close of the century when the Greek Revival introduced new fashions, encouraged fresh studies of antique prototypes, and perhaps made some modish people agree with Horace Walpole who had once said, in a letter to Sir Horace Mann (April 22, 1775), that "Adam, our most admired, is all gingerbread, filigraine, and fan-painting". But Walpole, who could seldom resist sharpening a phrase, was an inconsistent connoisseur of architecture and design, and would have been far less amusing and readable without the pungency of his prejudices. His reference to gingerbread meant gilding, for gingerbread cakes ornamented with gold leaf were sold at fairs, and Adam used gilding extensively and had transformed the character of gilded chairs. Hitherto such chairs had been heavy and overburdened with carved ornament; their shape still oppressed by the early Georgian corpulence that Kent's work had emphasized rather than mitigated; but the change of form that Adam introduced was as sweeping as the changes made by curvilinear design early in the century. His lighter and more subtle use of carved embellish-ment, his introduction of oval and shield-shaped backs, dispelled the ornate, overdressed look that had frequently marred even the most skilful of Chippendale's examples in the *Director*.

Demand for elegant gilded chairs increased, so did the number of master furniture carvers and gilders in London, and it has been estimated that by the 1790s there were over one hundred and fifty of them in business and more than thirty specialists in water-gild-ing in addition. The difference between the processes of water and oil gilding has been described in Chapter 6, and both were used, but, as Sheraton pointed out in *The Cabinet Dictionary*, the gilding of chairs was a branch "in some respects, conducted differently from the others in oil and water . . . though the principles of both are the same. The difference is chiefly in point of time, as the chair

Left: The anthemion motif, used in an oval chair back. (See illustrations on page 20). Like the lyre, it was one of the ornamental devices introduced during the Adam neo-classical revival. *Right:* A late eighteenth century American version of the lyre-back. *Drawn by Ronald Escott.*

branch requires the utmost dispatch, that the work may be kept clean, and quickly turned out of hand." Nearly two of the ten and a quarter pages he devoted to gilding were concerned with the methods used for chairs. (See Appendix II, page 289.)

Gilded chairs gleamed in every drawing room and boudoir, in bedrooms too; and when Lord Chesterfield was visited, half an hour before he died, by his friend and protégé, Solomon Dayrolles, the servant who obeyed the nobleman's last words, "Give Dayrolles a chair", almost certainly handed the visitor something gilded, most probably in the French taste. Many upholstered chairs in the Adam style were very close in design to those produced by Parisian makers, though more restrained in the use of carved

A bedroom chair, designed by Sheraton. From plate 30 of *The Cabinet Dictionary* (1803).

ornament, and the general resemblance of the two examples on plate 47 has already been mentioned. The frames were of mahogany, more rarely of satinwood, sometimes of beech, japanned in black and gold or in colours on a neutral ground, like grey. Sheraton describes the imitation of bamboo, which was used for chairs in the east. "These are," he said, "in some degree, imitated in England, by turning beech into the same form, and making chairs of this fashion, painting them to match the colour of the reeds or cane."

The form and finish of chair frames exhibited a new lightness of touch; when oval and shield backs were not upholstered they were animated by new treatments of splats and bars, that included ostrich plumes, lattice work, canework which sometimes surrounded a circular or oval plaque, motifs such as the lyre, the honeysuckle or anthemion, husks, carved draperies, elaborations of the vase and urn, as in the example on page 158, or radiating bars, like the settee on page 146. The older form of back, with vertical uprights and top rail, was reintroduced and given a new look, a rectangular tablet often breaking the top rail, delicately painted with wreaths and festoons of flowers, with classical scenes, or even inlaid with a Wedgwood plaque. So long as such decorative features were under the control of competent chair makers comfort was undisturbed; but after the turn of the century, when an appetite for novelty and the increasing influence of academic men of taste were beginning to destroy the graces of Georgian design, comfort was sacrificed. Early in the 1820s, Richard Brown made a critical comment about dining-room chairs. "This article has lately undergone a far greater improvement than any other branch of the cabinet art," he wrote, "insomuch that it now baffles the most skilful artist to produce any new forms: still, however, many chairs are very uncomfortable to sit upon, in consequence of the raised carved work on the splat and tablet of the yoke rail, though ease should be the great desideratum."

The impact of the Adam style on chair-makers is apparent in the later work of Thomas Chippendale and his son, also named Thomas, who carried on the business after his father's death in 1779. The published designs of Hepplewhite and Sheraton owe much to the example of Adam's designs, and this is particularly noticeable in the plates of *The Cabinet-Maker and Upholsterer's Guide*, made "from drawings by A. Hepplewhite and Co. Cabinet-Makers", and issued in 1788, two years after Hepplewhite's death, presumably by his widow, Alice, who was running the business at Redcross Street. New editions of this folio volume came out in 1789 and 1794, and in the third edition the section on chairs was revised, and examples of the new fashionable versions of the square-backed types were included. The oval, heart-shaped and shield-shaped backs, though represented in the *Guide*, were not originated by Hepplewhite. Like Chippendale's designs in the *Director*, and those by Ince and Mayhew in *The Universal System*, Hepplewhite's chairs and stools and settees reflected current trends in the chair-making trade. Heart-shaped and shield-backed chairs were being made outside of London; by Gillows, for instance, the Lancaster cabinet-makers to whom Hepplewhite had been apprenticed. That firm supplied a set of fourteen chairs with heart-shaped backs to the order of John Christian for the dining room of Workington Hall, Cumberland, between 1788 and 1790, and the design was recorded in the Gillow cost books. Incidentally, those chairs had stretchers, which indicated their north country origin, for comparable London-made types were without stretchers. The Lancaster business had been founded by Robert Gillow, a joiner, who had moved there from Great Singleton in the parish of Kirkham-in-the-Fylde and established himself about 1695. He prospered, was made a freeman of Lancaster in 1728, and his firm's records go back to 1731, when they were engaged chiefly in building and surveying. As those records have been preserved, we know far more about the Gillow family and business than we do about Hepplewhite. Richard Gillow, the son of Robert, was trained as an architect, and designed the Custom House at Lancaster, a building that showed, like the furniture made by the firm, the supremacy of the Adam style. During the middle years of the century, Gillows had been sending large quantities of furniture to London, and about 1761 they opened a branch there in the Tiburn Road, the former name of Oxford Street, on a site continuously occupied by the firm, which built up and maintained a flourishing business. (The firm is now represented by Waring and Gillow Limited.)

Hepplewhite's *Guide*, when it first appeared in 1788, included some 300 designs, engraved on 126 plates, preceded by these brief directions about proportions, materials and finish: "The general dimension and proportion of chairs are as follows: Width in front 20 inches, depth of seat 17 inches, height of the seat frame 17 inches, total height about 3 feet 1 inch. Other dimensions are frequently adapted according to the size of the room, or pleasure of the purchaser. Chairs in general are of mahogany, with the bars and frames sunk in a hollow, or rising in a round projection, with a band or list on the inner and outer edges." Seats for mahogany chairs should be "of horsehair, plain, striped, chequered, &c. at

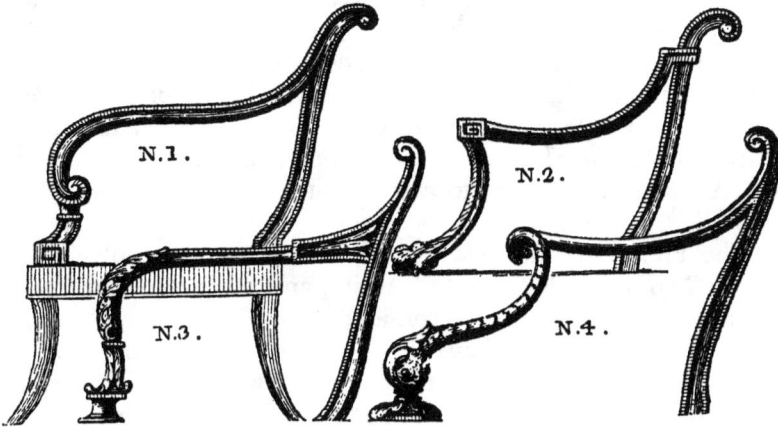

Four designs for chair arms by Sheraton, reproduced from plate 2 of *The Cabinet Dictionary* (1803). In the directions for execution, he said "Nos. 1, 2 and 4, whether made of beech or mahogany, should have the toe carved. No. 3 may have ornament painted, with carving." Such slender and elegant lines replaced the robust scroll-over arms of early Georgian chairs.

pleasure". Designs with splats in the form of plumes, variations on the vase motif, interlaced, looped or festooned, were described as "banister back" chairs, and those with stuffed backs were called "cabriole chairs". This accords with Sheraton's definition of a cabriole, quoted in the previous chapter, as an "armchair stuffed all over"; and this term, in current use during the latter part of the eighteenth century, appears in the *Bristol Journal*, for February 22, 1783, where an advertisement notifying a sale at St James's in London, included the items "Drawing room Cabriole Chairs and Soffa, cover'd with blue Morine. . . ." Another announcement in the same newspaper for April 16, 1783, reads thus: "For sale. Mrs Gordon, Abbots Leigh Court, Somerset. Sophas and Cabriole Chairs to match, in great perfection. . . ." The stuffed backs of cabriole chairs could be heart or shield-shaped. The term "banister back" apparently applied both to mahogany and japanned chairs, and the latter represented "a new and very elegant fashion", as painted or japanned work gave "a rich and splendid appearance to the minuter parts of the ornaments, which are generally thrown in by the painter". Japanned chairs could have a frame-work" less massy than is requisite for mahogany; and by assorting the prevailing colour to the furniture and light of the room, affords opportunity, by the variety of grounds which may be introduced, to make the whole accord in harmony, with a pleasing and striking effect to the eye. Japanned chairs should always have linen or cotton cases or cushions to accord with the general hue of the chair."

The Preface to the *Guide* begins with a correctly noble sentiment. "To unite elegance and utility, and blend the useful with the agreeable, has ever been considered a difficult, but an honourable task. How far we have succeeded in the following work it becomes not us to say, but rather to leave it, with all due deference, to the determination of the Public at large." But the humble opening sentences are cancelled out by a peevish air of superiority in the third paragraph, which asserts that "English taste and workmanship have, of late years, been much sought for by surrounding nations; and the mutability of all things, but more especially of fashions, has rendered the labours of our predecessors in this line of little use: nay, at this day, they can only tend to mislead those Foreigners, who seek a knowledge of English taste in the various articles of household furniture". Like Chippendale's *Director*, the *Guide* was intended to double the part of catalogue and copy book, and its usefulness to country makers is emphasized, though apart from a scale of measurements there are no technical notes like those Chippendale gave for his designs. The plates include single and armchairs, hall chairs, a clumsy winged easy chair, called a "saddle check", settees, sofas, stools, window stools, the combination of two chairs and a stool called a duchess, and specialized articles, like the adjustable foot rest for those afflicted with gout. Some of these are sparsely described. For example, "Two Barjur chairs, of proper construction, with a stool in the middle, form the duchesse, which is allotted to large and spacious anti-rooms: the covering may be various, as also the frame-work, and made from 6 to 8 feet long." (See page 147.) The bar-back settee or sofa "is of modern invention; and the lightness of its appearance has procured it a favourable reception in the first circles of fashion. The pattern of the back must match the chairs; these also will regulate the sort of frame-work and covering". (See page 146.)

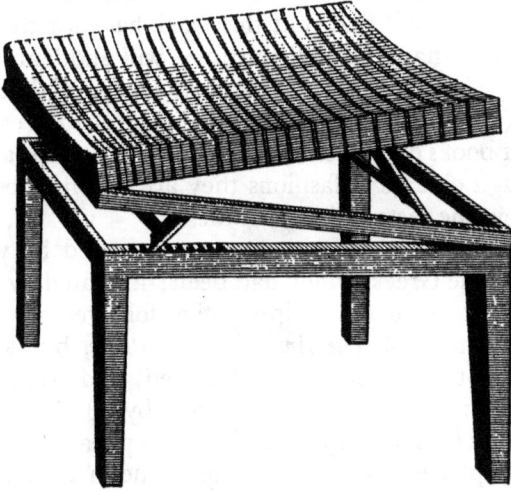

A gout or gouty stool, with an adjustable seat, designed for resting the feet of gentlemen afflicted with the complaint. From Hepplewhite's *Guide* (1788).

The Gouty stool, "the construction of which, by being so easily raised or lowered at either end, is particularly useful to the afflicted", was also known as a gout stool, a name used for a comparable design included in *The Prices of Cabinet Work* (1797 edition), and also by Boswell, for when he called on Mr Pitt in Bond Street during February, 1766, over twenty years before the *Guide* appeared, he found him attired "in black clothes, with white nightcap and foot all wrapped up in flannel and on gout-stool". (See above.) This was an accepted and quite ordinary item of furniture in a gentleman's household.

In order to keep in with "the first circles of fashion", tradesmen may have felt obliged to disparage their predecessors, for the critical remarks about earlier makers in the preface of Hepplewhite's *Guide* were amplified by Sheraton in *The Cabinet-Maker and Upholsterer's Drawing-Book*, which he published in four parts, between 1791 and 1794. His introduction was addressed to "Cabinet-Makers and Upholsterers in General", and he attacked the *Guide* by saying "notwithstanding the late date of Hepplewhite's book, if we compare some of the designs, particularly the chairs, with the newest taste, we shall find that this work has already caught the decline, and perhaps, in a little time, will suddenly die of the disorder. This instance may serve to convince us of that fate which all books of the same kind will ever be subject to. Yet it must be owned, that books of this sort have their usefulness for a time; and, when through change of fashions they are become obsolete, they serve to shew the taste of former times."

The "newest taste" in the 1790s was affected by yet another revival, this time Greek, which had been stimulated by the interest in Greek architecture and sculpture that followed the publication of the first volume of *The Antiquities of Athens*, by James Stuart ("Athenian" Stuart as he was nicknamed) and Nicholas Revett. Altogether four volumes were published by 1814, and in 1830 a supplement on *Athenian Sepulchral Marbles* appeared; but, as mentioned in chapter 2, the issue of volume one in 1762 was the real starting point of the Greek Revival. From the last decade of the eighteenth century until the early Victorian period the potent influence of that revival on architecture and furniture design—chairs, especially—was comparable to that exerted by Adam's classical revival thirty years earlier, though unlike the Adam style it was not accepted as a national form of taste. Interest in Greek prototypes for architecture, ornament and furniture developed at a time when the taste for Gothic was beginning to change from a polite antiquarian diversion that amused rich, worldly and fashionable people, into something sombre, almost sinister. A preference for Gothic architecture became an indication of serious purpose, of moral earnestness, of participation in a spiritual crusade against the covert paganism of all classic forms, whether derived from Greek or Roman sources, or edited by Renaissance architects and designers. This substitution of piety for gaiety was one of the causes of the "Battle of the Styles" in mid-nineteenth century architecture, that had such regrettable results for nearly all branches of design; but no warning shadows of such a futile conflict darkened the serenity of the Georgian scene in the 1790s, when Sheraton was a middle-aged man, establishing himself as a furniture designer and drawing master, and young Thomas Hope was completing his travels in Europe, North Africa and the Middle East, studying architecture and sculpture, collecting

An armchair for a drawing room, with a stuffed top rail and a square panel
in the back. "This chair would look well in mahogany," said Sheraton, "with
a brass bead round the stuffing to hide the tacks, &c. and which produces a
lively effect." Reproduced from plate 3 of *The Cabinet Dictionary* (1803).
Compare this design with the two cane-seated armchairs on plate 52.

antique objects and exotic ideas and preparing himself to be an
academic man of taste.

The most conspicuous effect of the Greek Revival on chair
design was the reappearance of the *klismos*, virtually unchanged in
form. English makers and designers interpreted the graceful lines
of this Greek chair with skill and sympathy, and adopted the
splayed, concave legs, which remained fashionable throughout the
Regency period. They were called sabre, scimitar, and, after 1815,
"Waterloo" legs, though the use of that last term brought a sharp
reproof from Richard Brown, who observed "that many cabinet-
makers, for the sake of notoriety, ridiculously give names to furni-

A Herculanium armchair, "so named on account of their antique style of composition", as Sheraton explained. This type was, he said, "peculiarly adapted to rooms, fitted up not only in the antique taste, but where apartments are appropriated for the purpose of exhibiting ancient or modern curiosities; and we particularly recommend them for the use of music rooms." From plate 7 of *The Cabinet Dictionary* (1803).

ture quite inconsistent, such as Trafalgar chairs, Waterloo feet &c." (Sheraton had celebrated Nelson's victory by designing some "Trafalgar" chairs of a highly complex character, with an anchor in the back and two dolphins, tied together with ribbon, serving as front legs.) The influence of the resurrected *klismos* is shown on page 15 and plates 7 and 55 to 58. Some of the derivative designs were heavy by comparison with the Greek prototype, though the elegance evolved in the fifth and fourth centuries BC was never wholly lost.

Sheraton's contributions to the "newest taste" in chairs were immensely varied though uneven in quality; his designs had a wide and sustained influence in the furniture trade, for his *Drawing-Book* attracted about 600 subscribers, including cabinet-makers and joiners, all over England, and a third edition was issued in 1802. We know more about Sheraton as a man than we do about Thomas Chippendale or Hepplewhite, who remains a shadowy figure, tenuously connected with Gillow; but we know that Sheraton was a deeply religious, humble, and unfortunately versatile man. His first book, published in Stockton in 1782, was *A Scriptural Illustration of the Doctrine of Regeneration*, and he appears on the title page as Thomas Sheraton, junior, describing himself as a mechanic; his last, published in 1805, the year before his death, was *A Discourse on the Character of God as Love*. According to the *Dictionary of National Biography* he was a zealous Baptist. His humbleness and uncommercial attitude to life are disclosed by the explanatory remarks he made after he had advocated the establishment of a public wood-yard, which "would greatly contribute towards the improvement of cabinet making in general, so that by such like institutions, in time, London might be a more famous market for every species of cabinet work, that Paris now is. [This was published in *The Cabinet Dictionary* in 1803 after the peace of Amiens had temporarily restored communication with France.] I mention these things," he continued, "with a view to the national credit, and the benefit of trade, and not from my own desire to recommend any extravagant steps in the purchase of grand furniture; for I can assure the reader, though I am thus employed in racking my invention to design fine and pleasing cabinet work, I can be well content to sit on a wooden bottom chair myself, provided I can but have common food and raiment wherewith to pass through life in peace."

His versatility is attested by Adam Black, founder of the publishing house of A. & C. Black, who came to England from Edinburgh as a young man to get experience of the London book trade, and lodged with Sheraton, whose home he described as "half shop, half dwelling-house". Sheraton was then living in great poverty, and in a diary addressed to his parents Black said he was "a man of talents, and, I believe, of genuine piety. He understands the cabinet-business—I believe was bred to it; he has been, and per-

A curricle armchair, designed by Sheraton. From plate 6 of *The Cabinet Dictionary* (1803). The name was suggested by a two-wheeled vehicle, that was described by William Felton in *A Treatise on Carriages* (1794), as "the chair-back curricle. . . ." (Chapter II, page 44.) A variation of the curricle armchair appears in the portrait of Henry Richard Vassal Fox, third Baron Holland, on plate 44.

haps at present is, a preacher; he is a scholar, writes well; draws, in my opinion, masterly; is an author, bookseller, stationer, and teacher. We may be ready to ask how it comes to pass that a man with such abilities and resources is in such a state? I believe his abilities and resources are his ruin, in this respect, for by attempting to do everything he does nothing."

This was the unpretentious and unbusinesslike man who gave his name to a style, entirely as a result of his published designs, for

"Drawing-room chairs", said Sheraton, who designed this example, "should always be the produce of studied elegance, though it is extremely difficult to attain to anything really novel. If those who expect the purest novelty in such compositions, would but sit down and make a trial themselves, it would teach them better how to exercise candour when they see designs of this kind." From plate 47 of *The Cabinet Dictionary* (1803).

although he was trained as a cabinet-maker, apparently he had no workshop of his own, and his trade card, issued from 106, Wardour Street, Soho, announced that T. Sheraton "Teaches Perspective, Architecture and Ornaments, makes Designs for Cabinet-Makers, and sells all kinds of Drawing Books, Etc." (Sheraton Street, between Wardour Street and Great Chapel Street, Soho, has been named after him; though he subsequently moved from that locality to 8, Broad Street, Golden Square, where he died in 1806.) Four single chairs are shown on the card, obvious products of the Greek Revival, robust descendents of the *klismos*, with lattice backs and stuffed seats. It was a small card, 2¼ inches by 3⅛ inches, a convenient size to leave with potential subscribers, for Sheraton apparently did his own travelling to collect subscriptions for his books. Apart from *The Cabinet-Maker and Upholsterer's Drawing Book*, already mentioned, he published, in 1803, *The Cabinet Dictionary*, from which various extracts have been quoted earlier, and a far more ambitious publication, *The Cabinet-Maker, Upholsterer, and General Artists' Encyclopaedia*, of which one volume only appeared in 1805. A collection of plates, drawn largely from his previous works, was published posthumously in 1812, entitled: *Designs for Household Furniture by the late T. Sheraton, cabinet-maker*. The *Drawing-Book* and *The Cabinet Dictionary* record not only his inventiveness as a designer, but his mastery of classic ornament, and his profound knowledge of materials and the technique of furniture making. He was primarily a designer, not a maker, though he had the advantage of being a practical craftsman, and his knowledge of ornament was reinforced by his personal experience as a carver. "Having possessed a strong attachment and inclination for carving, in my youth," he explained, "I was necessarily induced to make attempts in this art, and on succeeding in some degree, I was employed in the country occasionally in it, and therefore, from some experience, I make some remarks on the practice." Those remarks, which appear in *The Cabinet Dictionary*, classified the carver's work under four headings: architectural work, internal decorations, chair work and ship work. He said, "that the outline is the principal feature of good carving; and that on all occasions, every other thing must, if necessary be sacrificed for its preservation, particularly in bold works". Earlier he had written: "An adept in carving, is no mean person; and in reality requires more to qualify him thoroughly, than is generally apprehended; although many in this profession, as in all others, content themselves to know very little. A complete master in carving, ought to be acquainted with architecture, perspective, and, in some degree, with botany; nor should he be ignorant of the true effect of painting, nor of the structure of the human body; for, unquestionably, each of these sciences have something to do with carving. To these should be added an acquaintance with the antique ornaments."

A conversation chair designed by Sheraton on which the occupant sat facing
the back with his arms resting on the padded yoke rail.
From plate 29 of *The Cabinet Dictionary* (1803).

His chair designs in the *Drawing-Book*, accomplished, elegant,
and modish, were certainly not the work of a "mere plodding
artisan", but the creations of a craftsman accustomed to work in
the classic idiom, which recorded the fashions of the last decade of
the eighteenth century. He was a great designer, but always "a
back-room boy", handicapped by his imperfect education, his
wayward versatility, troubled perhaps by an unacknowledged
conflict between his religious enthusiasms and the dedication of his
gifts to the service of luxury, and working in an environment vastly
different from that of makers, well-established in the trade, as
Thomas Chippendale had been, and in a world apart from that of
fashionable architects like Robert Adam, or wealthy, well-
travelled amateur designers such as Thomas Hope.

G

The graces of the scroll-over arm are recalled by many of
Sheraton's chairs, and on page 165, four examples of his designs
for arms are reproduced from *The Cabinet Dictionary*. Although
many of the chairs in the *Drawing-Book* have a lightness of touch
and a refinement of line, some of Sheraton's later work was
eccentric, even clumsy, a deterioration that may have been due to
his failing invention, though possibly he was affected by the
incipient coarseness of early nineteenth century taste. Despite the
refinements of Regency chairs, and the slender beauty of line
introduced by the Greek Revival, there were indications of grossness in such works as *A Collection of Designs for Household Furniture
and Interior Decoration*, issued in 1808 by George Smith, upholder
and cabinet-maker to the Prince of Wales. Even when Sheraton
designed elaborate and unusual chairs, like the Herculanium and
the drawing-room model on pages 170 and 173, he never forgot
"that the outline is the principal feature of good carving", and
seldom used a chair, or any other article, as a framework for
supporting a load of ornament. The Herculanium armchair,
though ornate, is not uncomfortable; but the legs which terminate
in knurl feet lack the linear clarity of the cabriole or sabre types,
and have been so ill drawn that they appear to be structurally
unsound. Much depended upon the execution, said Sheraton,
"particularly in the carving part, and for the sake of proceeding
with certainty, a full-sized drawing ought to be made in order to
judge of the effect". The designs for Herculanium and drawing-
room chairs appeared in *The Cabinet Dictionary*, where the standard
of draughtsmanship in the new plates is far below that of the
Drawing-Book.

Sheraton's debt to the Adam style was manifest in many of his
designs, such as the armchair on page 169; while some of the
light and graceful chairs that were typical of the last decade of the
eighteenth century, like those on plate 52, owed their suave lines
and decorative character to the combined influence of both
designers, as much to the style that Robert Adam had created as
to Sheraton's inventive genius. Mahogany was still the principal
material for frames, except when beechwood was used for japanned
and painted chairs, and after 1800 rosewood became popular.
This dark, purple brown wood, which had a variegated figure and
a uniform grain, came from Brazil and the East Indies, and was

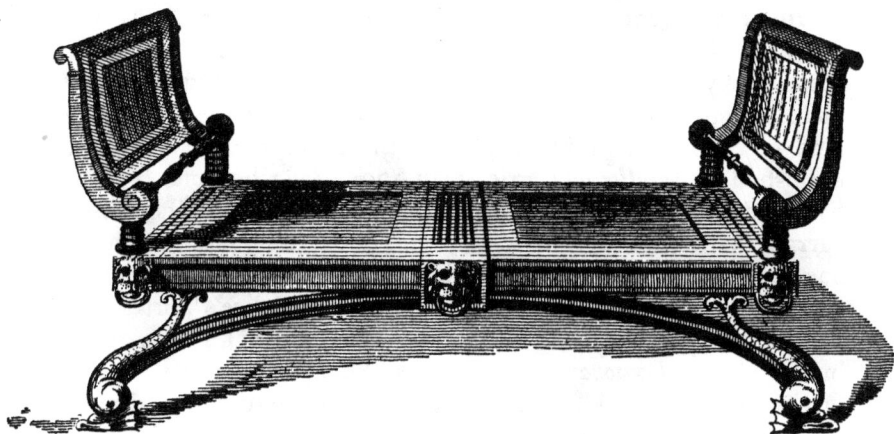

A double-ended backless seat, without cushions or upholstery, described by Sheraton as a Corridor Stool. From plate 29 of *The Cabinet Dictionary* (1803).

employed occasionally in the eighteenth century for case furniture; but during and after the Regency period its use increased, and its popularity was such that detailed directions for staining beech to imitate the colour and markings of rosewood were included by writers of technical books, like G. A. Siddons, whose *Cabinet-Maker's Guide* had reached a fifth edition by 1830. Sheraton's work has, with very little reason, been associated with satinwood, though he generally recommended mahogany for chairs. The name satinwood was applied to several different kinds of yellow wood from the West and East Indies, that were used chiefly for veneers but seldom for solid or case furniture, and not much for chairs until after 1800. The introduction of canework was an additional refinement suggested by Sheraton for "small borders round the backs of mahogany parlour chairs, which look neat", as well as for seats. "The cane used for the best purposes," he wrote, "is of a fine light straw colour, and this, indeed, makes the most agreeable contrast to almost every colour it is joined with. The more yellow kind is generally as strong and durable; but that which has lost either the white straw, or shining yellow colour, ought to be rejected, as having been damaged by salt water, or other accident, in its importation."

Under the general entry of ARM in *The Cabinet Dictionary*, Sheraton described and illustrated various types of arm-chair, occasionally specifying materials and finishes. Among these he included curricles, so called "from their being shaped like that kind of carriage". (William Felton, the coach-maker, who had published *A Treatise on Carriages*, in 1794, described one type of two-wheeled vehicle as "the chair-back curricle".) Sheraton's curricle had a concave back, and one of his designs is shown on page 172, while another chair of the same type, more emphatically decorative in the classic manner, appears in Fabre's portrait of Lord Holland reproduced on plate 44. Two examples were given in *The Cabinet Dictionary*, and for these Sheraton claimed "entire originality", and said that they were "well adapted for dining parlours, being of strong form, easy and conveniently low, affording easier access to a dining table than the common kind". There was a hunting chair, "stuffed all over, except the legs", which were of mahogany. "The slide out frame in front, when it is brought out to the full length, is intended to support the loose back cushion, which brings it even with the seat of the chair, and forms a temporary resting place for one that is fatigued, as hunters generally are." When the sliding front was omitted, the hunting chair was "made larger by a few inches each way". (His description of a bergère chair has been quoted earlier in this chapter.) A "tub easy chair, stuffed all over", was intended for invalids, "being both easy and warm; for the side wings coming quite forward keep out the cold air, which may be totally excluded from the person asleep, by laying some kind of covering over the whole chair". The winged easy chair had been shielding people from the draughts that whistled through English rooms ever since it was invented in Charles II's reign, and Sheraton, and other chair-designers and makers, amplified its comfort, sometimes at the expense of its former good looks. His design for a library or reading chair had been in use with little change of basic form since the early years of the eighteenth century and is shown on page 107 in Chapter 7, opposite its prototype; another example, *circa* 1735, in the Fitzwilliam Museum, Cambridge, is given on plate 41. One specialized type of chair was described under the entry CONVERSATION. "The manner of conversing amongst some of the highest circles of company, on some occasions, is copied from the French, by lounging upon a chair. Hence we have the term conversation chairs, which is peculiarly adapted for this kind of idle position, as I venture to call it, which is by no means calculated to excite the best of conversation." The design he gave for such a chair is reproduced on page 175. The occupant sat facing the back with his arms resting on the yoke rail, just as he would use the library or reading chair—a comfortable posture that saved his long-skirted coat from being crushed. More ornate suggestions for conversation chairs had been included in the *Drawing-Book*.

The Greek Revival stimulated Sheraton's rather heavy-handed designs for what he variously described as Grecian couches, sofas, and squabs, and an example of the latter is reproduced on plate 59, together with a far simpler and more graceful sofa with a scroll end, as delicate and precise as the volute on a Greek Ionic capital, which is in the collection at the Royal Pavilion, Brighton. "The stuffing part of these designs," wrote Sheraton, "is the chief difficulty in their execution, and doubtless requires upholsterers of taste and ability to finish them properly. The frames of these may be finished in white and gold, or in mahogany carved. . . . The scroles at the ends of the couches, are formed by deal kept lower than the carved work on the outside, to admit of some stuffing, which will bring the work nearly level with the moulding." Richard Brown, critically regarding the state of the trade and design some nineteen years later, said: "Although sofas as well as chairs have been allotted to the design and execution of one part of the trade exclusively, by which means chairs have received the highest improvement, yet sofas are as ridiculous and unmeaning in their forms as ever."

When Thomas Hope's *Household Furniture and Interior Decoration* appeared in 1807, his designs not only gave fresh impetus to the taste for chairs and furniture in the Greek Revival style, but loosed a lot of new ideas about the ancient world upon society and the furniture trade. Hitherto the ancient world had meant Greece and Rome; but Hope now introduced men of taste and modish furniture-makers to something much older, to the architecture and ornamental conventions of Egyptian civilization that had flourished and produced monumental art three thousand years before the city states of Greece or Rome were founded. He dramatized the results of his diligent studies and extensive travels, and made

Part of a design for the decoration and furnishing of a drawing room, by Thomas Hope, reproduced from his *Household Furniture and Decoration* (1807). The ends of the wall seat are ornamented with lion-headed recumbent sphinxes and a chimera, another winged, hybrid creature, appears on the side of the clumsy, box-like arm-chair—the sort of chair dreamed up on a drawing board. No accomplished chair-maker would have produced such a design.

his contemporaries conscious of this pre-Hellenic world of decorative art. Hope was a portent: unlike the master cabinet makers and chair makers who had published books of designs, unlike a trained and gifted architect such as Robert Adam, he represented the incursion of the amateur into furniture design.

There had been many amateurs of architecture in the eighteenth century, like Sanderson Miller, whose buildings in the "Gothick taste" were much admired; but though such amiable and accomplished gentlemen contributed to contemporary fashions, they did not change or improve them. Hope did both, and the neo-Greek style on the whole gained more than it lost from his work; the original pure lines of the *klismos* might be thickened and occasionally distorted, but he could create gracious shapes, like the scroll back chair with sabre legs on this page, and his introduction of Egyptian motifs could be as discreet as those which support the arms of the chair on plate 58. He was attracted by the sphinx motif, whether he used the Egyptian head, as on that arm-chair, or the winged lion, which adorns the end of the wall seat in the drawing room reproduced opposite "Is this Mr Thomas Hope? —Is this the man of chairs and tables?—the gentleman of the sphinxes—the Oedipus of coal-boxes—he who meditated on muffineers and planned pokers—Where has he hidden all this eloquence and poetry up to this hour?" asked Sydney Smith in astonishment, when reviewing a romantic novel that Hope had published anonymously in 1819. That sensational book, *Anastasius*, was at first attributed to Lord Byron, whose temper must have been brought to boiling point when the true authorship was revealed, for he had dismissed Hope in a contemptuous line as a

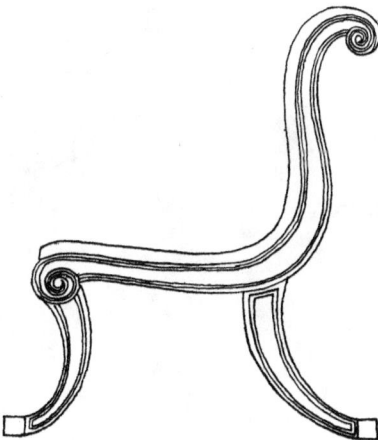

Profile of a chair with sabre legs and a scroll back, designed by Thomas Hope. The curves of the back and legs are complementary; they flow easily into each other without the abrupt break he gave to his version of the *klismos*, shown on plate 7, and low-seated chairs of this type contributed fresh grace to the Regency period. A variation of the form is shown on plate 60. Reproduced from *Household Furniture and Interior Decoration*, by Thomas Hope (1807).

"house-furnisher". (After the success of his novel he was known as "Anastasius" Hope.) "The gentleman of the sphinxes" certainly made Egyptian ornament fashionable; and because contemporary French Empire furniture was often decorated with Egyptian motifs, the misleading label of "English Empire" has been applied to furniture made during the Regency period. Except for the brief Peace of Amiens, England was cut off from France from 1793 to 1815, and while the French Empire style affected taste in the United States, the modes of the Regency developed during a time of national isolation. Chairs in that elegant age attained new graces, though occasionally in the later work of Sheraton and the plates of George Smith's *Household Furniture* (1808) there were hints of the corpulence to come.

In the eighty years, 1730–1810, covered by this chapter, we have been concerned chiefly with chair-making for the world of fashion, with an occasional glance at the work of country craftsmen; but while those craftsmen adapted and simplified and sometimes improved the chair designs of town-makers, they remained happily immune from the debilitating dictation of academic men of taste.

CHAPTER 9

SURVIVAL OF THE NATIVE ENGLISH STYLE, 1660–1900

C OUNTRY chair-makers, turners especially, conserved the native English tradition of design, and continued to develop and improve their distinctive chair styles throughout the seventeenth and eighteenth centuries, and far into the Victorian period. They worked independently, occasionally in such isolation that they were cut off from town life not only by distance, for roads were passable only in the summer months, but by time too, so many continued to use the same methods, materials and carved ornament that their fathers and grand-fathers had used, perhaps thinking the same thoughts, and certainly making much the same sort of furniture, especially seat furniture. We have forgotten today how remote and inaccessible many parts of the country were before the late eighteenth century, when roads were improved, mail coaches ran to time, and greater freedom of movement led to closer contact between towns and villages.

In many localities, especially in the west and north-west, joined stools and chairs and settles continued to be made throughout the early and mid-Georgian period, so that precise dating of well-preserved specimens of such furniture is difficult. This persistence of old forms may have been due partly to an ingrained and stubborn resistance to change—the "what was good enough for dad and grandad is good enough for me" attitude of mind, comfortably indolent and far healthier than romantic or antiquarian attempts to preserve or resurrect old shapes. Such traditional furniture was made for everyday use in farmhouses and inns and cottages where everyday life was much the same in 1750 as it had

G*

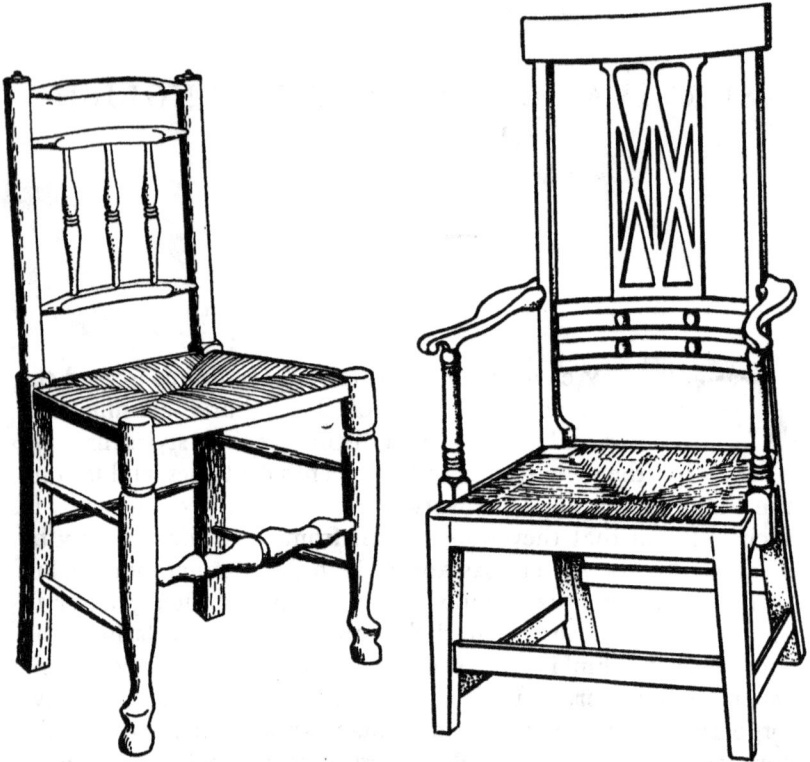

Two examples of chairs from country workshops, whose makers borrowed a little from town fashions, and edited them skilfully. *Left:* Cherrywood rush-seated, spindle-back chair, mid-eighteenth century. The turned front legs end in hoof feet, the back legs are square-sectioned, slightly splayed, and continuous with the turned back posts. Turned spindles connect the middle rails, and both of them and the yoke rail have a shallow concave depression carved out to increase the comfort of the sitter. Compare the treatment of this chair-back with the New England Carver chairs on plate 20. *Right:* Early nineteenth century rush-seated chair with painted frame. The pierced splat, linking the three lower rails with the yoke, is a simplified version of the lattice-back, which was used in various forms on chairs from 1790 to the Regency period.

been in 1650. The village carpenter or joiner who made seats as and when they were wanted, might be a sound craftsman, but he was very different from the country chair-maker, who invented new techniques, and was neither unaware of nor indifferent to contemporary fashions. These he heard about or actually saw when the local squire decided to refurnish his dining room or drawing room, and sent to the nearest town for chairs, as the mistress of Shalstone Manor House sent to Mr King of Bicester for walnut chairs in 1736; and after Chippendale's *Director* was published, and other copy books followed, the time-lag between the modes of town and country was shortened. During the first half of the eighteenth century news about fashions penetrated slowly; and while some ideas were picked up—the hoof foot for instance—neither then nor later was the serene common sense of country makers deflected from the task of using their materials to the best advantage, and exploring new ways of using them economically. They employed the woods of the countryside: ash, elm, beech, yew, and fruit woods like cherry and apple, also working in oak, occasionally in walnut, and, a decade or so after it was introduced, in mahogany. Even when copy books multiplied and those makers adopted and skilfully modified some contemporary fashions, the structure, shape and comfort of country-made chairs were only superficially affected, if at all, by what Lord This and Sir Somebody That might be ordering from Mr Chippendale or Mr Cobb or Mr Seddon, or by the antiquarian fancies that happened to engage the taste of Horace Walpole and his circle. Rural craftsmen were not only too remote, they were perhaps too innocent to fake-up imitations of the old turned chairs that had, so Horace Walpole imagined, an air of the cloister, and for which he was prepared to pay three-and-sixpence or five shillings apiece; the market for spurious antiques did not yet exist, perhaps because there was still plenty of mediaeval loot available for those who cared to seek it; and the country chair-maker, working in a living and lively tradition, had no inclination to reproduce the ideas of the past and as yet no economic reason to tempt him along that dead-end road.

The vitality of a craft may be assessed not only by the skill and inventiveness of those who follow it, but by their ability to relate their work to contemporary life, to the practical needs of the world as it is in their own day, not as it was the day before yesterday.

The simplest form of stick furniture consisted of turned spindles socketed into a shaped seat, forming legs and back, with the seat as the unifying structural member. The two basic types of Windsor chair are the hoop, or bow-back, and the comb-back. *Left:* A plain double bow back Windsor chair, with plain turned legs and a spur stretcher. Early nineteenth century. Compare with example at bottom of plate 63. *Right:* The most elementary form of comb-back Windsor chair. Mid-eighteenth century.

When chair-makers in small towns and the countryside acknowledged prevailing fashions, they chose and edited some appropriate features; made them their own, incorporating them as intrinsic parts of their design—a vase or baluster splat, cabriole legs, a type of foot. On page 184 two chairs are illustrated, separated in time by some fifty years, which exemplify this capacity for absorption. The first, dating from the middle years of the eighteenth century, has a cherrywood frame, a rush seat, a spindle-back, and turned front legs that end in hoof feet—a tribute to a fashion that was popular in the reign of Queen Anne, and indicative of that long time-lag between town and country modes. The second chair, much later in date, has a painted frame, drop-in rush seat, and a relatively high back with a pierced splat linking the lower rails with the yoke, a simplified version of the lattice-back that was used in various forms from the 1790s to the Regency period. The curved arms, scrolled at the ends and supported on turned columns jointed into the seat rail, are very much earlier in type; while the tapered front legs, splayed square-sectioned back legs, and heavy stretchers, had been in current use since the 1760s. These diverse features are congenially united by the maker's skill, and although the result would not, to quote Hepplewhite, have "procured it a favourable reception in the first circles of fashion", such a chair would have been welcome for its comfort and good shape in the parlour of a farmhouse or the snuggery of a country inn. Another example, mentioned in the last chapter, is the mahogany elbow chair on plate 43, which shows a country maker's restrained and graceful observance of the Gothic taste.

Quite apart from the large and varied family of spindle-back and ladder-back chairs, made with regional characteristics and little change in the basic form of the back or the shape of turned front legs and stretchers, was the prolific line of Windsors, originating at some time in the second half of the seventeenth century, though not mentioned by name until the early 1720s. The earliest dates given in *The Dictionary of English Furniture* are 1724, when Lord Percival, writing about a visit to the garden of Hall Barn in Buckinghamshire mentions a Windsor chair, and 1725, when seven japanned Windsor chairs were included in the library of the Duke of Chandos at Cannons. R. W. Symonds has quoted a sale catalogue of the furniture of Thomas Coke, sold on February 12, 1728, in the Great Piazza, Covent Garden. Lot 41 included: "Two cane Chairs, a matted Chair, a Windsor Chair, and a table. . . ."

Windsor has become a generic name for seat furniture of stick construction, and was probably in use much earlier than the dates just mentioned, dates which flatten a story, long accepted and cherished, that George III, finding chairs of this type in a cottage near Windsor where he was sheltering from the rain, thought them so comfortable that he ordered some to be made for himself, and thereafter they were called Windsor chairs in his honour. For over two hundred and fifty years the Windsor could almost claim to be the national chair of England, certainly the most expressively English in character and design, for it incorporated all the lessons turners and chair-makers had learned since the middle ages, was still linked with the mediaeval past, and closely akin to the work of the New England craftsmen who, with skills and traditions

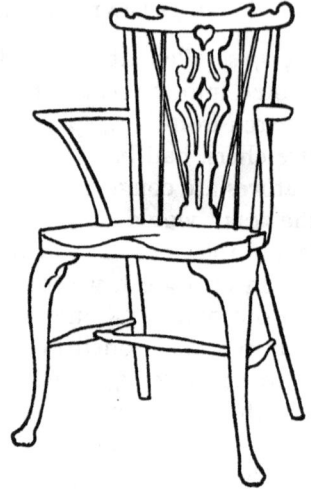

Left: Comb-back type with plain baluster splat and four cabriole legs. *Right:* Comb-back with pierced baluster splat, two stays forming a V-shaped brace for the back, and cabriole legs in front. Second half of the eighteenth century.

Left: Double bow-back type with pierced baluster, turned legs and spur stretcher. Late eighteenth and early nineteenth century. Compare this with the example on plate 63, top left. *Right:* Double bow-back, with pierced splat, cabriole front legs and spur stretcher. Second half of eighteenth century.

Left: Low-backed Windsor type known as a Smoker's Bow. Although this seems to have first appeared during the second quarter of the nineteenth century, its ancestor was most probably the corner or writing chair, like the example on plate 33. *Right:* Mendlesham or Dan Day variation of the Windsor type, called after a chair-maker of that name who worked at Mendlesham and Stoneham in Suffolk. Late eighteenth and early nineteenth centuries.

transplanted from old England, had perfected the Carver and Brewster types during the seventeenth century. (See plates 20 and 21.)

The extreme structural simplicity of the Windsor arises from the stabilizing function of the solid wooden seat, which unites the turned members that are socketed into it, while the stretchers, which perform a secondary stabilizing function, are socketed into the legs. The two main types of Windsor are the hoop-back and the comb-back, and the elementary forms of both are shown on page 186, while some of the refinements developed in both types are shown opposite. Sometimes the hoop-back is known as a bow-back; the arching back frame is the bow, the curve that gives concavity to the back is also called the bow, so armchairs with both are double-bows, like the examples on page 186 (top left), opposite (below), and plate 63. The bow, an early instance of the technique of bending wood by heat and pressure, is made of ash or yew, with back sticks and leg spindles of beech. Except

Left: Simple bow-back armchair with pierced baluster. *Right:* Wheel-back single chair, with V-shaped brace. Both types were made from the second quarter of the nineteenth century onwards. Compare with the example from Loudon's *Encyclopaedia* on page 195.

in the primitive types, like the comb-back on page 186, the back is inclined at a comfortable angle, and the saddle-shaped elm seat has shallow twin depressions that may well have followed contours impressed upon a clay mould. The beechwoods of Buckinghamshire supplied the material for the turned members—spindles for legs and stretchers, back and arm sticks—and the production of those components has been traditionally located in the Chilterns, and their assembly into chairs associated with the market town of Chepping or Chipping Wycombe, now called High Wycombe. Chair-making and turnery apparently flourished for a long time in the district, but Wycombe makers remained anonymous until the last quarter of the eighteenth century when two names are discovered, Samuel Treacher and Thomas Widgington, who, according to Sir Lawrence Weaver in *High Wycombe Furniture*, "seem to have been the Chippendales of the Windsor chair", and "they are commemorated in stained glass windows in the Mayor's Parlour in the Town Hall".

This suggests that chair-making was well-established in High Wycombe; but the industry is not mentioned in Lysons' *Magna Britannia*. The volume that includes Buckinghamshire, issued in 1806, records corn and paper mills, and describes the town as large and "much the handsomest in the county. . . ." By modern standards it was not large: the returns under the population act of 1801 showed a total population in town and parish of 4,248 inhabitants, of which 282 were employed chiefly in agriculture, and 724 in trade, manufacture and handicraft. That figure of 724 probably included some of the independent craftsmen, scattered about in the beechwoods. Those men, using pole-lathes and adzes, made chair parts in tens of thousands, which they delivered to workshops in the town, where they were assembled, loaded "in the white", without stain, polish or paint, on to farm wagons, and sent through the surrounding counties and up into the Midlands. They were known as "White Wycombes", and sold from door to door for a few shillings each. The turners who produced the spindles were called "bodgers", a local term that may not have become current until the early nineteenth century. A possible origin for it was once suggested to the writer by Mr L. John Mayes, the Borough Librarian of High Wycombe, who heard from an old paper-maker that "bodger" was first used by his fellow workers as a contemptuous name for turners, "bodging about in the woods and their poky little sheds in the town". The old man's final words to Mr Mayes were to the effect that paper making was a clean trade, and paper makers, who considered themselves to be highly skilled craftsmen, "allus did look down on they bodgers, dirty folk all of 'em, allus". Bodger is an old English word, sometimes used for a pedlar, and in this sense it may have been originally applied to the Buckinghamshire turners who peddled "White Wycombes" through the countryside. Boger or Bodger is also an English surname, and, according to Professor Ernest Weekley, both are archaic forms of Bowyer. In his *Dictionary of Archaic and Provincial Words* (1849), Halliwell includes the word Bodge, and one of its meanings was "To begin a task and not complete it", which certainly describes the function of the bodger, though there were exceptions, when one man did the complete job. Writing as late as 1929, Sir Lawrence Weaver said there were still chair-makers in Buckinghamshire "who buy trees as they grow, saw the trunks by hand into lengths suitable for the leg of a chair, split those great sections with an axe wielded with primeval skill, and then turn the leg of the chair on the spot, in the open air, with a pole lathe so simple that it might have made the balusters of the Ark. There were even lately bodgers who made the whole chair from the beginning. But that has practically ceased. In the main, these mediaeval survivals devote themselves to making legs. . . ." These were sent to High Wycombe and assembled "with other parts made solely by the machine. Oddly enough," Weaver concluded, "the machine cannot beat handicraft at making and turning a leg."

The basic shape of the Windsor chair, determined and perpetuated by structural character, allowed innumerable variations and refinements to be introduced, and throughout the eighteenth century makers in England and the American Colonies exhibited a vivacious ingenuity in their treatment of splat, legs, stretchers and, on the comb-back type, the yoke rail or comb-piece as it was called. In America especially that feature was elegantly diversified, occasionally following the outline of an Ionic capital with the ends in the form of delicately carved volutes. The two English examples at the top of page 188 illustrate the decorative possibilities of the comb-piece, and the splats of all four chairs on that page and those on the upper part of plate 63 show how that vertical member could be varied from the slim, restrained baluster to robust shapes with fret-cut ornamental patterns which may have owed something to the chair backs in Chippendale's *Director*. Comb-back Windsor chairs with baluster splats and cabriole legs are shown in Hogarth's drawing of *The Sleeping Housewife*. During the second half of the eighteenth century a Gothic type appeared, with the bow back replaced by a pointed arch and pierced balusters of Gothic character instead of sticks. As such chairs usually had cabriole legs in front, the turned work was then confined to back legs and stretchers. A few of the later eighteenth century examples had four cabriole legs, like the armchair at the top of page 188 on the left; more rarely a town maker would adopt the Windsor form, embellish the knees of the cabriole legs with lightly carved acanthus foliations, and use mahogany instead of yew or beech;

The Astley-Cooper chair, a Windsor type of high chair designed about 1800, by Sir Astley Paston Cooper, F.R.S. (1768–1841), the famous orthopaedic surgeon, to train children to sit upright. (Reproduced from *English Furniture for the Private Collector*, by Anthony Bird, by permission of the author, and the publishers, B. T. Batsford Ltd.) Compare this high chair with those shown in the family scene on page 243.

but such elaborations diverged from the main line of development. There were regional divergencies, like the Mendlesham chair on page 189, a type attributed to a maker named Daniel Day who worked at Mendlesham and Stoneham in Suffolk in the late eighteenth and early nineteenth centuries; and there were specialized types too, such as the Astley-Cooper chair shown above, designed about 1800 by Sir Astley Paston Cooper, the famous orthopaedic surgeon, for the purpose of training children to sit upright.

A low-backed type of Windsor, with arms and yoke rail continuous like the corner or writing chairs of Queen Anne's reign, was made in England occasionally but more frequently in the American Colonies, where it was associated by name with Philadelphia until the 1760s. This low-backed type was the progenitor of that most popular of all the variants of the Windsor, the smoker's bow, which first appeared in the second quarter of the nineteenth century, and may have originated in the north country. Some evidence suggests that from the heavily-built Windsors of that region a cut-down type was evolved, and such a chair is shown on plate 63, top right, which has the form of a smoker's bow up to the level of the arms and centre rail: remove the bowed top with the splat and sticks, so the centre rail becomes the yoke, and the smoker's bow is revealed. That chair of yew with an elm seat, dates from the 1830s. A little later, towards the middle of the century, the low-backed "Philadelphia Windsor" of the eighteenth century was revived in the United States, almost identical in design with the smoker's bow, and known as the Firehouse Windsor because it was used extensively in furnishing the quarters of the old volunteer fire companies of that time. Another name that became current still later in America was Captain's chair, derived apparently from the use of this type in the pilot houses of Mississippi steamboats and coastal craft.

The typical smoker's bow is shown on page 189, with its low back, the yoke rising a little above the level of the arms, joined to the seat by seven or eight turned bobbins or Roman spindles which incline outwards. The name presumably originated because of the bow-shaped back and the widespread use of the type in smoking rooms and bars. So great was its popularity that within a few years it was to be found not only in the public rooms of inns, in institutions, schoolrooms, cottage and farmhouse kitchens and parlours and in small suburban houses, but in that most staid of all apartments—the Victorian office. The comfort, strength, extreme simplicity of construction and consequent cheapness, commended the smoker's bow everywhere, particularly where furniture was liable to rough usage. The materials were the same as those used for other Windsors: elm seats, ash or yew bows, with arms and turned work in fruit wood or yew for the more expensive types, stained and varnished beech as usual for the cheaper. Surtees, who mentions "semicircular wooden-bottomed walnut smoking chairs" when describing Lord Scamperdale's grubby little parlour at Woodmansterne, probably had the smoker's bow type in mind, although John Leech, who illustrated *Mr Sponge's Sporting Tour*, showed his lordship and his toady, Jack Spraggon, wearing their "Stunner" tartans and sitting by the fire in a couple of cheap bow-back Windsor chairs.

The original "White Wycombes" of the early nineteenth century were of the plainest type, resembling the arm and single chairs on page 190, and the example on the opposite page, accompanied by structural details, reproduced from Loudon's *Encyclopaedia of Cottage, Farm, and Villa Architecture and Furniture* (1833). Loudon described the Windsor as "one of the best kitchen chairs in general use in the midland counties of England". After a rather laborious account of the structure, he gave the following details about finishes:—"These chairs," he wrote, "are sometimes painted, but more frequently stained with diluted sulphuric acid and logwood; or by repeatedly washing them over with alum water, which has some tartar in it: they should afterwards be washed over several times with an extract of Brasil wood. The colour given will be a sort of red, not unlike that of mahogany; and, by afterwards oiling the chair and rubbing it well, and for a long time with woollen cloths, the veins and shading of the elm will be rendered conspicuous. Quicklime slacked in urine, and laid on the wood while hot, will also stain it of a red colour; and this is said to be the general practice with the Windsor chair manufacturers in the neighbourhood of London."

Variations of the plainest Windsors were produced in great quantities, not only the wheel-back with its V-shaped brace, like the example on the right at the top of page 190, but far simpler

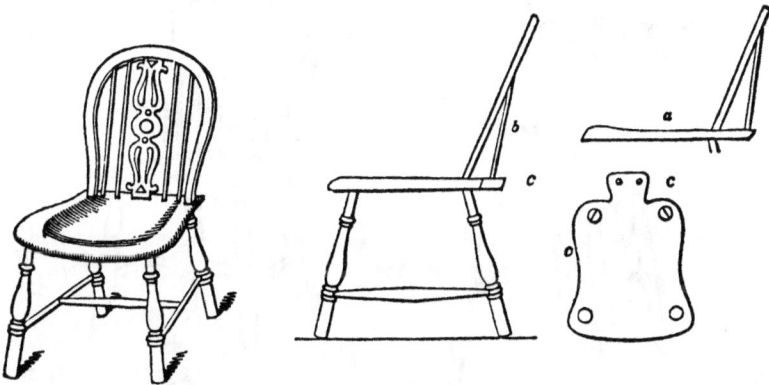

The early nineteenth century Windsor chair, with turned leg spindles, back sticks and back stays, pierced splat, shaped seat, and curved bow-back frame, made separately by different craftsmen, was assembled in a central workshop; anticipating the mass-production methods that were introduced with machinery. From Loudon's *Encyclopaedia* (1833), figs. 643–644.

The simplest types of nineteenth-century Windsor chairs changed very little during a hundred years. *Left:* Baluster-and-spindle chair. *Right:* Roman Spindle chair.

Left: The stick-back, with four slender spindles flanked by turned balusters. *Right:* The lath-back. During and after the second quarter of the nineteenth century, such chairs were to be found in nearly every kitchen.

A stick-back chair of the 1860's, illustrated by Eastlake in *Hints on Household Taste* (second edition, 1869), page 54. The Gothic arches cut into the yoke rail, and the lightly carved ornament on its surface, are far less effective in decorative character than the baluster-and-spindle and Roman spindle backs of the chairs on the opposite page.

types, with a plain version of the comb-piece into which sticks, spindles or laths are socketed, forming a slightly inclined back. These were primarily kitchen chairs, cheap, strong, and stained by the sort of methods Loudon described, and usually varnished, so the final result was treacly brown, which remained shiny until the varnish wore off: four examples are shown opposite, and they compare favourably with the rather self-conscious attempt at artistic improvement by Charles Lock Eastlake, reproduced above, who designed this variation and included it in his *Hints on Household Taste*. That work, first published in the 1860s, sold steadily, reaching a fourth edition in 1878, and promulgating the so-called "Eastlake style". The author highly praised the Windsor chair; that and the bedroom towel horse were, in his view, the only articles that had "been allowed to escape the innovations of modern taste. A careful examination of these humble specimens of home manufacture," he said, "will show that they are really superior in point of design to many pretentious elegancies of fashionable taste."

The early days of mechanical production had been disastrous for the design of furniture made to satisfy the expanding middle class and working class markets. Manufacturers with few exceptions were either crude business men or engineers or an insensitive combination of both, and their ideas, so far as they had any, stopped short at imitation. The cheapest materials were fed into machines to simulate articles previously made by highly skilled craftsmen, and about the only thing unmaimed by industrial change was the Windsor chair. For a long time the methods established and perfected since the late seventeenth century were undisturbed, but when at last the bodger's work was supplemented by mechanical assembly, and partly replaced by mechanical turning, the speed of production was increased, but the structure and design of the traditional Windsor were preserved. The weight and proportions of the turned members were not changed in order to save material, for the basic form of the chair was so perfectly adapted for mechanical production that skimping simply didn't pay, and in the furniture manufacturing trade—as in others—if a thing didn't pay it wasn't done. So the Windsor is the triumphant survivor of the native English tradition of chair design, because for over two and a half centuries it has represented the most economical and best use of materials.

CHAPTER 10

A SHORT HISTORY OF THE ROCKING CHAIR
1750–1900

FEW articles of furniture may claim to be habit-forming, and only one chair, the rocker, has imposed a soothing social habit upon a great nation, which provides a form of unoccupational therapy as an antidote to the hustle and speed associated with the American way of life, past and present. Although the rocking chair developed concurrently in England and America, it became a domestic institution across the Atlantic, where manners were more relaxed and postures less inhibited than in Georgian and Victorian England. Rocking chairs had existed before the thirteen American Colonies became the United States, and their invention has been attributed to Benjamin Franklin when he was still a British subject, at some time between 1760 and 1770, though an earlier origin has been claimed for them in Lancashire. Franklin is supposed to have used iron bends, which were, presumably, fixed to a wooden chair. Cradles with rockers had been known since the Middle Ages, probably much earlier, but the idea of fitting bends or rockers to the feet of chairs had not apparently occurred to anybody before the second half of the eighteenth century, or if it had was not practically applied, possibly because the aura of dignity and power that surrounded chairs in mediaeval times and long after forbade any tampering with their static majesty. The first rocking chair may conceivably have been a labour-saving device for mothers, to allow them to rock their babies while resting comfortably themselves.

The early rocking chairs were either ladder-back rush-bottomed country-made types, or Windsors, with bends connecting the back and front legs, curved gently to keep the rocking motion properly sedate; and for many years neither the angle of the back nor the shape of the seat was adjusted or in any way modified in recognition of a new function. Such recognition came only when the Boston rocker was designed, early in the nineteenth century, and the roll seat and roll arms were directly related to the curves of the bends, so the comfort of the chair was thus greatly increased. Apart from those refinements, the Boston rocker resembled a tall comb-back Windsor, with the comb-piece usually decorated with paintings or stencils of fruit and flowers. Rockers attained a popularity in America that was never approached in England; they were to be found in every parlour, one or more on every back porch, on the sidewalk outside stores and taverns; and the Boston rocker became and has remained a standard American type. In 1838 a builder named James Frewin, who had been travelling in the United States, contributed some notes on the Boston rocker to *The Architectural Magazine and Journal*. He described a richly carved mahogany example, which cost about £8, and a plainer variety in birch or elm that was sold at £2 10s. "In America," he said, "it is considered a compliment to give the stranger the rocking-chair as a seat; and when there is more than one kind in the house, the stranger is always presented with the best." The basic form even survived the pursuit of novelty that characterized the late 1890s, and, despite excessive attenuation, the example from Grand Rapids shown on page 205 is still recognizably a descendent of the Windsor type. Another type of American rocker had turned legs and stretchers, with back posts surmounted by knobs or finials, a rush seat and closely-woven canework or fabric filling the back instead of rails. This was descended, with some modifications, from the original ladder-back type shown opposite, and during the second half of the nineteenth century cheap varieties were exported to England where they were sold as Sinclair's "American Common Sense Chairs". An advertisement for them in *The Graphic*, dated May 17, 1884, reads as follows:—

" 'TAKE IT EASY.' Specially adapted for rest and comfort. Recommended by scores of gentlemen. The ladies are enthusiastic about them. Graceful, Easy, Fashionable, and Inexpensive. Visitors to the U.S. will recall the luxury of these chairs, which

The American ancestor of the rocking
chair, with ladder-back and rush seat,
the front and back feet connected by
"bends", which turned it into a rocker.
Drawn by Ronald Escott.

are to be found in every American home, and no family can keep
house without them. They are made in a variety of styles, so that
any one's taste can be suited. Try a 'Common Sense' easy chair,
and you will have solid comfort. Price of Rockers, from 25s. to 35s."

That was issued by the London agents, Richards, Terry, and
Co, 46, Holborn Viaduct, and the illustration that accompanied
it is reproduced on the next page, together with an example of one
in use, taken from Lady Barker's book, *The Bedroom and Boudoir*,
published in 1878. In *Plain or Ringlets*, which appeared in 1860,
Surtees mentions an "American rocking-chair" in one of the
bedrooms of Appleton Hall.

Dr Siegfried Giedion has recorded a United States Patent for an
improved rocking chair, taken out as early as 1831, that was
intended to increase resilience by inserting wagon springs between
the rockers and the seat. There were other departures from the
ancestral form, and during the 1840s some English manufacturers
had attempted to use cast iron for rocking chairs, but the material
was too brittle to withstand the strain to which the bends were
continually subjected, so steel or brass strips were used for the
frame, with a continuous upholstered seat and back, and padded
elbows, like the example at the bottom, left, on page 204. This
type of "brass rocking or lounging chair," was shown at the Great

The American rocking chair, with the high upholstered or canework back and
ball finials surmounting the uprights was popular in England during the last
quarter of the nineteenth century. *Above:* An example from *The Bedroom and
Boudoir*, by Lady Barker (1878), where it appears as part of the furnishing
suggested for the sick-room. (The mid-eighteenth century tripod table with
the bird-cage device which allowed it to be tipped up when not in use, is
described by the authoress as an "invalid table".)

Right: An advertisement for imported
American rockers, published by the
London agents, Richards, Terry and
Co. of 46, Holborn Viaduct, London,
in *The Graphic*, May 17, 1884, page
487. The prices were from 25s. to 35s.

Exhibition of 1851 by R. W. Winfield and Company of Birmingham, also an "improved iron rocking chair for the drawing-room, in gold, covered with French brocatel", by William Cunning of Edinburgh. "In this chair," said the makers, "the spine and back are supported, and the head and neck rest in a natural position." It was exhibited "as a useful invention for invalids and others". The rocking chair was still regarded as something of a freakish novelty; there were no references to it in the first edition of Loudon's *Encyclopaedia*, published in 1833, or in subsequent editions; that note in *The Architectural Magazine* had conveyed a faint air of surprise at the esteem in which it was held in America, and over a dozen years later it was not as socially acceptable in England, so its presence had to be excused on medical grounds. Chairs that were identical in design with those exhibited by Winfield and Company were presently associated with the name of a certain Dr Calvert, who called them "digestive chairs", and recommended them for the use of invalids and ladies. Married women were always supposed to be rocking their babies, but even when they were childless or unmarried, that levelling phrase "the weaker sex" was taken literally in those days, and as a consequence it was customary to equate ladies with invalids, so inevitably they were included as suitable beneficiaries of the alleged therapeutic properties of the "digestive" rocking chair. Dr Calvert never patented the design. His very identity is conjectural; though he may possibly have been Frederick Crace Calvert, F.R.S. (1819–73), the industrial chemist, who was interested in industrial design, and delivered one of the first Cantor lectures at the Society of Arts in 1864. As "digestive chairs" were not patented, any manufacturer could produce them, and several did, exporting them to the United States, where they were copied and marketed, though they never actively competed with the Boston rocker.

The most revolutionary design was the bentwood rocking chair, introduced and made in large quantities during and after the 1860s, by Michael Thonet (1796–1871), a gifted Austrian designer, who had exhibited bentwood furniture at the Great Exhibition. The length of the seat, the angle of the back, and the convoluted underframing gave greater stability and comfort than any other type. Two examples are illustrated on page 204, one with an ebonized frame and buttoned upholstery, the other, of slightly

Above: A bentwood rocking chair, reproduced from an advertisement by Oetzmann & Co., London, in *The Graphic*, March 31, 1883, page 331. "Stuffed all hair", it was sold at 42s. and "Ebonised and gold ditto, in velvet and satin, any colour, 72s. 6d".

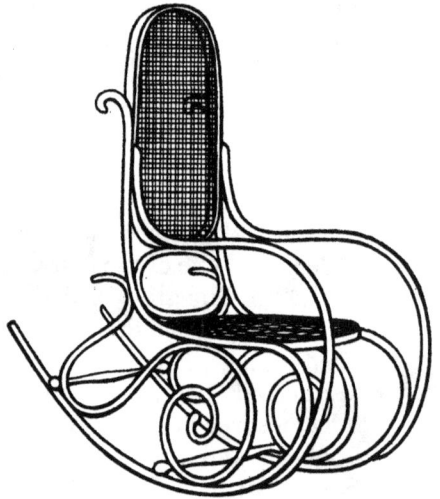

Left: Rocking chairs of this type with frames made from curved steel or brass strips, and upholstered seats and back, were shown at the Great Exhibition, 1851. *Right:* A variation of the bentwood rocker, with cane-work seat and back. The proportions are slightly different from those of the example above.
Drawn by Ronald Escott.

different proportions, stained brown and polished with close-mesh canework in seat and back. Sometimes the frames were in gold, more rarely in colours, and the usual finish was black or brown. These bentwood designs did much to popularize the rocking chair in England; Thonet's bentwood chairs, which continued to sell in thousands during the second half of the century, had already made the material and form of the frame familiar, and by the 1880s the bentwood rocker had become an accepted and popular item of furniture in the drawing-room and parlour. Although they were sold in America, Thonet's rockers never displaced the original Boston model, which has retained national loyalty for a hundred and fifty years. Bends were sometimes fitted to upholstered easy chairs, but seldom in England; such chairs were not true rockers, designed for their special function like the Boston or bentwood types; they were simply chairs adapted for rocking.

Late in the 1890s an entirely new form of rocker was produced

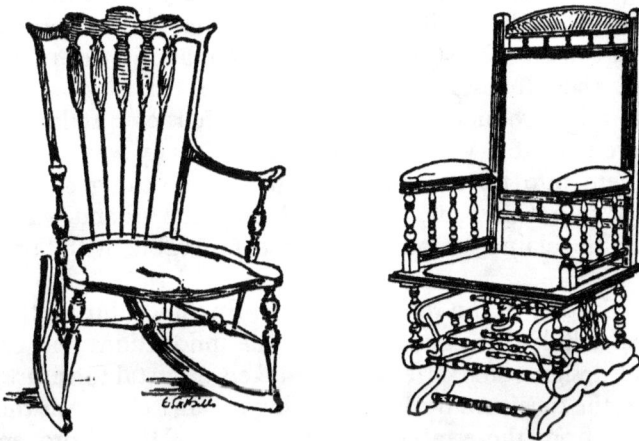

Left: An American rocker of the late 1890s, designed by Clarence R. Hills of Grand Rapids, which derives its character from a Windsor prototype. From *Furniture and Decoration*, February 1897, page 31. *Right:* The "swing" rocking chair, with a fixed base, introduced to the furniture trade by H. & A. G. Alexander & Co. Ltd. of Eastfield, Rutherglen, near Glasgow, and illustrated originally in *Furniture and Decoration*, April 1897, from which this simplified drawing has been made. See variation of the design on page 207.

by a firm of Scottish makers, H. & A. G. Alexander and Company Limited, of Eastfield, Rutherglen, near Glasgow. They called it the "Sanspareil" swing rocking chair, and it was shown at the International Furnishing Trades Exhibition, held in April 1897 at the Royal Agricultural Hall, London. There were no bends, the chair rocked on a fixed base which remained stationary, so it was "possible to sit in the chair and be gently rocked to and fro without shifting its position". The motion was described as "silent, smooth, and pleasant". The heavy underframing and the height of the seat allowed this type to be used also as a writing chair, that could be tilted back and kept at a comfortable angle without oscillating, like the example opposite from *Punch*, which has superficial differences in design from the original on page 205, but the same rocking principle. Compared with the Boston or bentwood chairs, it was complex and heavy.

Once the rocking chair was established in England it was not identified with either sex, and was equally acceptable in the drawing-room, parlour, boudoir, study, library or smoking-room. After the 1914–18 war its popularity declined, and although the frames of some of the steel tubular chairs made in the 1920s and '30s had enough resilience to permit a limited rocking motion, that was a by-product of their structural character and material: they were not fitted with bends or shaped in any way that would bring them into the rocking chair family. Rocking chairs with frames of thin steel rods, introduced since the second war, have indisputable claims to an elegance comparable with Thonet's design.

In the history of the rocking chair in England, during the century and a half that ended in 1900, the innovations and experiments in design came chiefly from makers of metal furniture, and not from the furniture trade. The swing rocking chair was the first departure from the established type; most of the improvements and changes of design in the nineteenth century came either from America or Austria, where the bentwood rocker originated. The rocker has never been quite the Englishman's chair; but it has been and is still America's national chair.

Mrs. Newlywed. "AND TELL ME—WHAT IS MY POPSY'S LITTLE WIFE TO HIM?"
Mr. Newlywed (thinking of the bills). "OH—VERY, VERY *DEAR!*"

This illustration, published in *Punch*, January 24, 1900 (page 68), shows a variation of the "swing" rocker; but the design differs only in minor detail from that on page 205. The fixed base and the height of the seat allowed this type to be used as a writing chair, which could be tilted back and kept at a comfortable angle without oscillating. Reproduced by permission of *Punch*.

H

CHAPTER II

DESIGN FOR COMFORT
1830–1900

VICTORIAN comfort depended partly on improved up-holstery, on soporific deeply-sprung armchairs, but chiefly on the conviction that comfort was a worthy end in itself, a morally irreproachable reward for the strenuous demands of a good and busy life. There was an element of national pride in this devotion to comfort, which encouraged a belief that the English alone possessed the ability to create comfortable homes. The grounds for that belief were explained with confidence and lucidity by Robert Kerr in his book, *The Gentleman's House*, which was published in 1864. "What we call in England a comfortable house," he wrote, "is a thing so intimately identified with English customs as to make us apt to say that in no other country but our own is this element of comfort fully understood; or at all events that the comfort of any other nation is not the comfort of this. The peculiarities of our climate, the domesticated habits of almost all classes, our family reserve, and our large share of the means and appliances of easy living, all combine to make what is called a comfortable home perhaps the most cherished possession of an Englishman. To dwell a moment longer on this always popular theme, it is worth suggesting that *indoor comfort* is essenti-ally a Northern idea, as contrasted with a sort of outdoor enjoy-ment which is equally a Southern idea, and Oriental. Hence the difference between the French habits, for instance, and the English. The French, like the modern Italians, represent the ancient Romans; while the English exhibit the old Gothic way by direct descent through the Saxons." What an English gentleman valued in his house was described as: "Quiet comfort for his family and guests,—Thorough convenience for his domestics,—Elegance and importance without ostentation."

The seventeenth century upholsterers and frame-makers who had created the winged easy chair were the pioneers of design for comfort, and their sense of style, and that of their Georgian successors, allowed standards of comfort to be progressively improved without injury to good proportions; but when that sense of style declined, as it did in the 1820s and '30s, the easy chair grew heavy and bloated, for the decline coincided with the invention and extended use of the coiled spring. The first patent for a coiled spring in a mattress and other upholstery was granted to Samuel Pratt, and signed and sealed on December 24, 1828 (No. 5668). Pratt described himself as a Camp Equipage Maker, of New Bond Street in the Parish of St George, Hanover Square, London. The springs shown in the diagram attached to the patent, did not differ much from those in use today. They were spiral, of iron or steel wire, twisted into circular or angular coils. The circular type was shaped like an hour glass, the other was triangular. These springs were attached to a foundation cloth of canvas or similar fabric, strengthened by whalebone or cane round the edges, and this reinforcing material was also sewn diagonally across the foundation cloth, so that it crossed at junctions, and was firmly sewn in position. The springs were sewn to the foundation cloth at spaced intervals, and a similar cloth was fixed on top, the springs being sewn to that also. The ends of the two cloths were then turned in to form a box for the springs, and the top padded. Two years earlier, in 1826, Pratt had patented a chair with spiral springs that gave resilience to a fabric-covered seat; but it was intended to prevent or alleviate sea-sickness, and was not a conscious contribution to increasing the comfort of easy chairs. Spiral springs had been known in the first half of the eighteenth century and used in the chamber horse, a device consisting of layers of such springs, separated by thin boards, enclosed in a leathern envelope that resembled a large concertina, the whole appliance being framed in mahogany. As the motions of horse riding could be performed upon it, the name "horse exercising machine" was sometimes used. In an advertisement published in *The London Daily Post and General Advertiser* on March 5, 7, and

10, 1739–40, Henry Marsh of Clement's-Inn Passage, Clare-Market, describes himself as the inventor, though he may have been only the first maker to advertise the device. There is no trace of his name at the Patent Office, either among the accepted official patentees, or among those who were merely granted a degree of protection for their inventions. Sheraton illustrates a chamber horse on Plate 3 of *The Cabinet-Maker and Upholsterer's Drawing Book* (3rd revised edition, 1802).

Five years after Samuel Pratt took out his patent for spiral springs, Loudon described their use for seats and bedding in his *Encyclopaedia*. "These springs," he said, "are placed side by side, on interlaced webbing, strained to a frame of the intended size of the bed, cushion or seat; they are then all confined by cords to one height, and covered by a piece of ticken or strong canvass, strained tightly over them." He concluded by saying: "The effect of spiral springs as stuffing has been long known to men of science; but so little to upholsterers, that a patent for using them in stuffing was taken out, some years ago, as a new invention. Beds and seats of this description are now, however, made by upholsterers generally, and the springs may be had from Birmingham by the hundredweight." He illustrated a double-cone spring, and was, presumably, referring to Pratt's patent, when he mentioned "a new invention". Well-sprung upholstery still had an air of luxurious novelty as late as the 1850s, for Surtees described Jack Spraggon sitting "cross-legged in an easy, spring, stuffed chair", while he collaborated with Mr Sponge in composing the account of the Puffington run.

The depth of seat demanded by spring upholstery affected the proportions and shape of the easy chair, so the legs were shortened, and the frame, while still an integral part of the design, seemed to be exercising a restraining function. Buttoned upholstery with the buttons deeply sunk exaggerated the curves and thickness of seat and back, like the examples on pages 211 and 213, reproduced from the second "improved" edition of *The Modern Style of Cabinet Work* (1832), a book as prophetic as Loudon's *Encyclopaedia of Cottage, Farm, and Villa Architecture and Furniture* (1833), for both gave a pre-view of Victorian design. The anonymous author of the first-named work explained in his preliminary "Address" that "As far as possible, the English style is carefully blended with Parisian

Easy chair with carved mahogany frame, stuffed arms and back, and silk lace on the side panels, matching the colour of the upholstery. Compare this with the example on page 213. From *The Modern Style of Cabinet Work* (London, 1832), plate 29.

taste: and a chaste contour and simplicity of parts is attempted in all the objects, which, being in some degree confined in dimensions and form, present rather a difficulty in the adaption of Grecian, Roman, and Gothic Ornaments". The "chaste contour" was occasionally sacrificed, not only to meet the requirements of bulging upholstery, but because the adaptation of classic ornaments was sometimes beyond the capacity of chair-carvers and frame-makers in the second quarter of the nineteenth century, though skill abounded and was lavished on furniture for the upper class market. The easy chairs above and on page 213 show that

Georgian graces were already on the way out, though they did not disappear altogether until after the Great Exhibition of 1851 had consolidated the confusion of ornament with design, and such compositions as "The Day Dreamer" easy chair showed how all sense of style had disappeared too.

That chair reveals much about Victorian taste, and epitomises the romantic, sentimental approach to design; for sentimentality had become as much a part of comfort as deeply-sprung upholstery. Armchairs and easy chairs were held in affectionate regard. In 1838, when she was twenty, Eliza Cook had written "The Old Armchair", and achieved fame on both sides of the Atlantic:

> "I love it, I love it; and who shall dare
> To chide me for loving that old arm-chair."

That couplet, which is all that most people can now remember of the poem, must have been recited and quoted millions of times in England and America in the mid-nineteenth century. If ever a chair was designed with the idea of inspiring love and affection, it was "The Day Dreamer". An illustration of it, reproduced from the *Official Descriptive and Illustrated Catalogue of the Great Exhibition*, on a slightly reduced scale, appears on page 215. The visible parts of the frame were made of papier mâché, and it was comfortably but strenuously upholstered, for the deeply-sunk buttons of the back produced not only an over-emphatic quilted effect, but an effect of strain, like a fat man about to burst out of very tight clothes. The symbolic character of the ornament was described in the *Official Catalogue* as follows:—

"The chair is decorated at the top with two winged thoughts—the one with bird-like pinions, and crowned with roses, representing happy and joyous dreams; the other with leathern bat-like wings—unpleasant and troublesome ones. Behind is displayed Hope, under the figure of the rising sun. The twisted supports of the back are ornamented with the poppy, hearts-ease, convolvulus and snow-drop, all emblematic of the subject. In front of the seat is a shell, containing the head of a cherub, and on either side of it, pleasant and troubled dreams are represented by figures. At the side is seen a figure of Puck, lying asleep in a labyrinth of foliage,

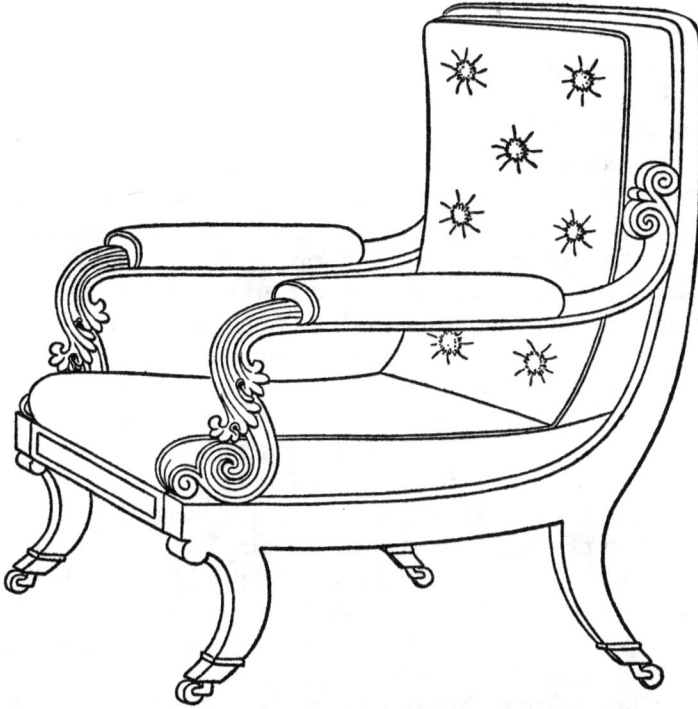

Easy chair, with scrolled arms, and stunted sabre legs. The Georgian graces are departing; so is the aptitude for good proportion; lines have coarsened; the design is portly rather than corpulent, but corpulence is on the way. From *The Modern Style of Cabinet Work* (London, 1832), plate 36.

and holding a branch of poppies in his hand. The style of the ornament is Italian."

From the 1830s onwards easy chairs acquired a robust and emphatically masculine character, nor was this modified until the late Victorian period, when they became less massive. During the second quarter of the century they were often upholstered in leather, stuffed all over so the frame was concealed, as in Hepplewhite's "saddle check" (page 157), and Sheraton's hunting chair. Mr Jorrocks had a "red morocco hunting-chair in the back drawing-room of Great Coram Street". *Handley Cross* was published in 1843; Sheraton's term was still current, and Leech's drawing of Jorrocks in the 1854 edition makes it clear that he was seated in the wider variety, "made larger a few inches each way", as Sheraton had specified.

The almost aggressive masculinity of the "stuffed all over" easy chair was modified later, when circular-seated types with voluptuous curves were developed, like the "Wolsey" on page 216, advertised by Oetzmann and Company in 1883 as "very soft and comfortable", and sold at £3 3s., or £3 17s. 6d., for an extra size. The depth of the seat has reduced the legs to mere feet, supported on castors; its size may well indicate an increasing tendency to stoutness in men, and from such a design elegance is perforce excluded. Far lighter but equally comfortable types known as lounging chairs had been introduced in the late 1840s and '50s, both in England and America, with long seats, an inclined back, open sides, and decorative ball turning. The two examples illustrated on page 219 anticipate a form that was later associated with the name of William Morris, whose firm produced a much simplified version of this long-seated easy chair. The long rectangular seat was ultimately adopted for the "club divan", a chair that rivalled the "grandfather" in popularity towards the end of the century. A detachable covering was used on the backs of easy chairs to protect them from being stained by the macassar oil used in hairdressing; but during the later Victorian period the anti-macassar became purely ornamental.

When the high-backed winged easy chair was reintroduced during the last quarter of the century, its popularity was increased by the sentimental name of "Grandfather", which became current at some time in the 1880s, shortly after "grandfather" was adopted as a term for long-case clocks. This had undoubtedly been suggested by the opening lines of Henry C. Work's song, "My Grandfather's Clock," which ran:

> "My grandfather's clock was too large for the shelf,
>   So it stood ninety years on the floor;
>   It was taller by half than the old man himself
>   Though it weighed not a pennyweight more."

As the upholstery of all varieties of seat-furniture became softer and deeper, the shapes of armchairs, sofas, divans, companion

Easy chair in papier mâché with buttoned upholstery, designed by H. Fitz
Cook and made by Jennens and Betteridge, of London and Birmingham.
This was shown at the Great Exhibition of 1851, and called "The Day
Dreamer". The name was explained, and the decoration described with
becoming seriousness. (See page 212.) Reproduced from the *Official Descriptive
and Illustrated Catalogue of the Great Exhibition of 1851*, Vol. II, plate 30.

H*

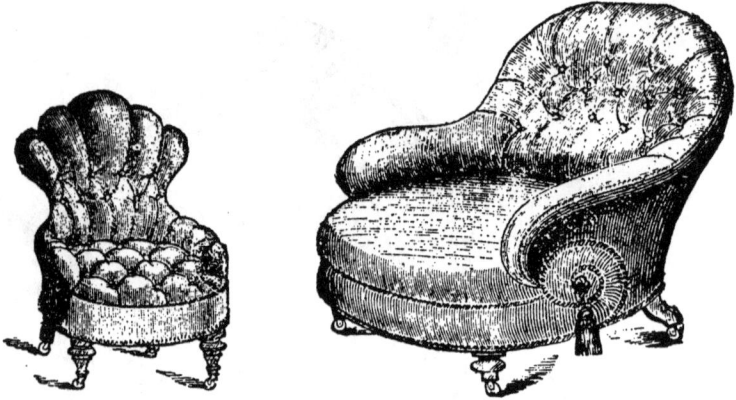

Left: The Prince of Wales' Lady's easy chair, advertised by Oetzmann and Company, of Hampstead Road, London. From *The Graphic*, August 25, 1883, page 194.   *Right:* The "Wolsey" easy chair, with a circular and very deep seat, arms and back inclined, and legs so short that they are little more than feet. Also by Oetzmann and Company and advertised in the same paper, March 31, 1883, page 331.

chairs and ottomans, became correspondingly obese, and far more relaxed postures were encouraged and permissible for adults, at least in the privacy of the home. Children remained unprivileged: they were expected to sit bolt upright, preferably in silence. A distinction between private and party manners, never alluded to, was now quietly accepted. Outwardly the Victorians valued dignity as much as their Georgian grandfathers and great-grandfathers, though ladies and gentlemen in the eighteenth century unconsciously enjoyed an advantage denied to their descendants, for they could be consistently dignified without the ever-present temptation to sprawl inelegantly that Victorian upholsterers provided in nearly every room; the Georgians might recline gracefully in a chair, or, like Horace Walpole, loll on a *péché-mortel*—they never lounged. That habit was roundly condemned in a short book on manners, etiquette, and general deportment, published in 1842, entitled *The Art of Conversation, with Remarks on Fashion and Address,* and written by Captain Orlando Sabertash. "There is a practice getting into vogue," he said,

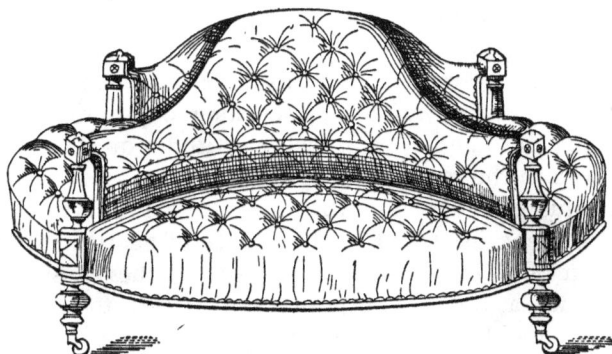

A circular ottoman, with buttoned upholstery, divided into four wide seats, and able to accommodate eight people. These relatively simple types were made in the early Victorian period: later they became more complicated. From a trade catalogue of an unknown maker, *circa* 1840–45.

The companion chair, to seat six persons, designed for the centre of a drawing room. From Tallis's *History and Description of the Crystal Palace, and the Exhibition of the World's Industry, 1851*. Edited by J. G. Strutt, Vol. II.

"almost into a sort of fashion, among young gentlemen who wish to impose upon the unwary, by *nonchalant* airs of affected ease and freedom from restraint, which I must here denounce as a breach of good manners, and a want of all just feelings of propriety;—I mean the practice of lounging in graceless attitudes on sofas and arm-chairs, even in the presence of ladies. All these vile and distorted postures must be reserved for the library-couch, or arm-chair, and should never be displayed in the society of gentlemen, and still less in that of ladies. In their own houses, ladies must submit to such conduct, as they cannot well leave a visitor to himself: at all times they should, if they have any respect for their own dignity, give the lounger the cut-direct, and go to some other part of the room. Once denounced, however, as vulgar and uncivil, the nuisance will cease of itself; for the guilty only offend, under the impression of being thought superlatively fine." He added that "Lounging is not a foreign vice, though foreigners take up the practice to an extravagant degree when mixing with English Society".

Easy chairs for ladies were light and small, compared with the male equivalent, a compromise between comfort and elegance; but they were well-upholstered rather than well-designed, and because the seat was low and the arms, in order to accommodate the crinoline, were either vestigial or dispensed with altogether, they looked squat, like the example with the buttoned shell back and seat on page 216, reproduced from an advertisement by Oetzmann and Company, published in *The Graphic* in 1883. The shape persisted, although by that date the crinoline was out and the bustle was in. That particular chair, called "The Prince of Wales", for no apparent reason, was described as "very comfortable", and sold at 32s., or 36s. for "superior ditto, all hair". An earlier type of lady's chair with a black japanned frame, a spoon back, and turned front legs, appears on the lower part of plate 61, an example that is not misshapen by concessions to comfort, although the front legs with their over-emphatic turning are incompatible with the curves and moulded detail of the back frame. The return of the high-backed winged easy chair was welcomed by such writers as Lady Barker, whose book, *The Bedroom and Boudoir*, appeared in 1878, and disclosed a trend of taste which rejected chairs that were "a mass of padded and

Above: An American easy chair, included by Andrew Jackson Downing in *The Architecture of Country Houses* (New York, 1850). He described it as a "lounge, better adapted for siesta, than to promote the grace or dignity of the figure". *Below:* An English lounging chair, illustrated in *The Adventures of Mr Verdant Green*, by Edward Bradley (who used the pen name of Cuthbert Bede), published 1853-56.

"Here is a chair of a pattern familiar to all travellers on the P. and O. boats," wrote Lady Barker, "and whose acquaintance I first made in Ceylon. It is essentially a gentleman's chair, however, and as such is sinking into an honoured and happy old age in the dingy recesses of a London smoking-room. Without the side-wings, which serve equally for a table or leg-rest, and with the seat elongated and slightly depressed, such a chair makes a delicious, cool lounge for a lady's use in a verandah." Like so many Victorian writers, her ideas about design and finish were impeccable. "It seems a pity," she said, "that sofas and chairs made of straw or bamboo should not be more used than they are. I mean, used as they come from the maker's hands, *not* painted or gilded, and becushioned and bedizened into hopeless vulgarity. They are only admissible *au naturel*, and should stand upon their own merits." From *The Bedroom and Boudoir* (1878), Chapter VII, pages 80–82.

cushioned excrescences". She illustrated a fine, mid-eighteenth century type of winged chair, and said: "If one *must* have large armchairs in a boudoir, or in a bedroom, here is one which is big enough in all conscience, and yet would go more harmoniously with an old-fashioned room than any fat and dumpy modern chair."

The high-backed winged chair was warmly welcomed and commercially recommended by the furniture trade during the last decade of the century; no "novel" or complicated variations of the framework and upholstery could wholly obliterate the basic excellence of the traditional design: not even the repellent practice of covering an easy chair or settee with velvet and large panels of oriental carpet. "The most fashionable type of easy chair at the present time is that known as the 'Fireside' or 'Grandfather'," said the anonymous writer of an article on easy chairs, published in *Furniture and Decoration*, October, 1897. "The elegance and comfort

The round-seated, open plaited basket chair, smaller than the croquet chair, which was semi-circular in plan, with arms and back continuous, and buttoned upholstery. This much simpler type had a loose cushion in the seat, and the shape had probably survived unaltered for centuries. From *The Adventures of Mr Verdant Green*, by Edward Bradley (published 1853–56), page 160.

By the 1890s the high-backed winged easy chair was always called a "grand-father", and variations of the traditional form resulted in shapes like this, which was illustrated, with three other designs and some laudatory descriptions, in *Furniture and Decoration*, August 1897. "The appearance of our present-day dining-room easy chairs is decidedly inviting," said the anonymous writer of the descriptive notes. "The prevailing designs seem to accord with one or two of the most comfortable types of lounges, to wit, the 'Grandfather' fireside chair and the 'Club' divan. Either of these favourite chairs, when properly proportioned and skilfully upholstered, makes a seat that may be described as the acme of luxurious ease. In point of coverings these dining-room chairs have of late years been conspicuous for a great diversity of colouring and material, and even in the seemingly stereotyped leather coverings many welcome innovations have been introduced. Thus, for example, where but a few years ago the limit of variety in this durable and always fashionable material was marked by a small range of crude colours and the absence or presence of buttoning on the seat and back, now-a-days the most charming dyes are available and the leather employed for furniture purposes is embossed with many beautiful and attractive patterns." The "Club" divan was an easy chair with an exceptionally long, rectangular seat.

of this kind of seat," he continued, "warrant the expectation that it will enjoy lasting favour, and it is therefore highly probable that easy chairs with high backs and side shoulders will long continue to be standard patterns among fashionable upholstery. . . . As a rule these chairs are made decidedly low in the seat so that they can be used only as luxurious lounges. The growing popularity of tall arm-chairs, such as those accompanying Sheraton and Chippendale suites, makes it probable that a stately 'Fireside' chair, if built upon similar lines, would prove acceptable. Such chairs could be employed at the head and end of the dining table, where their stately appearance would be peculiarly appropriate, whilst as chimney corner seats they would lose nothing of their usefulness."

Dining room easy chairs were the subject of another article published in that trade journal in August 1897, and plush, velvet, tapestry or leather were recommended as covering materials. One of the designs that accompanied the article is reproduced on page 222, and is very different from the "well-wadded leather arm-chair" in which the tall and portly Mr Bultitude is lying back when we meet him in Chapter One of *Vice Versa*. But Mr Bulti-tude's dining room in Westbourne Terrace was "furnished in the stern uncompromising style of the Mahogany Age" and the "sideboard, diner-wagon, and row of stiff chairs were all carved in the same massive and expensive style of ugliness". Anstey's classic story was published in 1882; the room he described was at least twenty years earlier, and probably arranged in accordance with the explicit directions for dining-rooms given by Robert Kerr in *The Gentleman's House*. "One feature which has always a sub-stantial and hospitable aspect in this apartment," he wrote, "is the unbroken line of chairs at the wall. Although it is not desirable to make a Gentleman's Dining-room like the Assembly-Hall of a Corporation or the Long-room of a tavern by carrying this prin-ciple to an extreme, yet it is not well when dinner waggons, cheffoniers, or whatever else, are placed at intervals in such number as to give the apartment the character of a Parlour. In fact, as much as possible, every chair ought to stand at the wall facing its place at the table; whereby, if no more, a species of association is kept up with the primary purpose of the room. If dinner waggons or cheffoniers are employed—which is commonly the case in rooms of any size—their best position, and most useful, is at the two end corners opposite the Sideboard. In superior rooms it is sometimes the practice to place the chairs, when not in use, not against the wall, but around the table. If this be done to leave the wall-space free for the display of objects of vertu, it is so far well; otherwise care has to be taken that there shall be some other sufficient reason apparent."

Easy chairs and armchairs were not, as Lady Barker assumed, invariably "fat and dumpy". At the time she wrote her book, three main divisions of taste had been established, which affected design and regulated demand. The enormously wealthy landed proprietors were in a class apart; but the three divisions of taste covered all sections of the great middle class; the working class in the towns being too poor to have much choice about anything. Firstly, at the top end of the market, were those who could afford to follow fashion, and supported every new style that came along with enthusiasm; secondly, and usually enjoying the same or a higher level of income, were the solid, "warm" people, whose homes, like the house at Dulwich to which Mr Pickwick retired, were "fitted up with every attention to substantial comfort, perhaps to a little elegance besides. . . ". As good plain Philistines they cared more for "substantial comfort" and were prepared to forego elegance. Those in the third and by far the largest division of taste were mainly concerned with getting the best of both worlds cheaply: comfort first, then just enough fashion to keep up with the Joneses, for the pursuit of status is as old as envy. Comfort was the common denominator of taste throughout the Victorian period, and by the 1860s chair-makers were producing designs that were comfortable without being clumsy, satisfying alike for those who wanted to lounge, to sit upright, or to curl up like Alice in Tenniel's illustration opposite. When Tenniel made that drawing for *Through the Looking Glass* in 1870, buttoned upholstery was as popular as ever, and on the armchair he depicted it was under far better control, confined by a bold, well-formed frame, with the scrolls that supported the arms and the curves of the back agreeably related. Such chairs with their rich red polished mahogany frames, represented the vernacular Victorian style that was happily free from ornamental debauchery. That style had followed a transitional period of fumbling compromise, which had lasted some

When Tenniel drew this picture of Alice curled up in a chair the date was 1870, and by that time Victorian chair-makers were catering for comfort without clumsiness. Buttoned upholstery, a robust, well-proportioned frame, a discreet use of carved ornament, and a happy relationship between the scrolled arm supports and the curves of the back, give this armchair an agreeable character. Rich, red polished mahogany would almost certainly have been used for the turned legs and exposed parts of the arms and back frame. This example of the vernacular Victorian style is far superior in design to the easy chair shown on page 213. Reproduced from *Through the Looking Glass*, by Lewis Carroll, by permission of Macmillan & Company Ltd.

Heraldic chair, "upon the surface of which are sculptured the arms borne by the ancestors of her most gracious Majesty in the Saxon line". Shown at the Great Exhibition of 1851, commended as "a work of considerable merit", and made by G. Shacklock of Bolsover, near Chesterfield. Reproduced from *The Art-Journal Illustrated Catalogue*, page 225.

A rustic chair of bog oak, made by G. Collison of Doncaster and shown at the Great Exhibition of 1851. The carver has remained in control of the design; the cresting on the back, the delicate openwork foliations below the seat and arms, are crisply executed, and robust, well-proportioned lines have been preserved. Compare this with Robert Manwaring's rural chair, on page 148, conceived nearly a century earlier. Reproduced from *The Art-Journal Illustrated Catalogue*, page 310.

227

fifteen years, from 1825 to 1840, when the last memories of the Greek Revival were effaced, and the virile lines of the true Victorian style emerged. That style developed independently and, uninfluenced by passing modes, continued to satisfy the people who valued solid comfort and liked to be cosy—the people in the second division of taste who ignored fashions whether they came from France, Turkey or Japan, or were generated by artistic coteries or collectors of antique furniture.

In that transitional period, before the vernacular style came to maturity, furniture in the Georgian Gothic taste was still being made, similar in character to the sofa and easy chair in the drawing-room of Eaton Hall shown on plate 60, with Gothic ornament used in a subdued manner; very different from the furniture Pugin had in mind when he condemned upholsterers who "seem to think that nothing can be Gothic unless it is found in some church". This was part of his general condemnation of the more unintelligent and insensitive exponents of the Gothic Revival, which appeared in his book, *The True Principles of Pointed or Christian Architecture*, published in 1841. "Hence your modern man," he continued, "designs a sofa or occasional table from details culled out of Britton's Cathedrals, and all the ordinary articles of furniture, which require to be simple and convenient, are made not only very expensive but very uneasy. We find diminutive flying buttresses about an arm-chair; every thing is crocketed with angular projections, innumerable mitres, sharp ornaments, and turreted extremities. A man who remains any length of time in a modern Gothic room, and escapes without being wounded by some of its minutiae, may consider himself extremely fortunate." Many of the ornate chairs made for display at the Great Exhibition of 1851 were "very expensive" and "very uneasy", like the Heraldic chair illustrated on page 226, but although such show pieces were exceptional, the intemperate praise given to their workmanship was enough to sanction comparable excesses. Fortunately the vernacular style was well-established before the Great Exhibition was opened.

During the formative years of the style, the debilitating influence of luxurious upholstery was largely confined to armchairs, easy chairs and sofas; the single chair, while sharing some of the comfort of improved springing and stuffing, was immune from the

Two drawing-room chairs. From *The Modern Style of Cabinet Work* (London, 1832), plates 31 and 34.

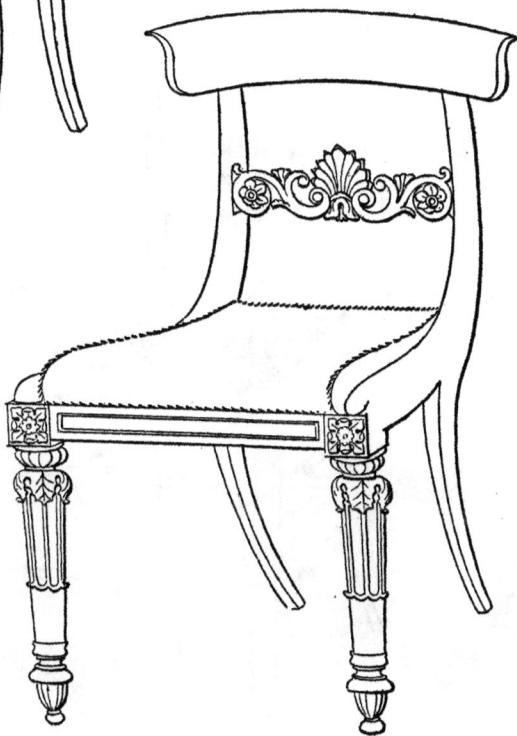

Two cane-seated bedroom chairs. From *The Modern Style of Cabinet Work* (London, 1832), plate 30.

Right: Drawing-room chair with stuffed back. *Below:* Parlour chair, described as "massive and plain". From *The Modern Style of Cabinet Work* (London, 1832), plates 32 and 34.

grossness of the larger forms of seat-furniture. For several years the memory of the *klismos*, as edited by Thomas Hope and his contemporaries, remained as a guide to good proportions. The two drawing-room chairs on page 229 show the process of change, for the upper example has the same characteristics as Hope's chair on plate 7 and the comparable design on plate 55, while the other has heavy turned legs instead of the elegant concave type, though they are still used at the back. Both chairs, also those on pages 230 and 231, are reproduced from *The Modern Style of Cabinet Work*, referred to earlier. The bedroom chairs on page 230 retain the gently curving line which gives continuity to the back legs and uprights—more graceful than the earlier light cane-seated chairs shown in Severn's portrait of Keats on plate 56 which have a pronounced break in the back line—while the turned front legs, slender stretchers and decorative back spindles exhibit the spontaneity and freshness of the native English style. At this stage of the transition from late Georgian to early Victorian the native tradition re-emerged and gave a vitality to chair design comparable with that animating the country-made Windsor types. Sometimes the results were as uncompromisingly masculine as "stuffed all over" easy chairs; "massive and plain" is the description of the parlour chair on page 231, although that particular example still had the classic Greek Revival form of back. The complete break with the classical Georgian past came with the introduction of the balloon back chair, and variations of this design were used in dining-rooms, drawing-rooms and parlours, with a lighter, completely round-backed type for bedrooms. These open circular-backed bedoom chairs were sometimes known as Quaker chairs, a name that appears to have been current in the furniture trade in the nineteenth century, though how it originated is unknown. The balloon type, with an elliptical back and a straight cross rail, like the middle example at the top of page 233, has recently been called a buckle back, presumably because of its likeness to a belt buckle, but that is a piece of dealers' jargon; nearly all variations of the type were covered by the term balloon back, even when the oval frame was filled by a stuffed panel. The three examples at the top of page 233 are from a trade catalogue issued about 1840, and below two obvious forerunners of the balloon back are reproduced from Loudon's *Encyclopaedia*. A slender and elegant development

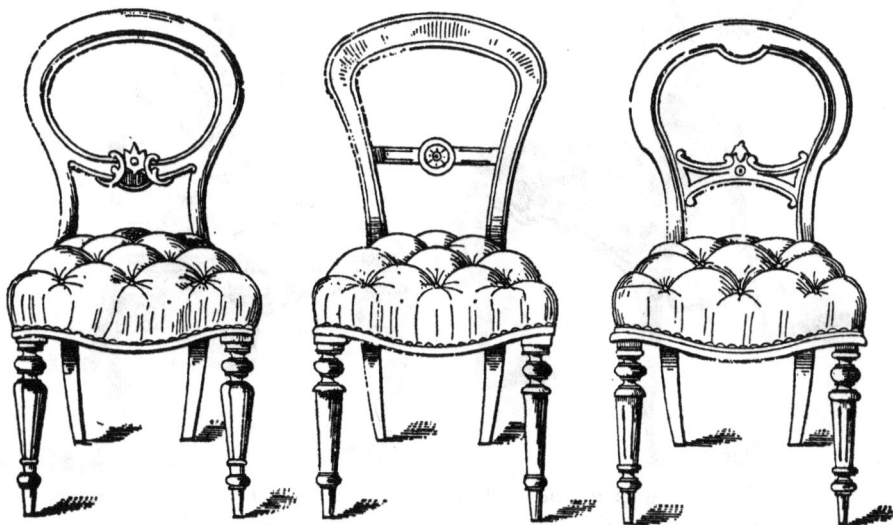

Above: Three balloon back dining-room mahogany chairs, with leather seats and buttoning, reproduced from a trade catalogue, *circa* 1840. *Below:* Drawing-room chairs in rosewood, which anticipate the early Victorian balloon back. Reproduced from Loudon's *Encyclopaedia* (1833), page 1063. (The chair on the left and the example in the centre above are sometimes called buckle back, which is certainly descriptive; but balloon back is the generally accepted term for all varieties of this type.)

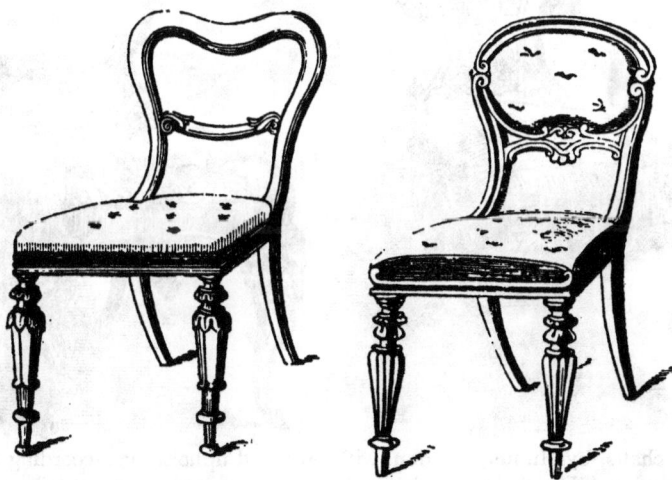

Left: Chair in papier mâché, with balloon-back. By Jennens and Betteridge, Birmingham and London. It was called the "Légère Chair". *Right:* Mahogany hall chair, with buttoned upholstered seat, by G. W. England, Leeds.

Two chairs, by Hunter, London, with buttoned upholstery. According to the description, "The chairs are of very elegant design, and are beautifully carved; they are, however, as remarkable for their comfort as for their elegance, and present all that is requisite for the beauty or the ease of the drawing-room."

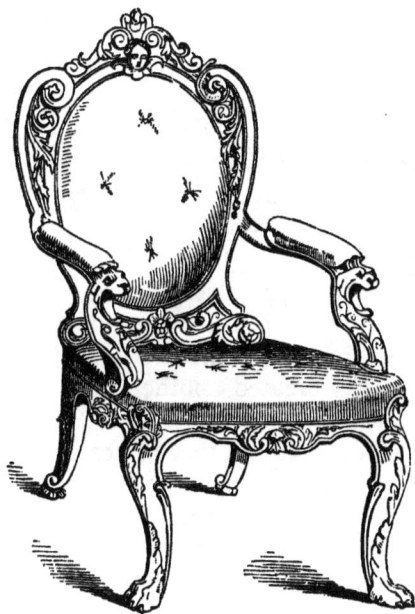

The chairs reproduced on this and the opposite page were all shown at the Great Exhibition of 1851, and included in *The Art-Journal Illustrated Catalogue*. *Above, left:* Armchair by Gillow, London. *Above, right:* Drawing-room chair, by Jackson and Graham, London. An adaptation of the balloon-back, with an oval upholstered panel. *Right:* Cane-seated papier mâché chair, by M'Cullum and Hodgson, Birmingham. Another example of an adapted early Victorian balloon back. Compare this chair with the more elaborate design on plate 61.

of the balloon type appears in the walnut bedroom chair at the top right of plate 61, with the centre and yoke rails of the back formed from cusps and foils, and the turned front legs slightly splayed. Chairs like this, made during the 1860s, were not ornamented; and their decorative quality, arising from a subtle grace of line, conclusively refutes the common belief that Victorian chair-makers were congenitally incapable of producing anything except oafish offerings to comfort. Apart from the distinctive style represented by the balloon back type, they created another style of light, cane-seated drawing-room chair made of papier mâché, japanned and delicately ornamented with inlaid mother-of-pearl and gold painted decoration. The example at the top left of plate 61 shows how the maker has taken full advantage of the ductile material to produce a graceful shape; the chair at the bottom of page 235 shows how that opportunity has been missed. Another variation of the balloon back appears in the papier mâché "Légère Chair" at the top left of page 234, shown at the Great Exhibition by Jennens and Betteridge, and an adaptation with an oval stuffed panel in the drawing-room chair by Jackson and Graham at the top right of page 235. The seven chairs illustrated on those two pages reveal the variety and uneven quality of the exhibits at the Crystal Palace in 1851; four of them are ill-proportioned, with indifferently carved decoration, badly chosen and unrelated to the frame. The examples at the bottom of page 234 by Hunter were highly praised for their comfort and elegance in *The Art-Journal Illustrated Catalogue*, from which they are reproduced: both are overloaded with carving far too heavy and profuse for the frames. The mahogany chair on the same page, top right, which resembles the type usually found in halls, is by England of Leeds, and the legs, seat rail and back have been separately conceived as ornamental features and casually assembled; while the armchair by Gillow at the top left of page 235 represents another assembly of odds and ends of classic ornament, used without taste or discretion.

The reappearance of rococo ornament in the 1850s, emphasized the vast difference between Georgian and Victorian chair-makers; for in the eighteenth century the rococo style had been edited with skill and judgment, but this no longer happened, and many Victorian drawing rooms were furnished with flimsy chairs that

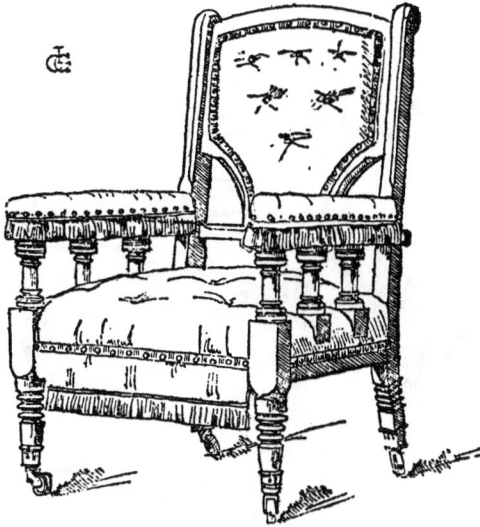

Drawing room arm chair in oak, designed by Charles Lock Eastlake, upholstered in velvet, and trimmed with silk fringe. Unlike the chair with Alice in
it on page 225, this is a deliberate attempt to break away from conventional
patterns; but is not the sort of design an accomplished chair-maker would have
produced; or anybody with a sense of style. From *Hints on Household Taste*
(second revised edition, 1869).

frothed with carved and gilded decoration. Chairs that were
described as Elizabethan, with spiral twisted legs, stretchers and
back posts, became popular in the 1840s and '50s, but they were
not remotely like Elizabethan chairs, and were adaptations of
Carolean chairs, but without the vigorous qualities of the prototype. Rosewood, black walnut and oak were all used for frames,
and the wood was polished and darkened, and mahogany—the
most favoured material—was given a reddish tinge by the use of
brick-dust. Charles Lock Eastlake, whose *Hints on Household Taste*
has been quoted in chapter 9, condemned the finishes used by the
furniture trade. "The present system of French-polishing, or
literally *varnishing*, furniture is," he said, "destructive of all artistic
effect in its appearance, because the surface of the wood thus
lacquered can never change its colour, or acquire that rich hue

"Few articles of furniture have received so much attention at the hands of designers as the chair frame, with the result that it becomes increasingly difficult to infuse originality thereto." That opening sentence of some notes on chairs, by Reg. Audley, appeared in *The Cabinet Maker and Art Furnisher*, March 1896, page 230. Five designs accompanied his remarks, of which one is shown above and another on the opposite page. Both examples are excessively fragile in appearance, with legs so attentuated that their ability to support any well-built man or woman seems doubtful. The stretchers are too slender to have a structural function and are apparently only ornamental. Of the design above, the writer said: "The back and arms . . . seem to suggest that the designer derived his inspiration from the works of Sheraton, though the legs are hardly in accordance with the traditions of that old master."

which is one of the chief charms of old cabinet-work." He believed that "Good artistic furniture ought really to be quite as cheap as that which is ugly. Every wretched knot of carving, every twist in the outline of a modern sofa, every bead and hollow executed by the turner's wheel, has been the result of *design* in some form or another. The draughtsman and mechanic must be paid, whatever the nature of their tastes may be; and no doubt as much thought, labour, and expense of material are bestowed on modern upholstery as would be necessary to ensure (under proper supervision) the highest qualities of which the cabinetmaker's art is capable."

He followed those criticisms by describing and illustrating a drawing-room chair of his own design, reproduced on page 237, which is not the sort of thing an accomplished chair-maker, or anybody with a sense of style, would have produced. Eastlake was an architect—from 1866 to 1877 he was secretary of the Royal Institute of British Architects—and like his Georgian predecessors recognized the responsibility of his profession for all branches of design, a responsibility forgotten or ignored by most of his contemporaries, and in the preface to his book he said: "Fifty years ago an architect would probably have considered it beneath his dignity to give attention to the details of cabinet-work, upholstery, and decorative painting." He was wrong: half a century before that was written, Thomas Hope's *Household Furniture and Interior Decoration* had been out for just a year, and architects still retained

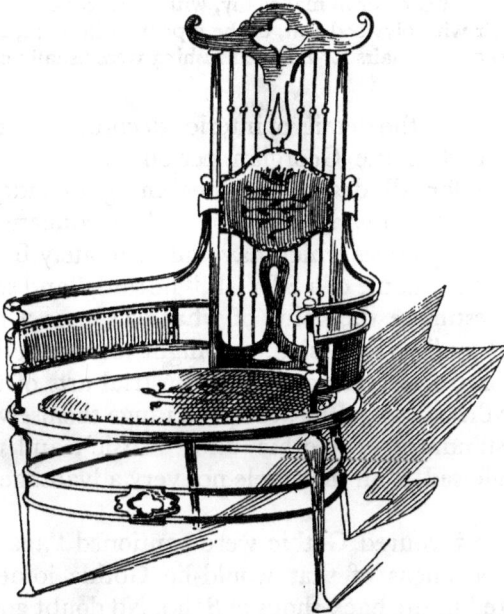

The influence of *Art-Nouveau* is apparent in this circular-seated, high-backed armchair. From *The Cabinet Maker and Art Furnisher*, March 1896, page 230. See opposite page, and compare with examples on pages 259, 260 and 261.

I

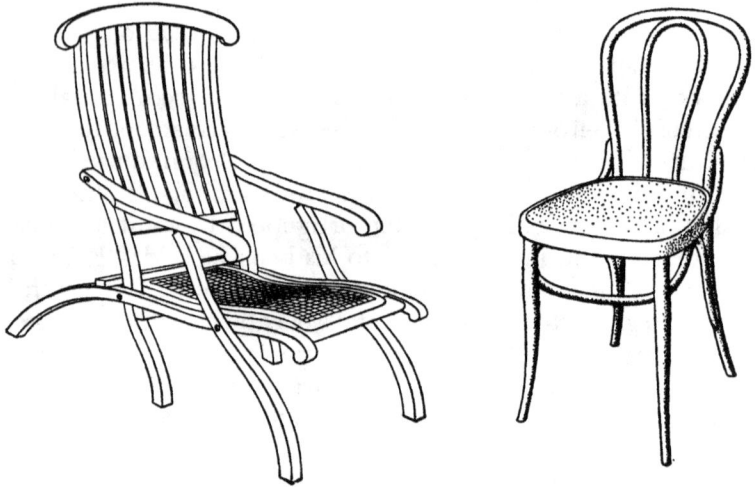

Left: Folding steamer chair in mahogany, with cane seat and slat back. *Right:* Bentwood chair with plywood seat, of the type used in shops, restaurants and hotels. Bentwood chairs for home furnishing were usually cane-seated.

a lively interest in the details of interior decoration and furnishing: but by the end of the Georgian period that sense of universal responsibility for all design was beginning to fade, and when Eastlake wrote it had vanished. "If people of education would but lay aside the prejudices which have unfortunately become identified with the very name of a STYLE," he said, "and set themselves seriously to estimate the value of what was once a national and unperverted *tradition* in design, we might look more hopefully on the future of architecture and the industrial arts of this country. As it is, our British amateurs are apt to range themselves under the respective standards of 'Gothic' and 'Classic'; and the result, it must be confessed, is on the whole not very advantageous to either cause."

Those who favoured Gothic were cautioned "against the contemptible specimens of that would-be Gothic joinery which is manufactured in the back-shops of Soho. No doubt good examples of mediaeval furniture and cabinet-work are occasionally to be met with in the curiosity shops of Wardour-Street; but, as a rule, the 'Glastonbury' chairs and 'antique' bookcases which are sold in that venerable thoroughfare will prove on examination to be nothing but gross libels on the style of art which they are supposed to represent." Eastlake was innocent enough to suppose that authentic examples of mediaeval furniture could be picked up at all: very little had survived: but he was right about the credulity that dealers exploited. The word "antique" was only then becoming generally accepted as a term for old furniture; before that the word "ancient" was used for articles made earlier than the eighteenth century, and the first English book on the subject, mentioned and quoted in chapter 4, was *Specimens of Ancient Furniture*, published in 1836, with drawings by Henry Shaw and descriptions by Sir Samuel Rush Meyrick. The taste for collecting antique furniture developed concurrently with the handicraft revival, which was fostered by the work and teaching of William Morris; and while the interest in old furniture stimulated the furniture trade to copy the work of the seventeenth and eighteenth centuries, more or less badly, the handicraft revival had no immediate or direct influence on industrial production, for it was conceived, preached and practised by a romantic mediaevalist who detested the age he lived in and reviled the mechanical achievements that had increased the wealth and greatness and ugliness of his country.

These aesthetic battles and competing forms of taste affected only a relatively small number of people; the majority simply wanted to be comfortable—young, middle-aged, and old alike—and they were catered for by the furniture trade without restraint. After the Great Exhibition the frame of nearly every type of seat was lost in layers of stuffing, and one of the most popular, the Chesterfield settee, was described by Rosamund Marriott Watson in *The Art of the House*, written in the late '90s, as that "obese, kindly-natured couch ... about as comely as a gigantic pin-cushion, and as little convenient in a room of moderate dimensions as an elephant. ..." (Defunct elephants did play an occasional part in Victorian furnishing, as we shall see later in this chapter.) Apart from Chesterfields and ottomans, there was an enormous array of lounging chairs conducive to those "vile and distorted postures" censured by Captain Orlando Sabertash, including light types in canework and wicker, with retractable foot-rests, and broad arms on which books, newspapers and glasses could stand,

Long, backless benches, with upholstered seats were often used in the mid-Victorian dining room for large parties, instead of individual dining room chairs. Reproduced from *Fun*, December 9, 1869, page 124. The scale is slightly reduced.

like the example on page 220, also adjustable "invalid furniture", and what were tactfully called "literary machines", which were book-rests used in conjunction with reading seats. A range of such devices is illustrated in John Carter's advertisement, reproduced on page 244. A reading seat was described in the supplement to the 1846 edition of Loudon's *Encyclopaedia* as "by no means elegant in form; but we can assert, from experience, that it is exceedingly comfortable to sit on; not only the back, but the head being supported by the peculiar form of the upper part of the end, or support for the back". This was a descendant of the day bed, which gave a studious air to indolence. Wicker and canework chairs could be used indoors or out, and a particularly expansive variety called a croquet chair, had an ample semicircular seat, continuous back and arms, and buttoned upholstery; the simplest form, with open mesh back and base is shown on page 221, and by

The high-chairs for the children at the family dinner were rather flimsy descendants of the Astley-Cooper chair; those for adults were interchangeable in design with bedroom or drawing room chairs. Reproduced from *Judy*, June 1, 1870, page 53. The scale is slightly reduced.

the end of the century combinations of wicker and upholstery had degenerated to a repulsive complexity. Commenting on the products of a firm that specialized in "novelties in upholstered wicker furniture", *The Cabinet Maker and Art Furnisher* said: "After artistic effect, stability of construction is the point first considered by this firm, and their productions certainly seem capable of successfully resisting any amount of ordinary wear and tear." The coverings included "art serge, plushette, tapestries, cretonne, and Oriental fabrics. . . ." (October, 1896.)

A six-legged folding chair, with a slatted or canework back and seat, was introduced during the 1850s, and was described in Heal's catalogues, 1858–60, as a folding Derby chair. Such chairs were used extensively on passenger liners, and the name Derby was changed to steamer chair. In *Cassell's Household Guide* (1875) a Derby chair is defined as a folding type without arms; when laths

Every inducement to relax and lounge, or, if suffering from indigestion, to take exercise the easy way in chairs "with horse-action" was provided by such makers as John Carter, who published this advertisement in *The Graphic*, November 17, 1883, page 503.

244

Invalid chair shown at the Great Exhibition of 1851 by James Heath, described in the *Official Catalogue* as an inventor and manufacturer of 4 Broad Street, Bath. This was the basic form of the "Bath" chair; a sedate vehicle that was the Victorian Englishman's chair in old age and infirmity when he went out of doors. It was not exclusively male. Devoted daughters, cowed nieces, and expectant nephews were to be seen in all the spas and seaside resorts, pushing or pulling some iron-willed and petulant old lady. The parades and promenades of Bath, Cheltenham, Leamington, Brighton, Eastbourne and Bournemouth would have seemed as odd and empty without Bath chairs as the streets of London without hansom cabs in the second half of the nineteenth century. The example shown here is particularly luxurious, even for a special "Exhibition" model. Intended for "Open air exercise", it was described as "very elaborately painted and gilt, combining an amount of luxurious elegance by no means inapplicable to work of this kind. On the side panels, and on the back, are paintings: the one indicated . . . is from the 'Aurora' of Guido". Compare this example with the strictly functional types shown on the opposite page in John Carter's advertisement. The Bath chair was a Victorian institution, less wasteful of man-power than the Georgian Sedan, not quite so private, but at least as elegant and far more comfortable.

Reproduced from *The Art-Journal Illustrated Catalogue*, page 211.

Smoker's chairs, with a drawer below the seat, containing a spitoon. Although the spitoon had been frowned on as an article of furnishing during the closing decades of the nineteenth century, spitting continued, and this device satisfied the Victorian gentleman's exacting standards of comfort, and allowed him to pretend that the habit had passed away. These examples, made by Tarn & Company, were illustrated in *Furniture and Decoration*, February, 1897, pages 26–27.

or slats were used for both seat and back, the cost was as little as 4s. 6d., and it was recommended for ladies when padded, cushioned, and "covered in chintz or worsted rep . . . ". A lath-backed cane-seated example is shown on page 240.

Bentwood chairs, which Michael Thonet had invented, were as good-looking and comfortable as the native Windsor, and were structurally as simple and easy to manufacture. The frames were of beech, bent by heat and steam treatment to the shape required, with seats of plywood or canework. Towards the end of the century rushes in various colours were occasionally used, an innovation described in *The Cabinet Maker* as "a novelty, and one which will, doubtless be appreciated as it merits". (March, 1896.) Bentwood chairs were ubiquitous; commended by lightness, grace of line, and comfort, they were to be found in every home, in hotels, shops, restaurants, public buildings and assembly rooms. They represented a triumph of industrial design and mass-production. Although the intense aesthetes of the '80s and '90s might reject such cheap and convenient chairs, they were a boon to householders with large families; and, like the gilded rout chairs which Georgian upholsterers hired out, as their seventeenth century predecessors had hired out imbrauderers' chairs of the "farthingale" type, bentwood chairs could be hired for parties from the confectioner who did the catering or from a furniture shop. Before they were available, long padded backless benches, seating three or four people, were hired when a large dinner party demanded more chairs than a middle-class household could muster. Such benches are shown in the illustration on page 242, reproduced from the extinct comic paper *Fun*. The pre-bentwood dining-room furniture in a modest household would usually consist of a set of balloon back chairs with flimsy versions of the Astley-Cooper high chair for the children, like those in the Sunday dinner scene from *Judy* on page 243. Although bentwood chairs were manufactured in England, they were outside the English tradition of design, and like the seventeenth century imbrauderers' chairs, were European and insusceptible to national fashions, though they became an almost indispensable item in late Victorian furnishing.

Specialized chairs included a type designed for the coarser aspects of pipe smoking, for by the '90s the spitoon or cuspidor had been banished, even from studies and smoking-rooms. For a time

I*

it had lingered on, disguised as a footstool with a hinged lid concealing the spitting pan in the recess below; but even the delicately allusive name of salivarium could not save it, and the smoker's chair which replaced it allowed everybody to pretend that the habit of spitting had passed away. That chair was described in *Furniture and Decoration* (February, 1897), as follows:—

"Under the seat of an ordinary standard chair, a club divan, or an upright arm-chair, is placed a drawer. This drawer is kept normally closed by means of spiral springs, and is brought forward by means of a cord, terminating in a small button. A pan (which for cleaning purposes is made removable) is contained within the drawer. Thus, when required, the spitoon may be drawn forward, and then released, when it returns to its place automatically." (Two variations are shown on page 246.)

Quite apart from chairs with specialized functions were the eccentric results of collaboration between chair-makers and taxi-dermists, designed to satisfy the taste of big-game hunters and other animal lovers who demanded realism and wanted their trophies or mementos to serve a practical purpose. Since the days of ancient Egypt representations of the legs, hooves and paws of animals, and the talons and wings of birds had been used either as decoration or for some integral part of seat furniture, and the actual skins of animals as well; but in the late Victorian period—not only skins but stuffed animals were used for some very odd chairs indeed. In an article on "Animal Furniture", which appeared in *The Strand Magazine* in 1896, William G. Fitzgerald described and illustrated several uses for real animals in the hearty type of furnishing favoured by travellers and Empire-builders. One of his examples was a porter's chair modelled from a young Ceylon elephant by Rowland Ward, the famous taxidermist, "in a perfectly natural position, but adapted for the use of a hall porter". Another was a tub-backed armchair covered by a tiger-skin with the head and paws "so arranged as to give the impression that the terrible animal is about to spring". Such furniture gave the owner a perfect opening for inflicting an anecdote on a captive audience, and the "tiger chair" had a gruesome past. It was made, according to the author of the article, "for a gentleman in the Indian Civil Service, and it is particularly interesting from the fact that the tiger was a dreaded man-eater, which had devastated

A variation of the cosy corner, from *Furniture and Decoration*, December 1897, where it is described as a "corner settle". The notes accompanying the design said: "Here we have remembered that familiar friend of yore—the 'high-low' sofa. In its new guise this antiquity lends itself admirably to the requirements of a cosy corner seat."

and appalled several villages in Travancore. The day it was shot, this brute came into a village in search of a dainty meal, and succeeded in carrying off a little white girl, ten years of age. This child was afterwards rescued, but she was so shockingly lacerated that she died the same night in the house of a missionary doctor". The author also mentioned chairs "which were supported by the four legs of a rhinoceros or zebra, or a favourite horse. But without doubt," he said, "the most original 'animal' chair I ever beheld was that which belongs to that mighty Nimrod, Mr J. Gardiner Muir, of 'Hillcrest', Market Harborough. This chair. . . . is made from a baby Giraffe, which, with its mother, was shot by Mr Gardiner Muir, near the Kiboko River, in British East Africa. The design is by Rowland Ward, of Piccadilly." Although no example was described or illustrated in Fitzgerald's article, apparently elephants had occasionally been hollowed out to form cosy corners.

Seats that fitted into the angles of rooms had been known in the middle ages; the angle settle could be regarded as the mediaeval ancestor of the cosy corner, but no conscious development of corner seating took place till the end of the nineteenth century. Hope's drawing-room interior on page 180 includes a seat that runs along two walls, with a loose cushion placed in the angle; but the Turkish corner, which later became the cosy corner, did not appear as a separate and distinct piece of seat-furniture until the late Victorian period. The name Turkish was used because the original form was an ottoman, extending as a continuous seat along two adjoining walls: when a high back was added, with oriental decoration, it was sometimes known as a Moorish corner. During the 1880s and early '90s, combinations of seats and shelves were fitted into recesses, particularly in libraries; thus resuming an old structural partnership between furniture and walls, before free-standing seats like settles had developed as independent pieces. The cosy corner had become independent of the wall at some time in the early '90s. The more substantial form had a tall back with buttoned upholstery, resembling a luxurious high-backed settle; and although it began as a discreet and secluded seat for two people, it ended as something far larger and more complicated, able to accommodate two couples, and surmounted by a superstructure of shelves and brackets for books

A typical late Victorian cosy-corner, with buttoned upholstery at the back. From *Furniture and Decoration*, November 1897, plate 588. Slightly reduced in scale. The uncosy mediaeval prototype was the angle settle, of the kind illustrated on page 43. Thomas Hope's design for a continuous seat on two adjoining walls on page 180 was a fortuitous anticipation of an upholstered corner, but the obvious progenitor was the mid-nineteenth century ottoman that fitted into an angle, an origin acknowledged by the term Turkish corner, by which the cosy corner was first known.

and ornaments, a small looking glass and sometimes a miniature cabinet with a glazed door. Two examples are shown on pages 249 and 251. That the original intention of providing a cosy, withdrawn nook for tender conversation or dalliance was never altogether lost is confirmed by three lines from a popular song of the late '90s:

> "My heart's in a whirl,
> As I kiss each curl
> Of my cosy corner girl."

Upholsterers had happily united cosiness and romance: a final triumph of design for comfort.

CHAPTER 12

CRAFT REVIVALISTS AND INDUSTRIAL DESIGNERS

1830–1930

———

ILLIAM MORRIS, who inspired the handicraft revival, was not a pioneer of the modern movement but a reactionary, detached from contemporary life, whose spiritual home was in the Middle Ages, and his chief contribution to chair design was to revive interest in the native tradition. The Editor of *The Cabinet Maker and Art Furnisher*, in an appreciation published after Morris died in 1896, said "that he blessed and made popular the old Wycombe rush-bottomed chair, and owing to that wholesome benison other inexpensive things, soundly constructed, have crept from the kitchen to the grander apartments". Morris and Company had made and sold rush-bottomed chairs with turned frames of birch, stained black, and these were acceptable in aesthetic households during the 1870s and '80s, and were described, illustrated, and strongly recommended by Robert W. Edis in the lectures he gave before the Society of Arts in 1880 which were subsequently expanded into a book called *Decoration and Furniture of Town Houses*. An elbow chair of this simple type, reproduced from Edis's book is shown on page 256, and was sold for 9s. 9d. "Whatever may be thought of its artistic merit, it is certainly comfortable for use, pleasant to look at, and cheap in price," said the author, who considered that it was "fitted for almost any room". Such chairs entered many homes, not only those of such exclusive and scrupulously artistic families as the Cimabue Browns, invented and mercilessly guyed by George du Maurier in *Punch*. Gradually the arts and crafts movement, which had grown out of the handicaft revival, was accepted as something respectable instead of cranky; simplicity in design became respectable too, and this led to a reassessment of the Windsor chair. Earlier in 1896, *The Cabinet Maker*, which reflected the views of the furniture trade and was the link between manufacturer and retailer, had published an article entitled "Arm Chairs on Wycombe Lines", which illustrated six variations of the Windsor type and read as follows:

"It is unnecessary nowadays to apologise for a chair because of its obvious relationship to those cheap and simple articles which used to be associated with the kitchen. Indeed, it is pretty evident that the sensible construction of the Windsor chair has outlived many rickety forms, more or less mortised, tenoned, dowelled, or 'braced', which were supposed to belong to a superior class. The spreading legs and useful listing of these primitive chairs have proved to be as wear-resisting as many more costly methods of framing up. There is no doubt that much money is wasted through some needy people affecting a 'drawing-room style' which is quite unfitted to their surroundings. The miserable attempts which one sees to get-up a 'stuffed suite of nine' for a few pounds is enough to make any lover of the genuine forswear ought but kitchen chairs. Unfortunately, since the old-fashioned parlour 'went out', and the drawing-room 'came in', many comely and well constructed patterns have been sent below stairs because they smelt of the kitchen. Now, thanks to common sense, they are 'coming up' again, and it is our pleasure to do what we can to encourage them." (The rest of the article was devoted to descriptions of the illustrations.)

Such views were an unacknowledged tribute to the teaching of Morris, whose indirect influence on the furniture manufacturing trade was growing, despite his avowed rejection of and contempt for industrial production. Even upholstery was affected, and in August 1897 an article about the design of couches appeared in *Furniture and Decoration and the Furniture Gazette* welcoming the introduction of thin stuffing, which "has not only created a novelty and helped to reduce the price of manufacture, but it has also an aesthetic value in that it compels the upholsterer for the first time in recent years to observe the golden rule of industrial art, viz., that we should ornament construction, and not construct orna-

Rush-seated armchair in oak, designed by Walter Cave, and shown by the Arts and Crafts Exhibition Society, 1896. An example of the Morris school of design, rather too insistent on sturdy simplicity, and without the lightness and grace of the Morris chairs on page 256 or the design by Ernest Gimson on plate 62. This is a product of self-conscious craftsmanship: as artificial in its deliberate crudity as the most extravagant product of the Rococo style, at the opposite extreme of taste. Reproduced from *The Cabinet Maker and Art Furnisher*, November 1896, page 119.

Two rush-seated chairs of birch, stained black, designed and made by Morris and Company, illustrated in *The Decoration and Furniture of Town Houses*, by Robert W. Edis (1881). The author described them as "comfortable, and artistic, although, perhaps, somewhat rough in make . . . ". The elbow chair, with the four decorative spindles between the centre and top rail of the back, is as light and graceful as the japanned chairs made in the last decade of the eighteenth century.

ment". The anonymous writer of the article was describing more than a novelty; thin stuffing was a revolution in technique, sponsored by a revolution in taste, and followed by a revolution in design. "It is necessary now that the system of thin stuffing has become prevalent," he continued, "to pay more careful attention to the frames of our couches than was commonly done a few years ago. The frames of some of the old-fashioned thickly-stuffed Chesterfield sofas bore little or no relation to the finished piece of upholstery. The lines of the wood formed merely a skeleton which was padded out and completely extinguished in an envelope of horsehair, flock, alva, shavings, or even cheaper and nastier fillings according to the wishes of the customer and the honesty of the

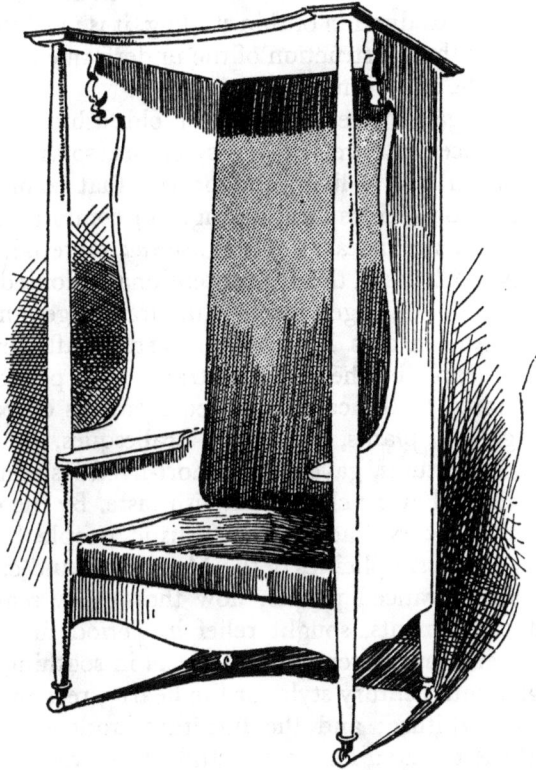

A hooded chair, designed by C. F. A. Voysey, and shown by the Arts and Crafts Exhibition Society, 1896. "How curiously old friends get promoted," wrote one anonymous critic. "William Morris brought the rush-seated chair from the kitchen to the drawing-room. Mr C. F. A. Voysey has carried the hall porter's chair upstairs and so purged it of its grossness that it now be welcomed in the daintiest of bedrooms." The settle, the winged easy chair, even the half-tester bedstead, have all contributed something to this comfortable, secluded, draught-proof seat. From *The Cabinet Maker and Art Furnisher*, November 1896, pages 117–18.

manufacturer. The construction of the article was completely hidden from the lay eye, and one of the primal laws of industrial art was outraged. Now-a-days, however, thanks in no small measure to the introduction of thin stuffing, it is possible, nay, it is imperative that the construction of the underframe shall manifest itself through the super-imposed upholstery."

The revolt against the grossness of old-fashioned Victorian upholstery reduced the weight of easy chairs, sofas and couches, revealed their structural lines, and proved that comfort did not depend entirely on springs and stuffing. But comfort was in abeyance when the feral fantasies of *art nouveau* materialized as the "Quaint" style. Chairs in this style intentionally flouted tradition: their shape usually outraged every structural usage, and whether they were produced at a high cost by artist-craftsmen or more flimsily and cheaply by the furniture trade, their purpose as seats was subordinated to the capricious requirements of exotic ornament. Wriggling plants, writhing arabesques, heart-shaped blossoms and apertures, gave to this short-lived fashion a restlessness that alienated every class of English taste. By the opening of the twentieth century "advanced" artistic people had revived their loyalty to the simplicities of the Morris arts and crafts school of design; less advanced people, now thoroughly scared of undisciplined experiments, sought relief in period furnishing and forgot the strenuous anarchy of *art nouveau* in soothing reproductions of eighteenth century styles or the hearty, reassuring solidity of Jacobean furniture; and the furniture trade expanded and encouraged the demand for "repro stuff" as it was called, to suit every section of the market.

A restatement of the principles of chair design, published in *Modern British Domestic Architecture and Decoration*, was a timely reminder that "a chair ought to be well *built*, and its structural qualities should be exemplified in two ways: first, the greatest possible amount of structural strength and dignity should be obtained with the smallest amount of wood; and, next, the wood must be handled expertly as wood, and not made to simulate the properties of any other material. For instance, to twist wood into interlacing and knotted forms that resemble ribbons, as Chippendale did in some of his early work, is precisely one of those fantastic vagaries of taste that a maker of furniture should take pride in

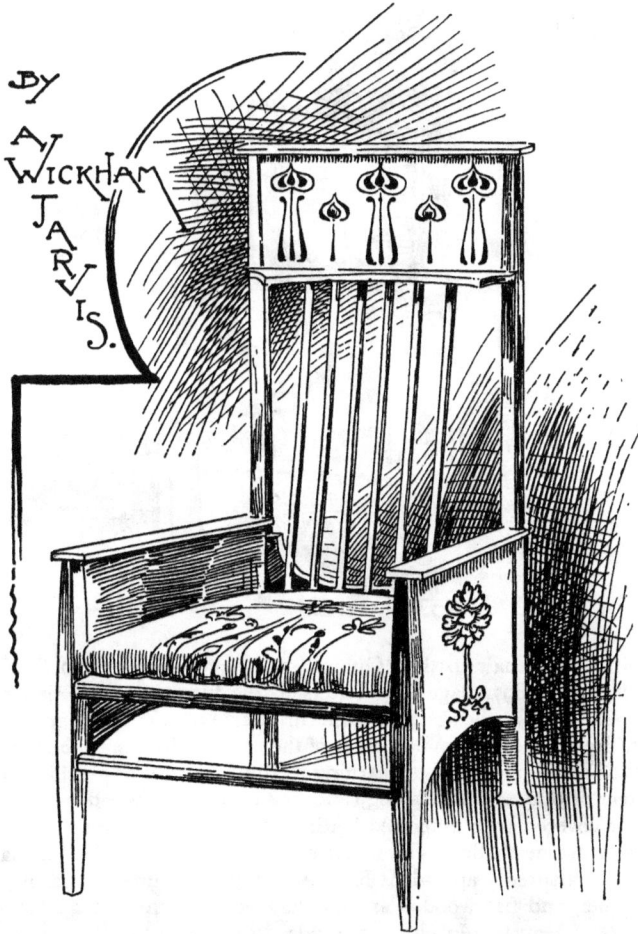

The influence of *Art Nouveau* inspired the "Quaint" style, which reduced standards of comfort in chair design. This example, by A. Wickham Jarvis, shown by the Arts and Crafts Exhibition Society, 1896, was illustrated in the November number of *The Cabinet Maker and Art Furnisher*, page 120, praised for its originality and criticised for its discomfort, as follows: "An attempt is made by an ingenious sloping *grille* to ease the body, which might, perhaps, be sorely tried by the square corners of the chair. It is certainly not a seat into which a tired thinker could 'throw' himself. But it is quaint and original, and the touches of gesso work and carving make it sufficiently pretty."

A drawing-room chair in the "Quaint" style, reproduced from *Furniture and Decoration*, May 1897, page 89. Writers in the furniture trade papers could seldom resist a dig at the aesthetes, and this design provided an opportunity for gentle satire. "Among a small section of the community," said the anonymous critic, "the satisfaction of the 'yearning for the beautiful' is a sufficient luxury in matters of domestic furnishing, and chairs, be they wooden-seated, rush-seated, or covered with embossed leather will be acceptable to the cult, provided they are aesthetic in form and colouring. To such folk," he said, this design "will assuredly appeal. It has the hieroglyphic tree carved in the back in low relief, and flat wooden arms, a flat wooden seat and an air of grim, austere loveliness pervades its subtle outline."

avoiding." (That was written and published in 1901.) The most complex and involved of Chippendale's designs was always under control; and, like other mid-Georgian makers and designers, he had attuned the rococo style to English taste, but rococo had classical roots, and *art nouveau* was rootless, for although it represented a genuine attempt to create a non-

Two chairs in the "Quaint" style, less decorative, but just as uncomfortable as the example on the opposite page. Every lesson of England's great tradition of chair-making has been discarded. Reproduced from *Furniture and Decoration*, January 1897, page 2.

historical style, it perished because it was ornamental and nothing else.

The contrast between chairs made by artist-craftsmen in the *art nouveau* style and the "Quaint" chairs produced by the furniture trade may be studied by comparing the examples on pages 255, 257, and 259, which were shown by the Arts and Crafts Exhibition Society in 1896, with those above and opposite, commercially manufactured in the following year. The rush-seated oak arm-chair on page 255, designed by Walter Cave is clumsy—an anticipation of "brutalism" in design—without the graces of the chairs by Morris and Company on page 256 or the agreeable proportions of the ladder-back rush-seated chairs by Ernest Gimson and Gordon Russell on plate 62. (Russell's work is, of course, very much later, and began in the 1920s.) The chair by A. Wickham Jarvis on page 259 is a restrained version of the "Quaint"

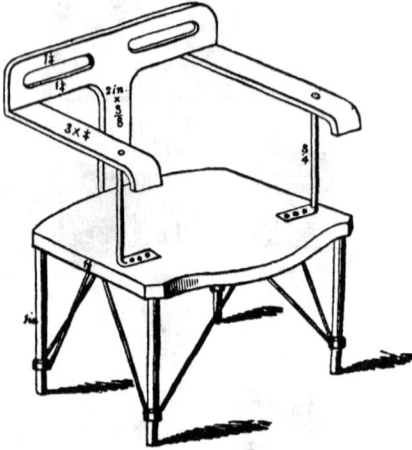

Design for an iron elbow kitchen chair, by Robert Mallet. From Loudon's *Encyclopaedia* (1833), Book I, Chapter III, Section IV, paragraph 639.

Design for a cast and wrought iron chair with a wooden seat, also by Robert Mallet. From Loudon's *Encyclopaedia*.

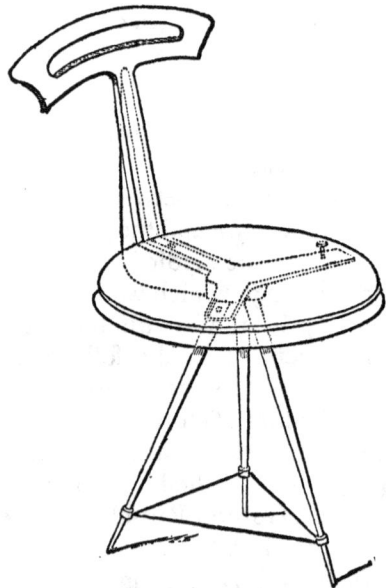

Two easy chairs produced by Sedley of Regent Street, London, and shown at the International Exhibtion of 1862. Flat metal strips are used in the example on the left, and cast metal for the frame of that on the right. Reproduced from *The Art-Journal Catalogue of the Exhibition.*

Metal chair with wire netting of close mesh on back and seat. Over thirty years separates this graceful design from Robert Mallet's crude experiments with iron and wood, which Loudon published in his *Encyclopaedia*; such chairs, used in gardens and parks, summer houses and conservatories, were not regarded as the progenitors of a new style. Reproduced from an illustration in *Judy*, August 19, 1868, page 170.

style, with a raked back that gives the illusion of comfort and a back rail which soon dispels the illusion, for it projects at exactly the right height to catch the neck at the base of the skull. The hooded chair on page 257, by C. F. A. Voysey, is a perfect draught-excluder, of mixed descent, for the sedan chair, half-tester bedstead, and winged easy chair have all contributed something to its character. Voysey was an architect and one of the earliest of what we now call industrial designers. He understood the significance of mechanical production, never surrendered to the sentimental obscurantism of the arts and crafts movement, and although influenced by *art nouveau*, recognised its ephemeral nature. He belonged to the modern movement in architecture and industrial design which was then finding expression through the work of men like Henri van de Velde, in Belgium, and Louis H. Sullivan and Frank Lloyd Wright in America, a movement that originated during the second quarter of the nineteenth century, and led ultimately to the new Western architecture of today. Men like Voysey who were prepared to supply working drawings for the mechanical production of their designs were exceptional at the beginning of the century, and very few designers of ability recognized the promise of a partnership with industry.

Traditional chair design was very much alive at High Wycombe where manufacturers were turning out large quantities of Windsor chairs, as they do still, and a new interpretation of the native style came from Ambrose Heal, who directed the design policy of Heal and Son of Tottenham Court Road, a furnishing business established in 1810, and, after the First War, Gordon Russell started to make furniture that continued and amplified the English tradition. During the opening decades of the century several highly accomplished artist-craftsmen were making furniture and rush-seated chairs in elm, ash, yew, English oak and English walnut; traditional types with ladder or spindle backs and decorative turning. Of these Ernest Gimson was the most outstanding, but the work of such artist-craftsmen was exclusive and costly, available only to a few wealthy and discerning patrons. The total rejection of industrial production by such gifted men inevitably restricted the market for what they made, but neither Heal nor Gordon Russell rejected industrial methods, and the pioneer work of Ambrose Heal established what is now a clearly identifiable early twentieth

Left: Hall-chair in cast-iron, designed by Henry W. Mason, and produced at the Lion Foundry of William Roberts at Northampton, and shown at the International Exhibition, 1862. Reproduced from *The Art-Journal Catalogue of the Exhibition. Right:* A garden seat cast at Coalbrookdale, *circa* 1870–75, which may well have been influenced by the work of William Morris. The ornamental forms resemble those produced by Walter Crane and his imitators. This design has the same mastery of motifs and material exhibited by the iron seat depicted in Gainsborough's painting of Mr and Mrs Andrews on plate 50, and is wholly different in conception from the incoherent muddle of ornamental odds and ends which emphasize the ill-proportioned lines of the hall chair. *Drawn by Marcelle Barton and reproduced by courtesy of the British Cast Iron Research Association.*

century style. He reintroduced a lattice-back type of chair; restored appreciation for the natural colour and marking of wood by renouncing stains and French polishing, and put his furniture within the reach of thousands of people, because he was an economic realist.

There was no economic realism about that odd, short-lived and sensational experiment, The Omega Workshops, which were opened in July 1913 at 33 Fitzroy Square, west of Tottenham Court Road, and lasted for nearly seven years. The workshops were inspired and directed by Roger Fry, a gifted painter with an international reputation as an art critic and historian, and a tireless propagandist for the work of young artists. The productions included textiles of cubist character, dress fashions, pottery, plain furniture, and ill-made chairs, covered with boldly painted patterns. A total preoccupation with colour was accompanied by an indifference to structural common sense; the Omega Workshops contributed nothing to furniture design; and the specimens of work exhibited fifty years later at the Victorian and Albert Museum suggested that, apart from pottery, the teams of artists responsible had confused decoration with design just as the Victorians had confused design with ornament.

When industrial designers of the 1920s and '30s began to study seating problems, they used metal and other industrially-produced materials, and although some nineteenth century furniture manufacturers had experimented with metal frames for chairs, the furniture trade was organized only for fabricating wood. Easy chairs with metal frames had been shown by Sedley of Regent Street at the International Exhibition of 1862, and the two reproduced on page 263 illustrate a good use of brass strips and a bad use of casting. Nearly thirty years earlier Loudon had published in his *Encyclopaedia* two designs for chairs with tubular metal legs, wooden seats and cast iron backs, which are reproduced on page 262. They were the work of a young Irish engineer named Robert Mallet (1810–81), who subsequently built the Fastnet Rock lighthouse, south-west of Cape Clear, and was also famous as a physicist and geologist. Both were intended for cottage kitchens; the back and elbows of the design at the top of page 262 were cast in one piece, with gas tubing for arm supports and legs; the other, below, has a circular seat, back and seat frame cast in one piece, and tubular legs with wire stays or stretchers. Mallet's training as an engineer gave him much the same approach to the problem as a modern industrial designer would have, and with the materials then available he produced "a machine for sitting in", logical enough, though destitute of civilized graces. During the 1860s light and comfortable metal chairs were made with seats and backs of close mesh wire netting, like the example at the bottom of page 263; but they were used almost exclusively for gardens and parks and summer houses, and were not recognized as serious contributions to contemporary design. Ironfounders cast chairs and garden seats as different in merit and character as those illustrated on page 265; but the furniture trade was wedded to wood, a marriage of economic convenience that remained undisturbed until the middle of the present century.

Chairs with frames of tubular steel were first introduced during the second quarter of the century, and the first ever made were designed by Marcel Breuer in 1925, when he was in charge of the cabinet-making class at the Bauhaus at Dessau. The first steel chairs were put on the market in England about 1930. The primitive forerunners designed by Robert Mallet in 1833 were probably never made; they represented an archaic phase, comparable with the early Greek chairs before the *klismos* was invented; but tubular steel chairs, like Thonet's bentwood chairs before them, were precociously mature, convenient and comfortable with their yielding seats and backs of leather or fabric, and a slight springiness imparted by the frame. The multiplicity of industrial materials now available—plastics and light alloys, rubber, latex foam upholstery—and a sophisticated sense of comfort, have given designers opportunities denied to the pioneers of the '20s and '30s, so that the early tubular models seem crude by comparison with the luxurious chairs of today. The examples on plate 64 show that some traditional devices, like the wings on easy chairs and settees, have survived, and that buttoned upholstery is used with discretion; but the established conceptions of comfort in seating have been amplified by what is now aptly called "dimensional abundance", which takes account of the tendency of modern people to fidget and constantly change their position when seated, and the large, luxurious chairs which accommodate this habit will, if they last long enough, disclose to our descendants the measure of our restlessness. Unfortunately, contemporary furniture has every-thing to lose from the passage of time: wood is enriched by age, and chairs in former periods were constructed to last, but today few things are made with posterity in mind, so the modern Englishman's chair may not survive to reveal the truth about him.

Perhaps this is just as well, because, as Jane Drew has put it in her paper on "The City of the Future", "We have become chair- and car-borne, with convenience a greater god than creation".

BOOKS AND REFERENCES USED OR QUOTED

CHAPTER I

A History of Egypt, by John Henry Breasted. (London: Hodder and Stoughton. Second edition. 15th reprint, 1939.)

The Art and Architecture of India, by Benjamin Rowland. (The Pelican History of Art: Penguin Books. 1953.)

The Art and Architecture of China, by Laurence Sickman and Alexander Soper. (The Pelican History of Art: Penguin Books. 1956.)

The Art and Architecture of Japan, Robert Treat Paine and Alexander Soper. (The Pelican History of Art: Penguin Books. 1960 edition.)

Furniture from Machines, by Gordon Logie. (London: George Allen and Unwin Ltd. 1947.) Section 1, pages 2–3.

"Natural Sciences: Anthropometrics." *The Architects' Journal Information Library*. February 6, 1963. Pages 315–325.

CHAPTER 2

A History of Egypt, by John Henry Breasted. (London: Hodder and Stoughton. Second edition. 15th reprint, 1939.) Chapter III, page 39.

The Practical Decoration of Furniture, by H. P. Shapland. (London: Ernest Benn Ltd. 1927.) Vol. II, Section III, page 17.

Egyptian Decorative Art, by Sir W. M. Flinders Petrie. (London: Methuen and Co., Ltd. 1895. Second edition, 1920.) Chapter III, pages 89–90.

The Revolutions of Civilization, by Sir W. M. Flinders Petrie. (London and New York: Harper & Brothers. Third edition, 1922.)

Discoveries in the Ruins of Nineveh and Babylon, by Austen H. Layard. (London: John Murray. 1853.)

A General History of Architecture, by Bruce Allsopp, F.R.I.B.A. (London: Sir Isaac Pitman & Sons Ltd. Reprint of second edition, 1962.) Part III, Chapter IV, page 42.

Analysis of Ornament: The Characteristics of Styles, by Ralph N. Wornum. (London: Chapman and Hall. Sixth edition, 1879.) Chapter VII, pages 59–60.

Household Furniture and Interior Decoration, by Thomas Hope. (London: Longman, Hurst, Rees and Orme. 1807.) Introduction, page 4.

The Rudiments of Drawing Cabinet and Upholstery Furniture, by Richard Brown. (London: Printed for J. Taylor, at the Architectural Library, 59 High Holborn. Second edition, 1822.) Appendix on "The Elucidation of the Principles of Drawing Ornaments", page 72. Preliminary Discourse, page x.

The Antiquities of Athens, measured and delineated by James Stuart and Nicholas Revett. Sponsored by the Society of Dilettanti. (London: Printed by John Haberkorn, 1762.) Four volumes issued between 1762 and 1814, and a Supplement on *Athenian Sepulchral Marbles*, in 1830.

Ancient Furniture: A History of Greek, Etruscan and Roman Furniture, by Gisela M. A. Richter, Litt.D., Curator of the Classical Department, the Metropolitan Museum of Art, New York. (Oxford: at the Clarendon Press. 1926.) Pages 45–53.

Illustrations of Ancient Art, selected from objects discovered at Pompeii and Herculaneum, by the Rev. Edward Trollope, F.S.A. (London: George Bell, 1854.)

The Decline and Fall of the Roman Empire, by Edward Gibbon. (London: New edition, 1807.) Vol. I, Chapter II.

Roman Silchester, by George C. Boon, F.S.A. (London: Max Parrish, 1957.) Chapter VII, page 162.

Furniture in Roman Britain, by Joan Liversidge. (London: Alec Tiranti Ltd. 1955.)

CHAPTER 3

A History of English Art in the Middle Ages, by O. Elfrida Saunders. (Oxford: at the Clarendon Press, 1932.) Chapter XIV, pages 174–75.

Westminster Abbey and the King's Craftsmen, by W. R. Lethaby. (London: Duckworth & Co., 1906.) Chapters I, XIII and XIV.

The Divine King in England, by Dr Margaret Alice Murray. (London: Faber & Faber, Ltd. 1954.) Chapter VI.

England as Seen by Foreigners in the Days of Elizabeth and James the First, by William Brenchley Rye. (London: John Russell Smith. 1865.)

An Apology for the Revival of Christian Architecture in England, by A. Welby Pugin. (London: John Weale. 1843.) Note 6, page 10.

Records of The Basketmakers' Company, compiled by Henry Hodgkinson Hobart, a former Clerk of the Company. (London: Dunn, Collin & Co. 1911.) Pages 6–7. (Also information supplied by Mr Cecil A. Rust, the present Clerk of the Company.)

A History of Domestic Manners and Sentiments in England During the Middle Ages, by Thomas Wright, with illustrations drawn from contemporary manuscripts by F. W. Fairholt. (London: Chapman and Hall. 1862.)

Furniture from Machines, by Gordon Logie, A.R.I.B.A. (London: George Allen and Unwin Limited. 1947.) Section I, page 1.

Wills and Inventories from the Registers of Bury St Edmunds. Quoted by John Henry and James Parker in *Some Account of Domestic Architecture in England*. (Oxford, Parker. 1859.) Chapter IV, pages 115–16.

The Complete Works of Chaucer, edited by Walter W. Skeat. (Oxford: at the Clarendon Press, 1925.) Troilus and Criseyde, Book III, line 964.

"The Craft of the Coffer Maker", by R. W. Symonds (*The Connoisseur*, Vol. CVII, January–June, 1941, page 100), also "The Craft of the Coffer and Trunk Maker in the Seventeenth Century" (*The Connoisseur*, Vol. CIX, January–June, 1942, page 40).

Furniture Making in Seventeenth and Eighteenth Century England, by R. W. Symonds. (London: The Connoisseur, 1955.) Chapter III. Note on page 69.

The Worshipful Company of Turners of London, by A. C. Stanley-Stone, C.C. (London: Lindley-Jones & Brother. 1925.) Chapter III.

The City of London Livery Companies, by Bryan Pontifex. (London: Methuen and Co. Ltd. 1939.)

CHAPTER 4

Harrison's Description of England, edited by Frederick J. Furnivall. (London: published for the New Shakespere Society by N. Trubner. 1877.) Part I, Book II, Chapter V, page 129.

Society in the Elizabethan Age, by Hubert Hall. (London: Swan Sonnenschien & Co. Ltd. Fourth edition, 1901.) Appendix to Chapter I, pages 149–50.

Anecdotes and Traditions, by W. J. Thoms. (Camden Society, 1839.) Extracts from the writings of Sir Nicholas L'Estrange are included. No. CXXVI, page 70.

Furniture Making in Seventeenth and Eighteenth Century England, by R. W. Symonds. (London: The Connoisseur. 1955.) Chapter III. Notes on illustrations, page 72.

"The Renaming of English Furniture", by R. W. Symonds. *The Antique Collector*, Vol. 19, No. 4, August 1948, page 128.

Farm and Cottage Inventories of Mid-Essex, 1633–1749. (Essex Record Office Publications, No. 8.)

Sylva, or a Discourse of Forest-Trees, by John Evelyn. (London, printed for John Martyn, 1679. Third edition.) Chapter VIII, section 4, page 50.

Aubrey's Brief Lives. Edited from the Original Manuscripts and with an Introduction by Oliver Lawson Dick. (London: Secker and Warburg. 1950.) "Ben Jonson." Page 178.

"The lamentable fall of Queen Eleanor." (Roxburgh Collection I, 225.) *The Roxburghe Ballads*, with short notes by William Chappell, F.S.A. (Hertford: printed for the Ballad Society, by Stephen Austin and Sons. 1874.) Vol. I, page 69. Also: "The Lamentation of a new-married Man." (Roxburgh Collection I, 216, 217.) Vol. I, page 36.

Industrial Organization in the Sixteenth and Seventeenth Centuries, by George Unwin. (Oxford: Clarendon Press. 1904.)

Diary and Correspondence of John Evelyn, edited by William Bray. (London: Hurst and Blackett. 1854.) Four volumes.

CHAPTER 5

Aubrey's Brief Lives. Edited from the Original Manuscripts and with an Introduction by Oliver Lawson Dick. (London: Secker and Warburg, 1950.) "Wenceslas Hollar." Page 163.

The Englishman's Food, by J. C. Drummond and Anne Wilbraham. (London: Jonathan Cape. 1939.)

Tobacco Cultivation in England, by Ronald Duncan. (London: The Falcon Press. 1951.)

The Social History of Smoking, by G. L. Apperson. (London: Martin Secker. 1914.)

K

Colonial Élites, by Ronald Syme. (Oxford University Press. 1958.) The Whidden
Lectures. III. "English America." Pages 47–48.

Farm and Cottage Inventories of Mid-Essex, 1633–1749. (Essex Record Office
Publications, No. 8.)

CHAPTER 6

Aubrey's Brief Lives. Edited from the Author's MSS, by Andrew Clark. (Oxford:
at the Clarendon Press. 1898.) Vol. II. "George Monk." Page 77.

"The Praise of Brotherhood." (Roxburgh Collection I, 338, 339.) Written
circa 1635–42. *The Roxburghe Ballads* (Hertford: 1874). Vol. I. Page 363.

Farm and Cottage Inventories of Mid-Essex, 1633–1749. (Essex Record Office
Publications, No. 8.) 134. Mark George of Writtle. June 20, 1685. Page
176.

The Cabinet Dictionary, by T. Sheraton. (London: Printed by W. Smith, King
Street, Seven Dials, 1803.) Entry CHAIR: pages 145–46.

The Every-Day Book and Table-Book, by William Hone. (London: Thomas
Tegg. 1841 edition.) Vol. II, columns 33, 34, 35, 901.

CHAPTER 7

The Cabinet Dictionary, by T. Sheraton. (London: 1803.) Entries: ARM-
CHAIR, page 19, and CABRIOLE, page 120.

Chats on Old Furniture, by Arthur Hayden. (London: T. Fisher Unwin. 1905.)

English Furniture and Furniture Makers of the Eighteenth Century, by R. S. Clouston.
(London: Hurst & Blackett, Ltd. 1906.) Chapter I, page 12.

"The Years of Mahogany: The Early Georgian", by Haldane Macfall. *The
Connoisseur*, Vol. XXIV, May–August, 1909.

"A Chair from China", by R. W. Symonds. *Country Life*, Vol. CXIV, No.
2964. November 5, 1953. Pages 1497–99.

The Drawings of William Hogarth, by A. P. Oppé. (London: Phaidon Press Ltd.
1948.) Notes on plate 95, page 58.

"Furniture in the Soane Museum", by R. W. Symonds. *Country Life*, Vol.
CVII, No. 2767. January 27, 1950.

The London Furniture Makers, by Sir Ambrose Heal. (London: B. T. Batsford
Ltd. 1953.) Entry WOLLASTON, page 206.

Hortus Jamaicensis, by John Lunan. (Jamaica: printed at the office of the St
Jago de la Vega Gazette, 1814.) Vol. I, page 472.

The Dictionary of English Furniture, by Ralph Edwards, C.B.E., F.S.A. (London:
Country Life Limited. Second, revised and enlarged edition, 1954.) Vol.
II. Entry MAHOGANY, page 295.

The Life and Work of James Gibbs, by Bryan Little. (London: B. T. Batsford
Ltd. 1955.) Chapter IV, page 50.

A Biographical Dictionary of English Architects, 1660–1840, by H. M. Colvin.
(London: John Murray. 1954.) Entry JOHN PRICE, page 474.

The Cabinet Dictionary, by T. Sheraton. (London: 1803.) Entries CHAIR, page 146, and CUBA WOOD, page 184.

The Purefoy Letters, 1735–53, edited by G. Eland, F.S.A. (London: Sidgwick & Jackson, Ltd. 1931.) Vol. I, pages 102–3.

An Essay Towards a Description of Bath, by John Wood, Architect. (London: the Second Edition, Corrected and Enlarged, 1749.) Vol. II. Preface, pages 2–6.

Sylva, or a Discourse of Forest Trees, by John Evelyn. (London: printed for John Martyn, 1679. Third Edition.) Chapter XXII, Section 15, page 111.

Anecdotes of Painting in England, collected by George Vertue and digested and published by Horace Walpole. (London: J. Dodsley. Third edition with additions, 1786.) Vol. IV. Pages 238–39.

The Way of the World, by William Congreve. Act IV. Scene V. (First acted, 1700.)

English Furniture Designers of the Eighteenth Century, by Constance Simon. (London: A. H. Bullen. 1905.) Chapter I, page 8.

"The Joys of Love Never Forgot." *The Gentleman's Magazine*, "Poetical Essays." March 1735. Vol. V, page 158.

The Journeys of Celia Fiennes, edited by Christopher Morris. (London: The Cresset Press. 1947.) Page 364.

"Moral Essays", by Alexander Pope. Epistle II, lines 169–70.

The Journeys of Celia Fiennes, edited by Christopher Morris. Pages 345–46.

Evelina, by Fanny Burney. (Originally published by Thomas Lowndes of 77, Fleet Street, London. January 1778.) Letter XLV.

A Complete Body of Architecture, by Isaac Ware. (London: 1767 edition.) Chapter XXI, page 316.

CHAPTER 8

The London Furniture Makers, 1660–1840, by Sir Ambrose Heal. (London: B. T. Batsford Ltd. 1953.)

Nollekens and His Times, by John Thomas Smith. (London: Henry Colburn. 1828.) Vol. II. "Recollections of Public Characters, sometime inhabitants of St Martin's Lane." Page 238.

The Gentleman and Cabinet-Maker's Director, by Thomas Chippendale. (London. The Third Edition, 1762.) Preface, and notes on Plates.

The Whitehall Evening-Post; or, London Intelligencer. From Thursday, June 26, to Saturday, June 28, 1760. No. 2228.

Thomas Chippendale, by Edwin J. Layton. (London: John Murray. 1928.) Pages 18–19.

Gillow Records. Entry: 1784–87, Estimate and Sketch Book, No. 153.

The Cabinet Dictionary, by T. Sheraton. (London. 1803.) Entry ARM, Arm-Chair, No. 5. Page 19.

The Cabinet and Chair-Maker's Real Friend and Companion, or, the Whole System of Chair-Making Made plain and easy, by Robert Manwaring, Cabinet-Maker. Engraved by Robert Pranker. (London. Printed for Henry Webley, 1765.)

Dictionarium Britannicum: Universal Etymological English Dictionary, by N. Bailey. (London: Second edition, 1736.)

Correspondence of Thomas Gray, edited by Paget Toynbee and Leonard Whibley. (Oxford: Clarendon Press, 1935.) Vol. II. Letter 231. December 29, 1756. Pages 490–91.

The Cabinet Dictionary, by T. Sheraton. (London. 1803.) Plate 17. (Entered in the list of plates as 16.)

The Cabinet and Chair-Maker's Real Friend and Companion, by Robert Manwaring. (London. 1765.) Final page of Preface.

The London Furniture Makers, 1660–1840, by Sir Ambrose Heal. (London: B. T. Batsford Ltd. 1953.) Pages 55 and 59.

The Builder's Companion and Workman's General Assistant, by William Pain, Architect and Joiner. (London: Printed for Robert Sayer. Third edition, 1769.) Page 89.

Letter by R. W. Symonds in the correspondence columns of *Country Life*. October 26, 1951.

The Letters of Horace Walpole, edited by Mrs Paget Toynbee. (Oxford: The Clarendon Press. 1905.) Vol. V. 1760–64. Letter 770. Page 99.

A Treatise on Carriages, by William Felton. (London. 1794.) Page 165.

Sunny Memories of Foreign Lands, by Harriet Beecher Stowe. (London: Sampson Low, Son & Co. 1854.) Letter III (April 16, 1853), pages 31–32.

The World, No. 12. March 22, 1753. (New edition, 1795. Dodsley, Pall-Mall.) Pages 69–70.

Jacob Faithful, by Frederick Marryatt. (London: 1834.) Chapter XV.

"Costly Elegance of Gilded Chairs", by G. Bernard Hughes. *Country Life*, Vol. CXXXIV, No. 3482. November 28, 1963. Pages 1398–99.

The Cabinet Dictionary, by T. Sheraton. (London. 1803.) Entry GILDING, pages 231–32. Entry BAMBOE OR BAMBOO. Page 22.

The Rudiments of Drawing Cabinet and Upholstery Furniture, by Richard Brown. (London: Second edition, 1822.) "Remarks about Dining Room Chairs", page 30.

Gillow's: A Record of a Furnishing Firm During Two Centuries. Anonymous. (London: Harrison & Sons. 1901.)

The London Furniture Makers, by Sir Ambrose Heal. (London: B. T. Batsford. 1952.) Notes on illustrations (Fig. 42), by R. W. Symonds. Pages 274–75.

A Biographical Dictionary of English Architects, 1660–1840, by H. M. Colvin. (London: John Murray. 1954.) Entry GILLOW.

Boswell on the Grand Tour: Italy, Corsica, and France, 1765–1766. Edited by Frank Brady and Frederick A. Pottle. (London: William Heinemann Ltd. 1955.) Entry for February 23, 1766. Page 309.

The Cabinet-Maker and Upholsterer's Drawing Book, by Thomas Sheraton, Cabinet-Maker. (London. Printed for the Author by T. Bensley. 1793.) Part III. "A Display of the present Taste of Household Furniture."

The Antiquities of Athens, measured and delineated by James Stuart and Nicholas Revett. (London. Printed by John Haberkorn. 1762.) Vol. I.

The Cabinet-Maker and Upholsterer's Guide, from drawings by A. Hepplewhite and Co., Cabinet-Makers. (London: published by I. & J. Taylor of the Architectural Library. 1788.)

The Rudiments of Drawing Cabinet and Upholstery Furniture, by Richard Brown. (London. Second edition, 1822.) "Preliminary Discourse", page xii.

The Cabinet Dictionary, by T. Sheraton. (London. 1803.) Entry CABINET, page 118.

Memoirs of Adam Black, by Alexander Nicholson. (London: A. & C. Black Ltd. Second edition, 1885.) Chapter I, pages 32–33.

The Cabinet Dictionary, by T. Sheraton. (London. 1803.) Entry CARVER, pages 135–37.

The Cabinet-Maker's Guide; or, Rules and Instructions in the art of Varnishing, Dying, Staining, Japanning, Polishing, Lackering, and Beautifying Wood, Ivory, Tortoiseshell, and Metal, by G. A. Siddons. (London: Printed for Sherwood, Gilbert, and Piper, Paternoster-Row. Fifth edition, 1830.) "To Imitate Rosewood." Page 30.

The Cabinet Dictionary, by T. Sheraton. (London. 1803.) Entry CANE, pages 126–27.

A Treatise on Carriages, by William Felton. (London: 1794.) Chapter II, page 44.

The Cabinet Dictionary, by T. Sheraton. Entries ARM and CONVERSATION, pages 17–18, and 177.

The Rudiments of Drawing Cabinet and Upholstery Furniture, by Richard Brown. (London. Second edition, 1822.) Page 38.

An Eighteenth-Century Correspondence. Letters addressed to Sanderson Miller of Radway. Edited by Lilian Dickins and Mary Stanton. (London: John Murray. 1910.) Chapters XVII–XIX.

CHAPTER 9

The Dictionary of English Furniture, by Ralph Edwards, C.B.E., F.S.A. (London: Country Life Limited. Revised and enlarged edition, 1954.) Entry, CHAIRS, WINDSOR, Vol. I, pages 319–20.

"The Windsor Chair", by R. W. Symonds. The first of two articles in *Apollo*, Vol. XXII, No. 128, August 1935, page 69.

High Wycombe Furniture, by Sir Lawrence Weaver. (London: The Fanfare Press, 1929.) Chapter I, page 11.

Magna Britannia, by Daniel and Samuel Lysons. (London. 1806.) Vol. I. Bedfordshire, Berkshire, and Buckinghamshire. Entry: HIGH, OR CHIPPING-WYCOMBE. Pages 674–75.

The Romance of Names, by Ernest Weekley. (London: John Murray. 1914.) Chapter XV, page 149.

High Wycombe Furniture, by Sir Lawrence Weaver. Chapter I, pages 17–18.

Field Guide to American Victorian Furniture, by Thomas H. Ormsbee. (Boston: Little, Brown and Company. 1952.) Pages 89–90.

Mr Sponge's Sporting Tour, by Robert Smith Surtees. (Original edition, 1853.) Chapter XXIV.

An Encyclopaedia of Cottage, Farm, and Villa Architecture and Furniture, by John Claudius Loudon. (London: Longman, Rees, Orme, Brown, Green & Longman. 1833.) Book I, Chapter III, Section IV, pages 319–20.

Hints on Household Taste, by Charles L. Eastlake. (London: Longmans, Green and Co. Second edition, 1869.) Chapter II, pages 53–54.

CHAPTER 10

"Notice of Two Rocking-Chairs", by James Frewin, Builder. *The Architectural Magazine and Journal*, edited by John Claudius Loudon. (London. 1838.) Vol. V, page 664.

Plain or Ringlets, by Robert Smith Surtees. (Original edition, 1860.) Chapter LIV.

Mechanization Takes Command, by Siegfried Giedion. (New York: Oxford University Press. 1948.) Page 402, Fig. 236.

Official Descriptive and Illustrated Catalogue of the Great Exhibition, 1851. Vol. II, pages 639, 746.

The Architect's Journal, September 1, 1949. Illustration and description of one of Dr Calvert's "Digestive chairs", owned by Mr C. F. Colt, and repaired by the late Ernest Race. Page 218.

Furniture and Decoration and the Furniture Gazette, Vol. XXXIV, No. 766, April 1897, page 72.

CHAPTER 11

The Gentleman's House; or how to Plan English Residences, from the Parsonage to the Palace, by Robert Kerr, F.R.I.B.A. (London: John Murray. 1864.) Part Two, First Division, Chapter III, page 77, Chapter I, page 73.

Encyclopaedia of Cottage, Farm, and Villa Architecture, and Furniture, by John Claudius Loudon. (London. 1833.) Book I, Chapter III, Section V, page 336.

Mr Sponge's Sporting Tour, by Robert Smith Surtees. (Original edition, 1853.) Chapter XXXVII.

The Modern Style of Cabinet Work, Exemplified in New Designs Practically Arranged. 72 plates, containing 227 designs (including fragmental parts). (London: published by T. King, 17 Gate Street, Lincoln's Inn Fields. Second edition, 1832.)

Official Descriptive and Illustrated Catalogue of the Great Exhibition, 1851. Vol. II, page 748.

Handley Cross, by Robert Smith Surtees. (Original edition, 1843.) Chapter VII.

The Art of Conversation, with Remarks on Fashion and Address, by Captain Orlando Sabertash. (London: G. W. Nickisson, 1842.) Pages 181–82.

The Bedroom and Boudoir, by Lady Barker. (London: Macmillan and Co. 1878.) Chapter VII, page 87.

Furniture and Decoration and the Furniture Gazette, October 15, 1897. Vol. XXXIV, No. 772. Page 201. No. 770. Page 157.

Vice Versa, by F. Anstey. (London: John Murray. Original edition, 1882.) Chapter I.

The Gentleman's House, by Robert Kerr. (London. 1864.) Part II, Division I, Section II, Chapter I, page 105.

The True Principles of Pointed or Christian Architecture, by A. Welby Pugin. (London: John Weale. 1841.) Page 40.

Hints on Household Taste, by Charles Lock Eastlake. (London: Longmans, Green and Co. Second edition, 1869.) Chapter III, page 75. Chapter VI, pages 156–58. Preface, pages ix and x. Chapter II, pages 57–58.

The Art of the House, by Rosamund Marriott Watson. (London: George Bell and Sons. 1897.) Chapter V, page 75.

Cottage, Farm, and Villa Architecture, and Furniture, by the late J. C. Loudon. (London: Frederick Warne and Co. A New Edition, edited by Mrs Loudon. 1846.) Supplement, pages 1287–88.

The Cabinet Maker and Art Furnisher, Vol. XVII, No. 196. October 1896. Page 109.

Catalogues of Heal and Son, Tottenham Court Road, London. 1858–60.

Cassell's Household Guide to Every Department of Practical Life: being a Complete Encyclopaedia of Domestic and Social Economy. (London: Cassell & Company Limited. New and Revised Edition, 1875.) Vol. I, page 126.

The Cabinet Maker and Art Furnisher, Vol. XVI, No. 189. March 1896. Note on "Bentwood Furniture", page 242.

Furniture and Decoration and the Furniture Gazette, February 15, 1897. Vol. XXXIV, No. 764. Page 27.

" 'Animal' Furniture", by William G. Fitzgerald. *The Strand Magazine*, September 1896. Vol. XII, pages 273–80.

CHAPTER 12

"The Late William Morris", by the Editor, *The Cabinet Maker and Art Furnisher*, November 1896. Vol. XVII, No. 197, page 133.

Decoration and Furniture of Town Houses, by Robert W. Edis, F.S.A., F.R.I.B.A. (London: Kegan Paul and Co. 1881.) Lecture 1, pages 28–29.

The Cabinet Maker and Art Furnisher, May 1896. Vol. XVI, No. 191, page 288.

Furniture and Decoration and the Furniture Gazette, August 1897. Vol. XXXIV, No. 770, page 153.

Modern British Domestic Architecture and Furniture, edited by Charles Holme. (London: Offices of "The Studio". 1901.) Pages 17–18.

An Encyclopaedia of Cottage, Farm, and Villa Architecture, and Furniture, by J. C. Loudon. (London. 1833.) Page 320.

An Enquiry into Industrial Art in England, by Nikolaus Pevsner. (Cambridge University Press. 1937.) Part I, pages 42–44.

Furniture from Machines, by Gordon Logie. (London: George Allen and Unwin Ltd. 1947.) Section 12, page 119.

"Luxury Seating", introduction to "Design Review". *The Architectural Review*, April 1962. Pages 265–66.

"The City of the Future", a paper delivered by Jane Drew, F.R.I.B.A., before the Royal Society of Arts, February 28, 1962. Printed in *The Journal of the R.S.A.*, Vol. CX, No. 5072, July 1962.

The premises of a chair and cabinet maker in St John's Street, West Smithfield, reproduced from the *Gentleman's Magazine*, October 1814. The design of the chairs displayed for sale on the pavement is over half a century earlier than the date of the engraving. The name Bailey is not included in Sheraton's trade list, or in Sir Ambrose Heal's *London Furniture Makers*, and this was probably a small business, selling second-hand furniture as well as making new articles. By 1814, furniture retailers and second-hand dealers may have been trying to establish the belief, later so widely accepted, that they were also makers, with busy workshops just behind their showrooms.

APPENDIX I

ADAM, Robert (1728–92). Architect and furniture designer, second and most famous of the four sons of William Adam (1689–1748), of Maryburgh, Fife. In partnership with his brothers, James and William. Designed complete schemes for the interior decoration and furnishing of houses, employing contemporary cabinet and chair-makers. Appointed Architect of the King's Works, 1761. *Works in Architecture of Robert and James Adam*, covers every aspect of the Adam style. Vol. I, 1773, II, 1779, III, published posthumously, 1822.

CHIPPENDALE, Thomas (?1718–79). Cabinet-maker and chair-maker. Baptized at Otley Parish Church, Yorkshire, June 5, 1718. Died 1779, buried in St Martin's-in-the-Fields, London, on November 13th of that year. First cabinet-maker to publish a book of designs: *The Gentleman and Cabinet Maker's Director*, 1754; second edition with same contents, 1755, third with additional plates, 1762. It is not known when he first came to London, but in 1745 he was living in Conduit Court, Long Acre, and in 1752 at Somerset or Northumberland Court in the Strand. He moved to 60 St Martin's Lane in 1753 or 1754, and may then have taken into partnership James Rannie, *q.v.*, a cabinet-maker. Rannie died in 1766, and Chippendale continued his business alone until 1771, when Thomas Haig joined the business, which then became known as Chippendale, Haig and Company. After his death, the business was carried on by his eldest son, Thomas, *q.v.*

CHIPPENDALE, Thomas Junior (1749–1822). Eldest of the famous Thomas Chippendale's eleven children by Catherine Redshaw. Continued the business of Chippendale, Haig and Company, after his father's death in 1779. (Haig withdrew from the firm in 1796.) The premises at 60 St Martin's Lane were retained, and Sheraton includes the name of Thomas Chippendale, Upholsterer, at that address in his list of makers in *The Cabinet Dictionary* (1803). Chippendale was made bankrupt in 1804, but re-established the business, opened a second shop at 57 Haymarket in 1814, and moved to 42 Jermyn Street in 1821. He was a member of the Society of Arts, and exhibited pictures at the Royal Academy between the years 1784 and 1801. A very rare small quarto *Book of Designs*, by Thomas Chippendale, Junior, is preserved in the Victoria and Albert Museum.

COBB, John (d. 1778). Upholsterer and cabinet-maker, with premises at the corner house of St Martin's Lane and Long Acre, which became No. 72 in the latter part of the eighteenth century. He was in partnership with William Vile, *q.v.*, and traded at that address as Vile and Cobb. After Vile's retirement in 1765, Cobb continued the business until he died in 1778. He enjoyed the patronage of George III, and many members of the nobility. He is one of the few makers of whom we have a personal description. In *Nollekens and his Times*, John Thomas Smith (1766–1833) tells us that Cobb was excessively haughty, and was, perhaps, the proudest man in England. He used to dress superbly, and would strut through his workshops in his beautiful and costly clothes, issuing orders to his workmen. The extent of his pomposity is disclosed by Smith's account of an occasion when George III gave him a lesson in common courtesy. "One day, when Mr Cobb was in his Majesty's library at Buckingham-house, giving orders to a workman, whose ladder was placed before a book which the King wanted, his Majesty desired Cobb to hand him the work, which instead of obeying, he called to his man, 'Fellow, give me that book!' The King, with his usual condescension, arose, and asked Cobb, what his man's name was. 'Jenkins,' answered the astonished Upholsterer. 'Then,' observed the King, 'Jenkins, you shall hand me the book.' " Smith states that he had the information about Cobb from "Banks, the cellaret maker".

DARLY, Mathias (d. ?1780). A designer and engraver, who published (1750–51) a work entitled *A New Book of Chinese, Gothic and Modern Chairs*, an indifferent performance, but one that justifies his inclusion in this list as it was the first English book specifically concerned with chairs. He engraved most of the plates for Chippendale's *Director* and for *The Universal System of Household Furniture*, by Ince and Mayhew.

DAY, Daniel. Chair-maker who worked at Mendlesham and Stoneham, in Suffolk, during the late eighteenth and early nineteenth centuries. He gave his name to a variant of the Windsor type. (See page 189.)

EASTLAKE, Charles Lock (1836–1906). Architect, furniture designer, and exponent of the revived "Early English" or "Modern Gothic" style. He was not, apparently, an artist-craftsman, for he employed other makers to carry out his designs. In 1868 he published *Hints on Household Taste*, which gained immediate and considerable popularity in England and America, and went into four editions in ten years. In that book he included several designs for furniture of plain shape and mediaeval construction, which generated the so-called "Eastlake

Style", but no actual pieces made from his designs have ever been traced. Secretary of the Royal Institute of British Architects, 1866–77, Keeper of the National Gallery, 1878–98. He was the nephew of Sir Charles Lock Eastlake, the painter, who had been President of the Royal Academy in 1850.

THE GILLOW FIRM. (Founded 1695.) The firm of Gillow was founded at Lancaster by Robert Gillow, a joiner, in 1695. He had moved there from Great Singleton in the parish of Kirkham-in-the-Fylde; he flourished and was made a freeman of Lancaster in 1728. The firm's records go back to 1731, and at that time their work was chiefly building and surveying. Richard, the son of Robert, was trained as an architect, and designed the Custom House at Lancaster in the Adam style. A London branch was opened in 1761, in what was then the Tiburn Road and is now Oxford Street. The firm had been sending increasingly large quantities of furniture to London, and the business continued to prosper during the rest of the eighteenth century, throughout the nineteenth, and continuously occupied the Oxford Street site. The firm is now represented by Waring and Gillow Limited.

GIMSON, Ernest (1864–1919). Artist-craftsman and architect. The son of Josiah Gimson, an engineer, he was trained at Leicester Art School, and articled, in 1881, to Isaac Barradale, a Leicester architect. In 1884 he met William Morris, and was greatly influenced by his teaching. He came to London in 1886, and subsequently settled at Pinbury in Gloucestershire, where he practised as a cabinet-maker, chair-maker, and designer and worker in metal, plaster, and embroidery. In 1903, he moved to the neighbouring village of Sapperton. He died on August 12, 1919.

HAIG, Thomas (d. 1803). The date of his birth is unknown. He died in 1803 and was buried at St Martin's-in-the-Fields. Cabinet-maker, upholsterer, and Thomas Chippendale's partner, 1771–79, having previously acted as clerk to James Rannie, q.v. After Chippendale's death he continued in partnership with Thomas Chippendale junior. He retired from the firm in 1796.

HALLETT, William (1707–81). One of the most eminent of fashionable Georgian cabinet-makers, who was established in 1732 at Newport Street, removing in 1752 to premises in St Martin's Lane, adjoining those of Cobb and Vile. Among his clients were such wealthy noblemen as the Earl of Leicester and Lord Folkestone. He was able to retire from his prosperous business at the age of 62. He may possibly have had some association with Cobb and Vile.

HEAL, Sir Ambrose (1872–1959). Artist-craftsman, designer and maker of furniture, and chairman of the firm of Heal and Son Limited, which had been established as an upholstery and bedding business in 1810. After serving his apprenticeship to cabinet-making, 1890–93, he entered the firm in 1893, becoming managing-director in 1907 and chairman in 1913. He directed the design policy of the business, and the influence of his well-made, simply-designed furniture was considerable during the first quarter of the century. He re-introduced the lattice-back type of chair, and continued and enlarged the scope of the native English style, which, apart from Windsor chair developments, had become submerged in the Victorian period. He was knighted in 1933; appointed a Royal Designer for Industry; and awarded the Gold Albert Medal of the Royal Society of Arts in 1954. His publications included: *London Tradesmen's Cards of the Eighteenth Century*, 1926; *The Signboards of Old London Shops*, 1947; and *London Furniture Makers, 1660–1840*, 1953.

HEPPLEWHITE, George (died 1786). Cabinet-maker and chair-maker, whose name has been given to a distinctive style of light and elegant furniture that was fashionable in the last quarter of the eighteenth century. Little is known about him, and no pieces of furniture made by him or his firm have ever been identified. He was apprenticed to the firm of Gillow, *q.v.* in Lancaster, came to London, opened a shop in Redcross Street, St Giles's, Cripplegate, and died in 1786, his business being carried on by his widow Alice. A book of some 300 designs "from drawings by A. Hepplewhite and Co., Cabinet-Makers" was published in 1788, two years after his death; a second edition was issued in 1789 and a third in 1794. Ten designs in *The Cabinet-Makers' London Book of Prices*, published in 1788, are inscribed with the name Heppelwhite, spelt like that.

HOPE, Thomas (1770–1831). Art collector, author, architect and furniture designer, he was the eldest son of John Hope, a wealthy merchant of Scottish descent whose family had for several generations lived in Amsterdam. He had studied architecture and travelled extensively as a young man to pursue his studies in Syria, Egypt, Turkey, Greece, Spain, Portugal and France. He came to England in 1795, having been compelled to leave Holland with his family when the

French occupied that country, settled in London, bought and decorated a house in Duchess Street, Cavendish Square, and acquired Deepdene in Surrey as a country home. He accommodated his large collection of antique vases and sculpture in these two houses. His published works are *Household Furniture and Interior Decoration* (1807); *Anastasius, or Memoirs of a Modern Greek, written at the close of the eighteenth century*, issued anonymously in 1819; *Origin and Prospects of Man* (1831), and an *Historical Essay on Architecture* (1835), the last two works appearing after his death. His published designs helped to expand the taste for the neo-Greek style and Egyptian ornament.

INCE, William. Cabinet-maker and upholsterer, in partnership with John Mayhew, *q.v.*, and in business from 1759–1803. Ince was apprenticed to Mr West, a cabinet-maker in King Street, Covent Garden. The dates of his birth and death are unknown, but his marriage is recorded, for he and his partner Mayhew were married to two sisters on the same day, February 20, 1762, at St James's Church, Piccadilly. The firm had premises in Broad Street, Golden Square, Soho, also in Marshall Street, Carnaby Market. The partners collaborated in producing *The Universal System of Household Furniture*, consisting of over 300 designs, of which all but the last six were engraved and signed by Mathias Darly, *q.v.* The plates were issued between 1759 and 1763, and in that year presumably the book was published, though no date appears on the title page. It was dedicated to George Spencer, the fourth Duke of Marlborough.

KENT, William (?1685–1748). Architect, landscape-gardener, painter and furniture designer, born at Bridlington, Yorkshire, and said to have been apprenticed to a coach-painter in Hull. He had many patrons, of whom the chief was the Earl of Burlington. He designed the interior decoration and furnishing of several great houses, and his designs for furniture, particularly chairs, were bold and florid. Some of his furniture is included in John Vardy's book published in 1744 under the title of *Some Designs of Mr Inigo Jones and Mr William Kent*.

LANGLEY, Batty (1696–1751). Architect, designer, and author of technical works on architecture and building practice. He was born at Twickenham, Middlesex, and his brother Thomas was also born there in 1702. About 1740, he established a school or academy of architectural drawing at Meard's Court, Dean Street, Soho, assisted by his brother who was an engraver, and in that year published *The City and Country Builder's and Workman's Treasury of Designs*, which included some plates on furniture, some of them copied from the work of Continental designers. He published a large number of books for the practical guidance of builders and woodworkers, and invented five Gothic orders, which were condemned by Horace Walpole who said: "All that his books achieved, has been to teach carpenters to massacre that venerable species. . . ." One of his later books, issued in 1751, *The Builder's Director, or Bench-Mate*, contained many details of Gothic ornament and mouldings, and as his books had a wide circulation in the country-side, many craftsmen who were joiners, cabinet-makers or chair-makers, as occasion demanded, may have picked up their knowledge of Gothic ornament from his plates.

LINNELL, John (died 1796). Carver, cabinet-maker and designer, possibly the son or nephew of William Linnell, *q.v.*, whom he succeeded at 28 Berkeley Square, in 1763. Many of his designs for furniture are preserved in the Victoria and Albert Museum.

LINNELL, William (died 1763). Carver, cabinet-maker and uphol-sterer, established at 28 Berkeley Square. His patrons included Sir Richard Hoare, for whose house at Barn Elms he supplied a quantity of furniture between 1739 and 1753. He was succeeded by John Linnell, *q.v.*

LOCK, Matthias. Carver and designer. Dates of birth and death unknown. Trade cards are engraved with the date, 1746, and give addresses in Tottenham Court Road, and Nottingham Court, Castle Street, Long Acre. In collaboration with Henry Copland, he published *A New Drawing Book of Ornament* (1740), and various other works, largely concerned with the interpretation of the Rococo style. Both Copland and Lock worked for Thomas Chippendale the elder, *q.v.*, and may have been responsible for some of the designs in the *Director*.

MANWARING, Robert. Cabinet and chair-maker, and a contemporary of Chippendale. Dates of birth and death unknown. His first book, *The Cabinet and Chair-Maker's Real Friend and Companion, or the Whole System of Chair-Making made plain and easy*, was published in 1765, and at the end of the Preface he gives his address as Hay-Market. *The Chairmakers' Guide* appeared in 1766. Many of his designs for chairs were heavy and overloaded with ornament, especially those he described as Chinese and "Rural".

MAROT, Daniel (1662–1752). Architect, furniture designer, and engraver, born in Paris, and son of Jean Marot (1620–79), also an architect and engraver. He was a Huguenot who left France the year before the Revocation of the Edict of Nantes and settled in Holland, where he entered the service of the Stadtholder, who, when he became William III of England, appointed Marot as one of his architects and Master of the Works. A folio volume of Marot's furniture designs was published at Amsterdam and entitled *Oeuvres du Sieur D. Marot*, and he is described on the title page as "Architect de Guillaume iii, Roy de la Grande-Bretagne". The upholstered chairs and stools included in the plates show French and Dutch influence, and strongly resemble English chairs of the late seventeenth and early eighteenth centuries, which Marot's work may well have affected. He visited London between 1694 and 1698, was partly responsible for planning the gardens at Hampton Court, and may have influenced some of the interior decoration and furnishing of the Palace that was being largely rebuilt by Sir Christopher Wren.

MAYHEW, John (died 1811). Cabinet-maker and upholsterer. Partner of William Ince, *q.v.*, and joint author of *The Universal System of Household Furniture*. Details of their business are given under the entry for Ince.

MORRIS, William (1834–96). Artist-craftsman, designer, poet, author, romantic mediaevalist, and social reformer, who initiated the handi-craft revival and founded the firm of Morris, Marshall, Faulkner and Company in 1862. The company consisted of D. G. Rossetti, Philip Webb, *q.v.*, Burne-Jones, Madox Brown, Faulkner and Marshall, and was prepared to undertake carving, church decoration, stained glass, metal-work, fabrics and furniture. Morris rejected contemporary industry, detested machinery, and turned his mind back to an imaginary golden age of mediaeval craftsmanship. As his reactionary teaching and influence deflected attention from the need for industrial design and thus hindered its development, the claim that he was a pioneer of the modern movement is fallacious. He was educated at Marlborough and Exeter College, Oxford, and afterwards became a pupil of George Edmund Street, the architect, but gave up the idea of following that profession, and devoted most of his time to the revival of crafts that had declined or were about to disappear. One of the effects of his influence was to restore respect for chairs of simple design, and examples produced by Morris and Company were light and agreeable versions of traditional country-made turned work. The impact of his ideas was far greater in Europe, particularly in the Scandinavian countries, than in England.

PUGIN, Augustus Welby Northmore (1812–52). Architect, designer, mediaevalist and champion of the Gothic Revival. An artist of outstanding genius who almost alone of the Gothic Revivalists could design buildings and decoration with the vitality of mediaeval work. He was the son of August Charles de Pugin (1762–1832), a refugee from the French Revolution, and a gifted artist who published two illustrated works on Gothic architecture. From an early age Pugin, the younger, was interested in Gothic art, and his designs for the interior decoration, fittings and furniture of the new Houses of Parliament were inspired by the spirit of the last phase of native English Gothic. He published illustrated works, advocating a return to Gothic design, and criticizing classic architecture and the growing ugliness of industrial towns: *Contrasts* (1836); *The True Principles of Pointed or Christian Architecture* (1841); and *An Apology for the Revival of Christian Architecture in England* (1843).

RANNIE, James (died 1766). Cabinet-maker and upholsterer, and the first partner of Thomas Chippendale the elder, *q.v.* The partnership began about 1755. Nothing is known about Rannie, who seems to have been a well-established business man before his partnership with Chippendale.

RUSSELL, Sir (Sydney) Gordon (born 1892). Designer, artist-craftsman, founder of the Russell Workshops, later Gordon Russell Limited, at Broadway, Worcestershire. Original member of the Council of Industrial Design, 1944, and Director, 1947–59. C.B.E., 1947; knighted, 1955; Royal Designer for Industry, 1940, and Master of the Faculty 1947–49; and first Fellow of the Society of Industrial Artists. Awarded Gold Albert Medal of the Royal Society of Arts, 1962. His early furniture continued the native English style, and under his direction Gordon Russell Ltd. produced robust examples of turned chairs with ladder backs and rush seats; but unlike the artist-craftsmen of the William Morris school, he did not reject mechanical production, and the example of his work had a profound effect, after a time-lag of several years, not only on other contemporary designers, but on the furniture trade as a whole. Gordon Russell's great contribution to twentieth-century furniture-making was in the nature of research work in design, and during the 1920s and 1930s he was the pioneer of English design as Sir Ambrose Heal had been the pioneer in the opening decade of the century. His work was not economically isolated like Gimson's, hand-made for a few wealthy people, but reached an increasingly large market and thus influenced contemporary taste.

SEDDON, George (1727–1801). Cabinet-maker and founder of a large business that flourished during the second half of the eighteenth century. He set up for himself about 1750 at London House, Aldersgate Street; after 1763 and until 1770, at No. 158, from then until 1784 at 151, and thereafter at 150. Contemporary references suggest that the business was not only of considerable size, employing over four hundred skilled men, but was the most eminent cabinet-making and upholstery firm in London.

SHEARER, Thomas. Furniture designer, about whom nothing is known apart from the engraved plates in the *Cabinet-Makers' London Book of Prices*, published in 1788. Most of those plates were re-issued in that year as *Designs for Household Furniture*, under Shearer's name.

SHERATON, Thomas (1751–1806). Cabinet-maker and furniture designer, born at Stockton-on-Tees, who settled in London about 1790. Although trained as a cabinet-maker, he was primarily a designer, whose fame rests on his published works, of which the first and most influential was *The Cabinet-Maker and Upholsterer's Drawing Book*, originally issued in four parts between 1791 and 1794. *The Cabinet Dictionary*, 1803, contains a large number of useful and instructive definitions, and a great deal of practical information about the technique of cabinet and chair-making. Only about a quarter of his last work, the *Cabinet-Maker, Upholsterer and General Artists' Encyclopaedia* appeared just before his death. No pieces of furniture have been traced to him, and it is doubtful whether he ever had a workshop; his trade card, with the address of 106 Wardour Street, Soho, announced that he taught perspective, architecture and ornaments and made designs for cabinet-makers, and sold "all kinds of Drawing Books". He moved later to No. 8, Broad Street, Golden Square. (See pages 171 to 176.) His name has been identified with the style of furniture that was fashionable during the 1790s and the opening years of the nineteenth century.

VILE, William (died 1767). Upholsterer and cabinet-maker, in partnership with John Cobb, *q.v.*, with premises at the corner of St Martin's Lane, and Long Acre. The superb quality of Vile's work, of which much has been identified, gives him pre-eminence among eighteenth-century cabinet-makers. He was the senior partner of the firm, and after his death Cobb carried on the business. (See entry Cobb.)

VOYSEY, Charles Francis Annesley (1857–1941). Architect, furniture designer, one of the first men to appreciate and understand the significance of industrial design, and a true pioneer of the modern movement. Although some of his work was linked with *Art Nouveau*, he was boldly experimental, and soon abandoned the complexities of that purely ornamental style. His designs for chairs were plain, simple and extremely comfortable, and he advocated a natural finish for wood. Although influenced by the teaching of William Morris, he soon outgrew it, and never succumbed to mediaeval romanticism. He was one of the first authentic modern designers.

WEBB, Philip (1831–1915). Architect and designer of furniture, who met William Morris after he had entered G. E. Street's office. He designed the Red House at Upton, Kent, for Morris, and afterwards became chief designer for the firm of Morris, Marshall, Faulkner and Company. He used bold and vigorous naturalistic motifs, and designed in addition to furniture, metalwork of various kinds, table glass, stained glass, and patterns for wallpapers and fabrics.

APPENDIX II

The Gilding of Chairs. From *The Cabinet Dictionary*,
by Thomas Sheraton. Entry on Gilding.

Gilding chairs. This branch of gilding is, in some respects, conducted differently from the others in oil and water already mentioned, though the principles of both are the same.

The difference is chiefly in point of time, as the chair branch requires the utmost dispatch, that the work may be kept clean, and quickly turned out of hand.—Hence the japanners' gold size is of a composition that dries rapidly, and requires the gold to be laid on in the most expert and ready manner. And for this purpose, in narrow fillets, which it chiefly consists of, the leaves of gold may be cut off singly, and cut upon the cushion with the paper under it, and another blank leaf being laid over the gold, and turned over as the narrow slips of gold are laid on, so that the tip is not wanted, and the work is executed with proportionably greater swiftness. And it is necessary to begin rather sooner in this than in the other oil gold size, on account of its drying quicker, and it need not be pressed down with cotton till the whole of the chair is covered, and then pass the cotton over the whole. All the japan part of the chair ought to be finished, before the gilding be entered upon, that the gold may not be disturbed in handling, and not merely for this reason, but that the lines or fillets of gold may be trimmed up, by japanning the uneaven edges with a colour suitable to the ground, especially if the gilding be any part of it flowered work, for it is impossible to gild the outlines so clean as to require no help by the pencil dipped in the ground colour; and moreover, it should be noticed, that in some cases of small flower or leaf work, it is best to lay on the gold without regard to the outline, and afterwards draw upon the gold, and pick in the ground of the outline. In sizing over for the gold, it should be so coloured, as to distinguish the sizing work from the ground of the chair; for the size of itself bears no material colour. A little red lead, vermillion, or ochre, will generally do; or if for a dark ground, mix with the size a little white lead. The japanners' gold size may be made by pulverizing gum animi and asphaltum, of each 1 ounce; red lead, litharge of gold, and umbre, of each 1 ounce and a half, mixing them with a pound of linseed oil, and boiling them, observing to stir them till the whole be incorporated, and appear, on growing cold, of the consistence of tar. Strain the mixture through a flannel, and keep it stopped up in a bottle. Another more simple may be made of 1 pound of linseed oil, 4 ounces of gum animi; powder the gum, and mix it gradually with the boiling oil. Let it continue to boil, till it be of the consistence of tar, and then strain it as before.

In gilding chairs with burnished gold, it is not necessary to make the operation so tedious as in picture or glass frame gilding; for the chairs are usually primed with whiting, and the japan laid upon it, forms a base for the gold; it is generally sufficient to give only a coat or two of the bole size, and then lay on the gold as in other works. The gold in chair work ought to be varnished to secure it, and the best varnish for this purpose is copal, diluted a little with the spirit of turpentine, that it may dry quick, and be more transparent over the gold, which it injures very little when it is thoroughly dry.

Pages 231–32.

APPENDIX III

Painting Furniture. From *The Cabinet Dictionary*,
by Thomas Sheraton. Of Painting in General. Chapter 4.

Of Painting Furniture

The principal thing which constitutes this a distinct branch of painting, is the general use of size and varnish colours, by which it is performed with much greater dispatch and effect. Yet the prices allowed in the country, at least in many parts of it, are so poor, that the painter can hardly distinguish furniture from common oil painting.

Of Painting Chair-seats

Rush-bottom chairs ought always to have their seats primed with common white lead, ground up in linseed oil, and diluted with spirits of turpentine. This first priming preserves the rushes, and hardens them; and, to make it come cheaper, the second coat of priming may have half Spanish white in it, if the price require it. The third coat should be ground up in spirits of turpentine only, and diluted with hard varnish, which will dry quick; but should not be applied till the priming be perfectly dry. Of this, probably the seats may require to have two lays, to make the work firm. A very small quantity of turpentine varnish may also be used for cheapness, and to keep the spirit varnish in a more flowing state; but the less it is used the better, since it is of such a quality as makes it very subject to turn soft and clammy by the heat of the body, when the chairs are used to sit on; especially, for some time, at their first use. They who use any kind of water colour for rush bottoms, entirely deceive the purchaser, for it rots the rushes, and by the sudden push of the hand upon the seat, the colour will-frequently fly off. All the other parts of chairs are primed with Spanish white, and glove leather size, as in any other mode of size painting. Sometimes once over may do, but when the work requires well finishing, three times, which should be rushed, or glass-papered down, for the beauty of the japan depends much upon the well-finished sizing; and it is better when the last coat of sizing is of white lead; upon such a ground, any colour may be laid with advantage, as it will always help the effect of the varnish colours, and particularly bright greens and straws.

To shorten the description, the reader should observe, that all kinds of colours are to be ground in spirits of turpentine, and no more of it than what is wanted for present use, as it presently dries, and will require as much spirits to grind it as at the first. And the same must be observed in all the varnish colours, and for more reason, for when it is left to stiffen, or set in pots, it is entirely wasted.

Of Painting Chairs

In painting chairs with a green ground, common verdigrise may be used; and, as it is extracted from copper, it is of a drying quality, and is much helped in colour by being partly diluted with good turpentine varnish, and partly copal; which will presently dry, if laid on thin, which it always should be. But if, in laying on the last coat of green, the tool be dipped into white hard varnish, in a separate pot, before it is put into the green, this will assist much in speedy drying. The green may be compounded to any shade by means of white lead, and king's yellow, both of which must first be ground in turpentine out of the dry colours; see also *Green* in the dictionary. A straw colour is best compounded of white lead, king's yellow, and a little Oxford ochre; and as the king's yellow is a slow drying colour, the more the tint imbibes of this, the more it is requisite to lay it on in white hard varnish. Black grounds for chairs, are generally made of lamp black; but the black will bear the best out on a white ground, prepared as before. This colour is of a greasy or oily quality, and a bad drier; consequently, requires a strong size priming. Some burn the lamp black, to take away the oil out of it; but this occasions a great waste, and does not always succeed in drying much sooner. It is sometimes mixed with ivory black, which helps it to dry, but is too dear for common chair work. When cheapness is not so much regarded, it should be ground up in turpentine, very fine, but previously sifted from the grit to which it is subject, and then laid on in white hard varnish, very thin, and repeated. But to help the black, a little varnish composed of asphaltum, black rosin, and the drying linseed oil, which was formerly mentioned, may be used in diluting the lamp black, after being ground in turpentine; for observe, lamp black never comes up to its proper colour so well, as when impregnated with something of linseed oil in it. If this asphaltum varnish be used with white lead and lamp black, ground in pure turpentine, it may be applied to chairs as the first priming; and a second, without white lead, will prepare the chairs for the last coat, which should be in white hard varnish only.

Pages 422–25

APPENDIX IV

Decoration of Chairs. From *The Cabinet Dictionary*, by Thomas
Sheraton. Of Drawing Lines on Chairs. Chapter 8.

As black chairs look well when ornamented with yellow lines, it may
be proper to give some directions as to the mixture of the colour, and
the manner of drawing these. King's yellow and white flake, with a
trifle of orange lead, ground finely up in spirits of turpentine very thick;
for if there be too much of the turpentine, the yellow will wash to the
ground, and produce a bad line. After grinding, it should be as a
paste; in which state it will admit a proper quantity of copal varnish
in diluting it. No other will produce so good a line, and therefore the
best of it should be procured, as the expence will soon be saved in time.
The thickness of this mixture, should not be more, when diluted with
copal, than will permit it to run very freely from the pencil that is
filled with it, when it is pressed against an upright surface; for except
it will run from the pencil in such a position, it will not freely leave the
pencil when it is pressed on a level surface, which position almost
every thing is placed in when it is to be run with lines. The kind of
pencil should be of camels hair, very long; some half inch, and three-
quarters, or one inch long in the hair, according to the thickness of the
line to be drawn. The pencil being well primed with this colour, which
should be kept in a deep hole, bring it to a fine point, on a flat marble
stone; and, in drawing the line, apply the fore-finger to some straight
angle of the work, and at the same time, keeping the pencil between
the first finger and the thumb, draw steadily along, and the quicker
the better the line will be drawn, if the colour be in proper order. Any
other necessary deviation from this general rule, must be learned from
experience and practice, which alone can supply the defects of every
theory in this art. In ornamenting japanned furniture, no person can
proceed further than to do it by lines, except he has previously been
taught, or has practised ornamental drawing himself.

Pages 425–26.

THE PLATES

The sixty-four plates follow the historical sequence of the twelve chapters, and supplement the illustrations in the text. The first eight are concerned with structural and stylistic developments in the ancient world, which directly or indirectly affected the design and character of English chairs during and after the end of the sixteenth century. Some American examples have been included on plates 20 and 21, to show how the technique of turning was improved by New England craftsmen, and how closely their work was related to forms evolved by turners in twelfth century Europe.

The Dutch example on plate 25 illustrates a type of chair that was in common use in England, the Low Countries, France and Northern and Central Europe during the first half of the seventeenth century; and the French armchair on plate 47 is included for purposes of comparison with a design by Robert Adam. One plate only, the last, has been given to contemporary design in the present century, and that has been included because it illustrates how a brilliant designer, like the late Ernest Race, could re-interpret traditional forms, using modern materials and production techniques with results as characteristically English as the Windsor chairs on plate 63, or the country-made types on plates 32 and 43.

PLATE 1. Seated statues of an Egyptian noble and his wife. XVIII Dynasty, *circa* 1450 BC. The front and back legs of the chair are derived from animal forms; the seat is slightly dipped, the back is very slightly inclined, and the junction with the seat is curved. Those concessions made to the contours of the body are too small to allow any relaxation from a position of upright dignity.

Reproduced by permission of the Trustees of the British Museum.

PLATE 2. Low-backed Egyptian chairs, with back and seat joined by a curve. From the upper part of a stele showing the deities Amen-Rā and Mut, and Herakhti and Isis seated at an altar. New Kingdom, *circa* 1200 B.C.

Right: A crude Egyptian forerunner of the joined chair, with a high raked back with four slats, and a seat of woven string. The front view is shown on plate 3 opposite. New Kingdom, *circa* 1250 B.C. *Both illustrations reproduced by permission of the Trustees of the British Museum.*

PLATE 3. *Left:* Folding wooden stool with duck's head terminals, turned rests, and dipped seat supports. Inlaid with ivory and ebony. From the tomb of Ani at Thebes. XVII–XIX Dynasty, *circa* 1300 B C

Below left: Front view of high-backed wooden joined chair. (See plate 2 opposite.) *Circa* 1250 B C. *Right:* Low chair of acacia wood with lion's paw feet on turned and grooved bases. The panelled back is inlaid with ivory and ebony: the seat is of plaited string. From Thebes. New Kingdom, *circa* 1250 B C. *All three illustrations reproduced by permission of the Trustees of the British Museum.*

PLATE 4. The Assyrian King Ashurnasirpal enthroned. The throne is a cushioned stool, which has a shallow dipped seat carved with ram's heads, a stretcher decorated with volutes, and ring-turning on the feet. The footstool rests on boldly carved lion's paws. *Circa* 1260 B C. *Reproduced by permission of the Trustees of the British Museum.*

PLATE 5. *Above:* Seated figures from the Parthenon frieze. The arm of the chair is supported by a sphinx, the legs and back uprights are turned. Reproduced from *The Antiquities of Athens*, by Stuart and Revett. Vol. II, plate XXIV. *Right:* Macedonian medal, one of a group of four, showing seated figure on chair with ball-turning. From *The Antiquities of Athens*, Vol. III, plate V.

PLATE 6. Seats in the Theatre of Dionysos, Athens, 340 BC. *Photographs by the author.*

PLATE 7. *Right:* The *klismos*, the elegant form of chair perfected by Greek designers. Compare the sweep of the legs with the seats on the lower part of plate 6 and the drawing on page 12. From the grave-stone of Xanthippos: Athenian, *circa* 430 B C. *Reproduced by permission of the Trustees of the British Museum. Below, left:* Thomas Hope's version of the *klismos*. The subtle continuity of the splayed back legs and back uprights has been abruptly broken at seat level. From *Household Furniture and Interior Decoration* (1807), plate 4. *Below, right:* A group of figures, showing a *klismos*, from an Athenian sepulchral urn. From *Athenian Sepulchral Marbles*, Supplement to *The Antiquities of Athens* (1830), plate 2.

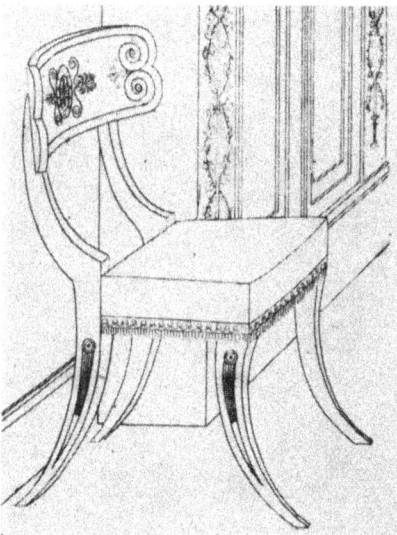

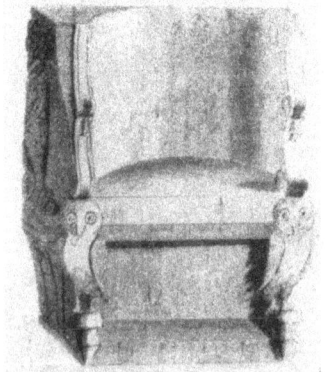

PLATE 8. Side and front views of marble chair, with carved owls supporting the seat. Reproduced from *The Antiquities of Athens*, Vol. III, page 19.

PLATE 9. A wicker or basket-work chair is shown at the left of this Romano-British sepulchral monument to Julia Velva. Basket-making was probably one of the oldest crafts in Britain, pre-Roman in origin, and surviving through the Dark Ages to flourish in mediaeval times. The monument is in the Archaeological Museum at York. *Reproduced by permission of the Royal Commission on Historical Monuments (England). Crown copyright reserved.*

PLATE 10. A carving from Chartres Cathedral, twelfth century, showing a turned chair with rising, ball-topped front posts, resembling the mid-seventeenth century "Carver" and "Brewster" chairs of New England. (See plates 20 and 21.) Reproduced from *The English Chair: its History and Evolution.* (London: M. Harris and Sons, 1948 edition.)

PLATE 11. Late fourteenth century portrait of King Richard II in Westminster Abbey. The pierced arms of the throne, the tracery carved on the
back, and the finials with crockets are closely related to contemporary Gothic
architecture. *Photograph by the Victoria and Albert Museum. Reproduced by permission
of the Dean and Chapter of Westminster Abbey.*

PLATE 12. A school scene from a mid-fourteenth-century manuscript in the Bodleian Library, Oxford. The schoolmaster is seated on a chair, constructed from turned spindles, that anticipates the design of the eighteenth century ladder-back type. *Circa* 1338–44. MS. Bodley. 264, fol. 123v.

Two high-backed late fifteenth century thrones or chairs of state, far more elaborate than the relatively modest throne on plate 11. A circular three-legged stool of the simplest construction is shown at the right. From an illuminated French manuscript in the British Museum. (Harl. 4372. F.12.) *Reproduced by courtesy of the Trustees of the British Museum.*

PLATE 13. Detail from the Throne in the House of Lords, designed by A. W. N. Pugin, *circa* 1846. No other Gothic Revivalist of the nineteenth century could give the fire of life to mediaeval design; Pugin alone could respond to the spirit that had inspired the craftsmen of that time, and through his work we gain our last glimpse of the English Middle Ages. (See page 40.) *Reproduced by permission of the Ministry of Works: Crown copyright reserved.*

PLATE 14. A high-backed settle from a fifteenth-century manuscript in the Bodleian Library, Oxford. The finials on the back uprights and arm posts resemble those of the angle settle shown on page 43. MS. Bodley 283, fol. 59R.

PLATE 15. A King seated in an X-framed chair. From *La Bible Historiale*, an illuminated manuscript in the British Museum, *circa* 1470. (Royal 15D, III.) This is a much lighter type than the coffer-makers' chair in Winchester Cathedral shown on plate 22 or the example from York Minster on page 45. The material that forms the seat and back is attached to the frame, and the round-headed nails on the stretcher suggest that the frame was covered with some fabric, such as velvet. *Reproduced by courtesy of the Trustees of the British Museum.*

PLATE 16. *Left:* Board-ended oak stool, early sixteenth century. This example is incomplete, as the pierced underframing is missing at the back.

Right: An oak joined chair, second quarter of the sixteenth century. The linen-fold motif is used on four of the panels, and the upper panel of the back is carved with Renaissance ornament. (See drawings on page 46.)

Both examples on this plate are reproduced by courtesy of the Victoria and Albert Museum, Crown Copyright.

PLATE 17. An oak joint stool, mid-seventeenth century, with turned legs of a very simple pattern. The sides of the seat are decorated by a struck moulding, the ends by shallow carved serrations; a more elaborate struck moulding is used on the seat rail. The heads of the dowels that secure the joint of leg and seat rails are shown in the detail below. *In the possession of the author.*

PLATE 18. *Left:* Joined armchair in oak, with an arch enclosing a diamond incised on the back panel, scrollwork on the cresting derived from architectural motifs, and simple turning on the front legs and arm supports. *Circa* 1630. *In the possession of Mrs Grace Lovat Fraser.*

Right: Joined armchair in oak, inlaid with various woods, cresting and brackets carved with foliage, and fluted front legs and arm supports. *Circa* 1600. *Reproduced by courtesy of the Victoria and Albert Museum, Crown Copyright.*

PLATE 19. *Right:* Turned chair in oak and ash, with triangular seat, an elaborate development of the simpler types shown on page 51. Early seventeenth century. *Reproduced by courtesy of the Victoria and Albert Museum. Crown Copyright.*

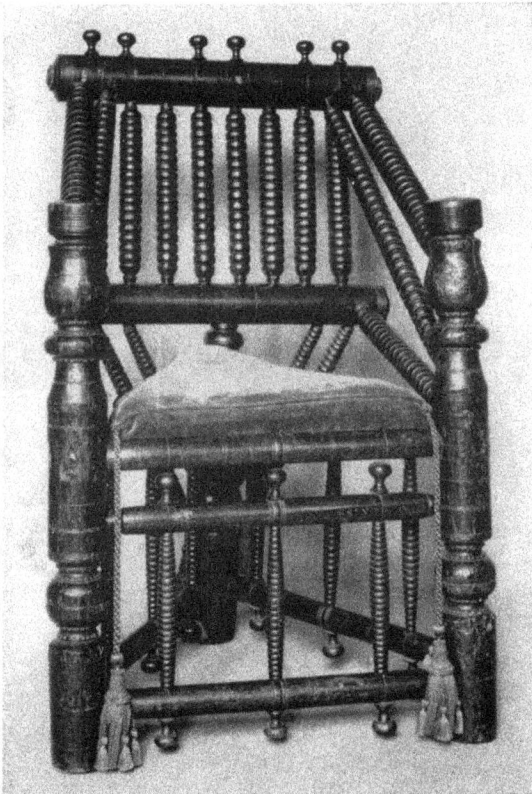

Left: Turned chair, probably of East Anglian origin. *Circa* 1600. *Reproduced by permission of the Syndics of the Fitzwilliam Museum, Cambridge.*

PLATE 20. *Above:* New England chairs of the Carver type, in maple and ash, middle to late seventeenth century. *Right:* Armchair with carver type back. *Reproduced by permission of the Metropolitan Museum of Art, New York.* (Upper subject, Gift of Mrs Russell Sage, 1909; that on the right, Rogers Fund, 1941.)

PLATE 21. A Brewster type of turned chair, Massachusetts, *circa* 1650. *The Metropolitan Museum of Art, New York.* (Gift of Mrs J. Insley Blair, 1951.) Compare this example, and those on the plate opposite, with the twelfth-century prototype on plate 10.

PLATE 22. *Left:* Oak chair with X-shaped frame, originally covered in blue velvet, garnished with nails. *Circa* 1550. In Winchester Cathedral. Compare with chairs on plate 15 and page 45. *Copyright, "Country Life".*

Right: Armchair with X-shaped frame, covered with crimson velvet, with footstool to match. *Circa* 1610–20. Formerly the property of Archbishop Juxon. Variations of this type are shown on the opposite plate and page 52. *Reproduced by courtesy of the Victoria and Albert Museum, Crown Copyright.*

PLATE 23. The meeting in old Somerset House, August 18, 1604, of the eleven Commissioners who assembled to ratify a treaty of Peace and Commerce between the kings of England and Spain, and the archdukes of Austria. They are seated on high-backed X-framed chairs, varying in type like those shown in the small drawings. The painting is attributed to Marcus Gheeraedts. *Reproduced by courtesy of the Trustees of the National Portrait Gallery.*

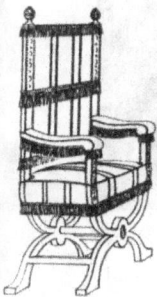

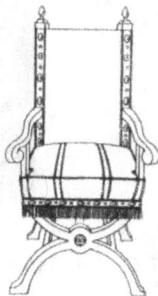

PLATE 24. Portrait of the Countess of Derby, painted about 1635, probably by Gilbert Jackson. The chair on which her left hand rests is a richly uphol-stered variety of back-stool, sometimes called an imbrauderers' or upholsterers' chair, and in general use throughout Europe and England. Compare with the example from Knole on page 57, and the much simpler specimen on the plate opposite. *Reproduced by courtesy of the Victoria and Albert Museum, Crown Copyright.*

PLATE 25. "The Housewife at Work", a painting by Nicolas Maes, dated 1656. The chair beside the housewife is a plainly covered back-stool, garnished with nails, of a type extensively used in England during the first half of the seventeenth century, and in the Low Countries, France and Northern and Central Europe. This sort of standardized frame could be upholstered richly, like the example on the opposite plate, or with austere simplicity, like this Dutch example. *Reproduced by courtesy of the Trustees of the Wallace Collection.*

PLATE 26.   *Above, left:* Turned and joined walnut chair, *circa* 1650. *Reproduced by courtesy of the Victoria and Albert Museum, Crown Copyright.*

Above, right: Oak chair upholstered in leather, with boldly carved scrolls on the front stretcher. One of a set of twenty-four. (Chetham's Hospital, Manchester.)

Right: Turned walnut and embroidered chair, *circa* 1660: the embroidery about 1641–55. From Denham Place, Buckinghamshire. Compare with the chairs on plates 24, 25, and page 57. *Reproduced by courtesy of the Victoria and Albert Museum, Crown Copyright.*

PLATE 27. *Right:* Oak chair-table, or "table-chairwise", with turned front legs and arm supports, carved and decorated with applied ornament. *Circa* 1650–60. *Below:* The hinged back swung over to form a table. (See circular-backed example on page 65.) *Reproduced by courtesy of the Victoria and Albert Museum, Crown Copyright.*

PLATE 28. *Above, left:* Carved and turned walnut chair with caned seat and back, *circa* 1675.

Above, right: Carved and turned walnut armchair, with caned seat and back panels, scrolled front legs and stretcher and arm supports. *Circa* 1670.

Right: Elaborately carved walnut armchair with caned back and seat. *Circa* 1680–90.

All three subjects reproduced by courtesy of the Victoria and Albert Museum, Crown Copyright.

PLATE 29. *Above:* Carved walnut day-bed with caned seat. *Circa* 1685. *Below:* A pair of "Sleeping Chayres", with gilded frames, the front feet carved in the form of recumbent sea-horses. Both chairs are covered in cherry-coloured brocade, and the backs are fitted with iron ratchets, so they may be let down. (Ham House, Surrey.) *Both subjects reproduced by courtesy of the Victoria and Albert Museum, Crown Copyright.*

PLATE 30. *Left:* A carved walnut single chair with caned back and seat, one of a pair. End of the seventeenth century.
Below: Carved beech wood stool, with scroll legs that foreshadow the cabriole form, *circa* 1685.
Both subjects reproduced by courtesy of the Victoria and Albert Museum, Crown Copyright.

PLATE 31. *Above:* Oak settle at Trinity College, Oxford, *circa* 1715. The turned front legs and arm supports are traditional survivals, and the carving on the front stretcher and top rail are Carolean in character. *Copyright, "Country Life".*

Left: Early eighteenth-century oak settle, with ball feet terminating the front legs, and a panelled back. Probably the work of some small country joiner, who, like the more accomplished maker of the other example on this plate, still used a much earlier form of arm.

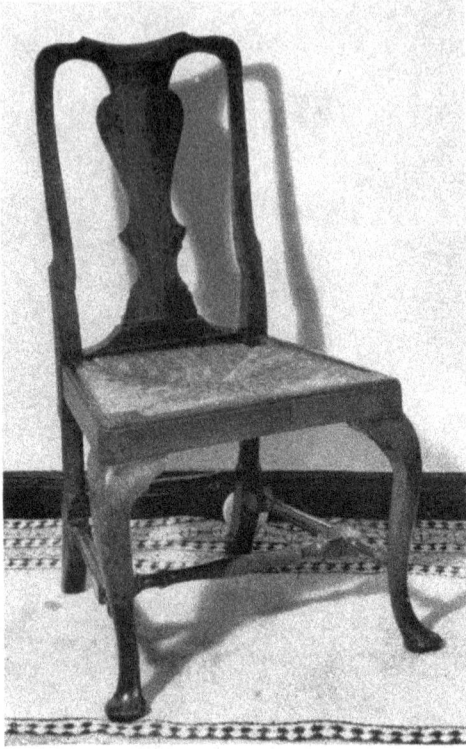

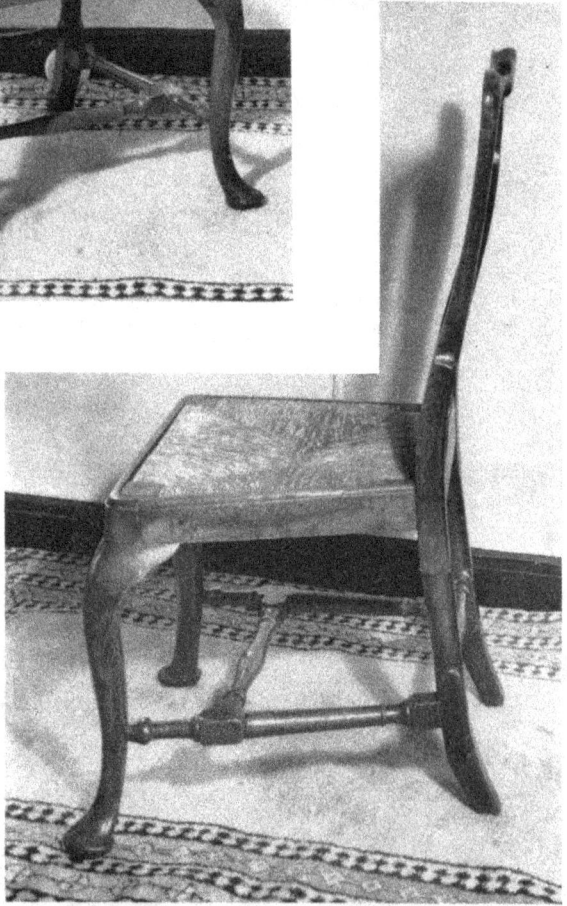

PLATE 32. Early eighteenth century single chair in walnut, with cabriole legs in front, splayed back legs, turned stretchers, and a back gracefully curved to invite a relaxed, comfortable posture. Compare this example of curvilinear design with the rigidity of the examples on plates 28 and 30. *In the possession of the author.*

PLATE 33.   *Right:* Walnut arm-chair with upholstered seat and back, scroll-over arms and cabriole legs, *circa* 1710. *Reproduced by permission of the Syndics of the Fitzwilliam Museum, Cambridge.*

Left: Walnut writing chair, with fan-shaped seat, cabriole leg in front, three turned legs, continuous with the back uprights, and vase-shaped splats. *In the possession of Julian Gloag.*

PLATE 34. *Above:* Self-portrait, by William Hogarth. This engraving shows a bended-back armchair with scroll-over arms, that was obviously part of the furnishing of his studio. (The original painting, in the National Portrait Gallery, is dated 1758.) There is some reason for assuming that he also possessed some bended-back single chairs.

See pages 100 and 101.

Right: A country-made chair in cherry-wood, with an early eighteenth-century form of back, and underframing of a much later type. (Compare this with the examples on page 96.) *In the possession of Mrs Frances J. Custance.*

PLATE 35. Portrait of Benjamin Hoadly, by William Hogarth. The chair has a high, inclined upholstered back, with carved cresting decorating the curved top rail. The back legs are splayed, the front legs, of a heavy cabriole form, are clumsy, a defect shared by the scroll supports of the arms. *Reproduced by permission of the Syndics of the Fitzwilliam Museum, Cambridge.*

PLATE 36. Carved walnut settee with upholstered seat and back. First quarter of the eighteenth century. The arm supports spring outwards from the seat rail, with a boldness that contrasts sharply with the unemphatic curves of the cabriole legs; indeed, contrast seems to have been the designer's aim, which he has achieved without disrupting the proportions or diminishing the grace of the design as a whole. The arms scroll over to terminate in the heads of eagles; the foliage on the knees of the legs, and the shells that rise into the seat rail, are delicately carved, and the claw-and-ball feet vigorously rendered. The upholstered back, enclosed by a slender moulded frame, has an elegant outline.

Reproduced by courtesy of the Victoria and Albert Museum.

PLATE 37.   Walnut armchair, upholstered in red velvet. First quarter of the eighteenth century. Lightly carved shells decorate the knees of the cabriole legs, with scales on the lower part and talon-and-ball feet. *Reproduced by courtesy of the Victoria and Albert Museum.*

PLATE 38. Pinewood armchair, carved and gilt, with X-formed front legs, lion-headed arm terminals, and acanthus scrolls on the cresting and below the seat. The design is probably by William Kent, and is almost identical with a pair of such armchairs attributed to him, formerly at Devonshire House. Upholstered with the original cut velvet brocade, from the Spitalfields manufactory. *Circa* 1730. *Reproduced by courtesy of the Trustees of the Wallace Collection.*

PLATE 39. Carved mahogany armchair, with a wide seat, *circa* 1730. (See page 98.) *Reproduced by courtesy of the Trustees of Sir John Soane's Museum. Copyright, "Country Life".*

PLATE 40. Prince George Frederick, Prince of Wales (later, King George III), and Prince Edward Augustus. The frame of the settee is gilt, and seat and back are upholstered in a pale rose coloured material. *Reproduced by courtesy of the Trustees of the National Portrait Gallery*. (An outline drawing of the frame is shown below.)

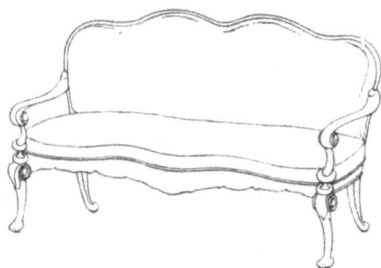

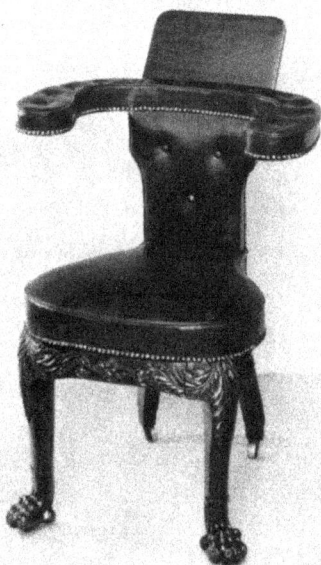

PLATE 41. *Left:* Mid-eighteenth century mahogany single chair, with pierced back splat, and drop-in seat. The front legs follow a much earlier cabriole form. *In the collection of the late Robert Atkinson, F.R.I.B.A. Right:* Mahogany library or reading chair, *circa* 1735. *Reproduced by permission of the Syndics of the Fitzwilliam Museum, Cambridge.*

Left: Mahogany chair with underframing in the Chinese taste. *Right:* This example resembles American variations of the Chippendale type—notably those from Philadelphia—which retained the cabriole leg and claw-and-ball foot. *In the collection of the late Robert Atkinson, F.R.I.B.A.*

PLATE 42. Mahogany chair, one of a set of six, *circa* 1760. The modified rococo treatment is confined to the back: a plain underframe, with square-sectioned front legs and splayed back legs, supports the stuffed seat. *Reproduced by permission of the Syndics of the Fitzwilliam Museum, Cambridge.*

PLATE 43. A country-made elbow chair in mahogany with a drop-in seat and a triple lancet splat, a restrained and graceful tribute to the Gothic taste. *Circa* 1765–70. *In the possession of the author.*

PLATE 44. *Left:* Robert Adam, portrait by an unknown artist. He is seated in a mahogany armchair, covered in a soft green fabric, garnished with brass-headed nails, of the type Chippendale called French. (See page 134 also example on plate opposite. Details of arm and back shown below.) *Right:* Henry Richard Vassall Fox, third baron Holland, painted by Francois Xavier, Fabre, 1795. The chair appears to be a mahogany curricle, upholstered in dark red leather, garnished with brass-headed nails. *Reproduced by courtesy of the Trustees of the National Portrait Gallery.*

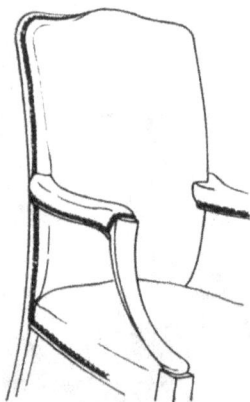

Right: The curricle shown in Lord Holland's portrait probably looked like this; resembling the curricle by Sheraton on page 172 in general form though differing in detail. *Drawn by Marcelle Barton.*

PLATE 45. *Right:* Mr Wilson and Mrs Mattocks in the characters of Ben and Miss Prue in *Love for Love*. The chair has an oval lattice-back and carved cresting. *From a contemporary print, published in 1776.*

Below, left: A "French" chair with a plain mahogany frame, of the type shown in the portrait of Robert Adam opposite. The upholstery is modern.

Below, right: An oval backed elbow chair with a painted and decorated frame. Compare this with the chair designed by Robert Adam on plate 47. *In the collection of the late Sir Albert Richardson, K.C.V.O., PP.R.A., at Avenue House, Ampthill, Bedfordshire.*

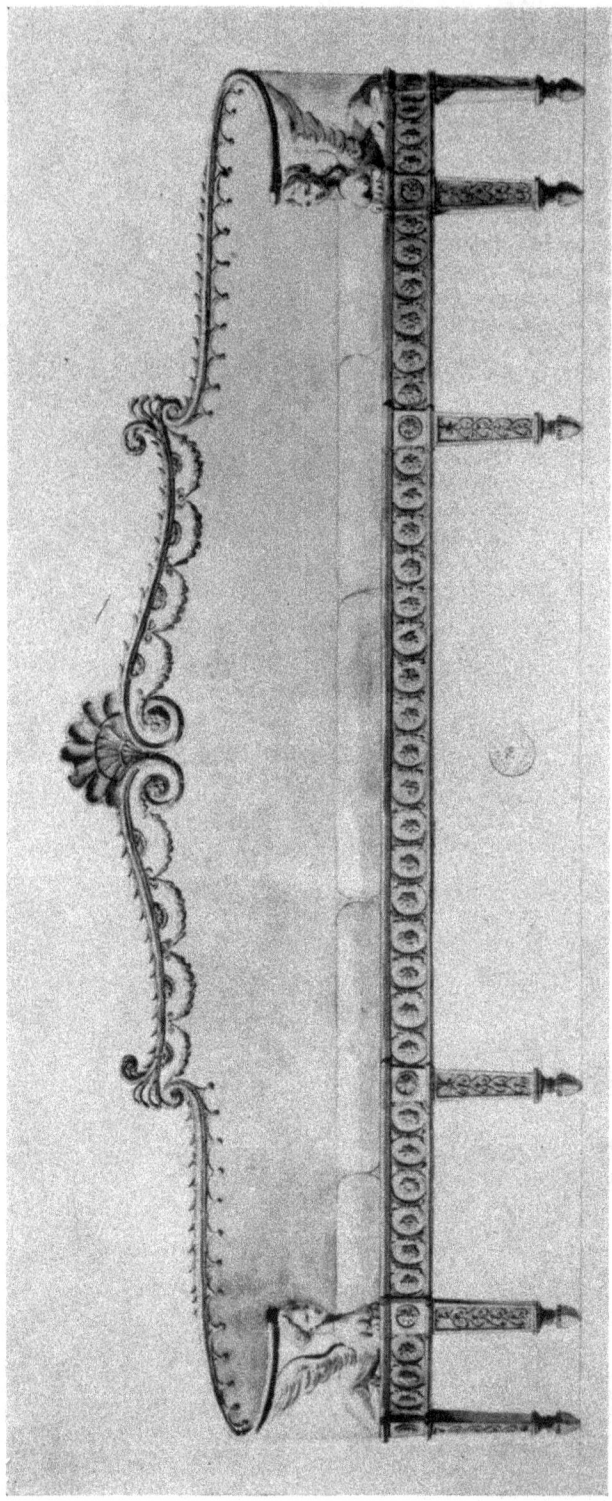

PLATE 46. Sofa designed by Robert Adam for **Mr** President Dundas, 1770. *Reproduced from the original drawing by courtesy of the Trustees of Sir John Soane's Museum.*

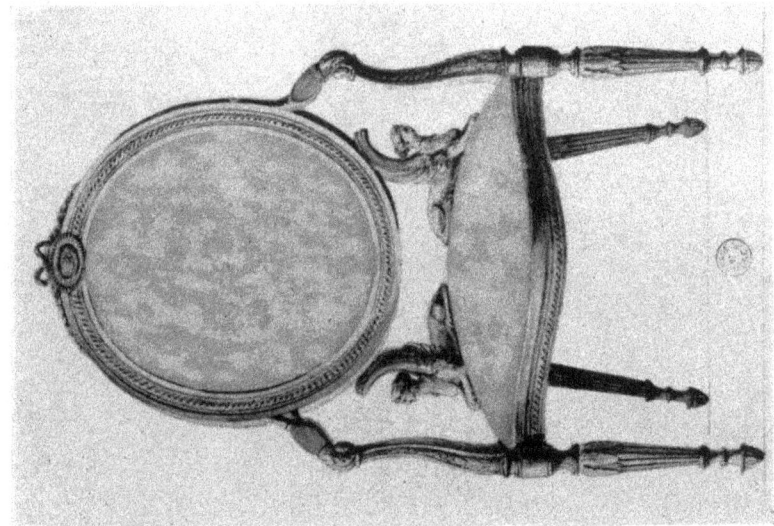

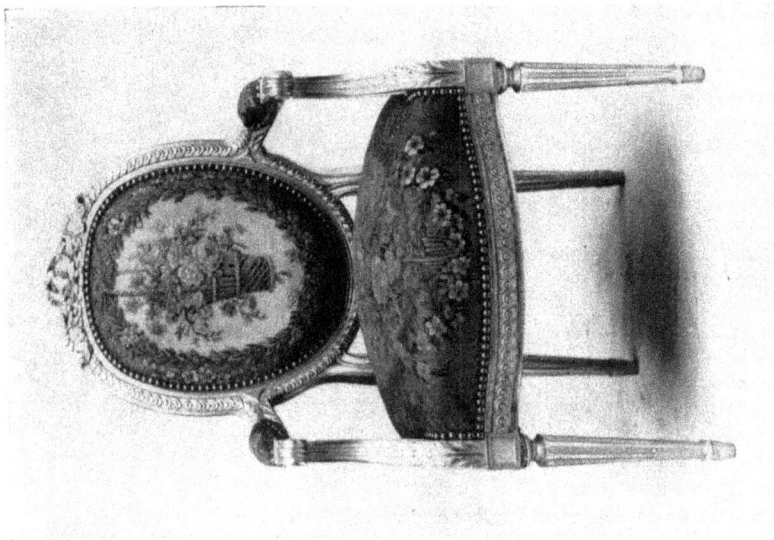

PLATE 47. *Left*: Chair designed by Robert Adam for the bed chamber of Osterley House, Middlesex, 1767. *Reproduced from the original drawing by courtesy of the Trustees of Sir John Soane's Museum. Right*: Armchair in birch wood, carved, gilt and upholstered in Beauvais tapestry. French, Louis XVI period. *Reproduced by courtesy of the Trustees of the Wallace Collection.*

PLATE 48. Two sofas designed by Robert Adam. *Above:* For Lord Scarsdale, 1762. *Below:* For Sir Laurence Dundas, 1764. *Reproduced from the original drawings by courtesy of the Trustees of Sir John Soane's Museum.*

PLATE 49.   *Above:* Mahogany settee, upholstered with buttoned leather, *circa* 1785. Hatfield House, Hertfordshire. *Copyright, "Country Life".* The technique of buttoning, used extensively by coach-builders for the inside of vehicles, was adopted later for first-class railway compartments, together with some of the features of high-backed easy chairs. *Below:* "The Return", painted by Abraham Solomon, 1855. *Reproduced by courtesy of The Museum of British Transport.*

PLATE 50. The iron garden seat in this portrait of Mr and Mrs Andrews by Gainsborough has a rococo fluidity of line, and is painted dark olive green. Only the left-hand part of the picture is included. *Reproduced by permission of the Trustees of the National Gallery.*

PLATE 51. *Above:* The trade card of John Stubbs (1790–1803), depicting examples of rustic and garden furniture. A hoop-backed Windsor chair appears in the top left-hand corner, a ladder-back rush seated chair on the extreme right. *Reproduced by courtesy of the Trustees of the British Museum. Below:* Charles James Fox, painted by Karl Anton Hickel, 1793. The wooden garden seat is painted apple green. (See page 151.) *Reproduced by courtesy of the Trustees of the National Portrait Gallery.*

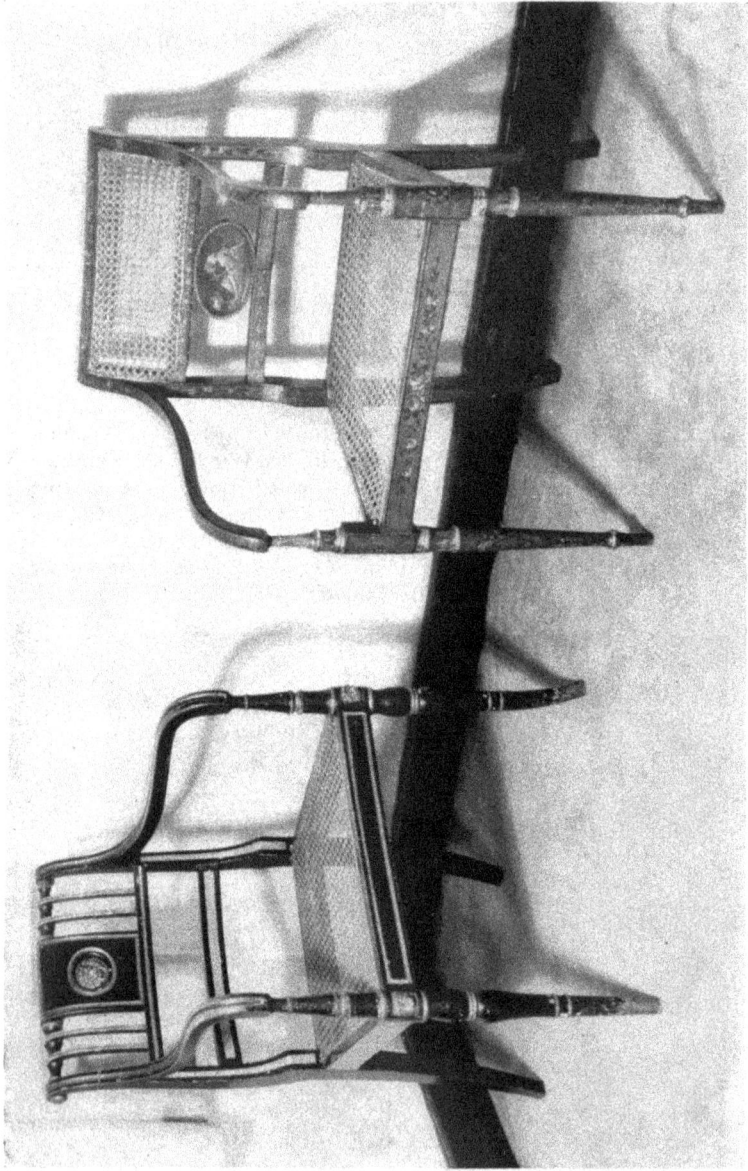

PLATE 52. Two armchairs, *circa* 1790–95. *Left*: Frame japanned black, decorated with gold. *Right*: Frame painted and decorated with floral motifs. Both chairs have a resemblance to the Sheraton design on page 169.

PLATE 53. Two of a set of six small chairs in mahogany with ormolu mounts and sabre legs. The lunette in the back, formed by the upper semi-circle, is filled by a diagonal metal grille, gilded. In the King's Library, Royal Pavilion, Brighton. *Reproduced by courtesy of the Brighton Art Gallery.*

PLATE 54. *Above:* A gilt scroll-back chair, with turned and reeded front legs, and swept back legs. *Circa* 1810. In the King's Bedroom, Royal Pavilion, Brighton. *Right:* One of four gilt seats carved in the form of a shell supported by a dolphin. *Circa* 1805. In the Music Room, Royal Pavilion, Brighton. *Reproduced by courtesy of the Brighton Art Gallery.*

PLATE 55. Frederick Augustus, Duke of York and Albany (1763–1827), from the panel by Sir David Wilkie, painted in 1823. The sabre legs of the mahogany chair are not so emphatically concave as Thomas Hope's design on plate 7, but the memory of the *klismos* survives, a little blurred and thickened, but still recognizable. *Reproduced by courtesy of the Trustees of the National Portrait Gallery.*

PLATE 56. Portrait of John Keats (1795–1821), painted by Joseph Severn. The influence of the Greek Revival is still apparent in the two cane-seated chairs. *Reproduced by courtesy of the Trustees of the National Portrait Gallery.*

PLATE 57. Three early nineteenth century mahogany single chairs with turned front legs. They are much simpler in design than the examples in the portrait of Keats on the opposite plate.

PLATE 58. *Left:* Cane-seated mahogany armchair. *Circa* 1810. *In the collection of the late Robert Atkinson, F.R.I.B.A.* *Right:* Mahogany armchair. *Circa* 1830. *In the author's possession.*

Left: A late version of the Greek Revival form. *Circa* 1830–40.
Right: Small mahogany chair. *Circa* 1810–20.

PLATE 59. A scroll-end sofa, japanned black, decorated with gold lines, and covered in peach velvet, in the South Drawing Room of the Royal Pavilion, Brighton. *Circa* 1805. *Reproduced by courtesy of the Brighton Art Gallery*. This is a refined version of Sheraton's design for a "Grecian Squab", shown below, and reproduced on a slightly smaller scale from *The Cabinet Dictionary* (1803).

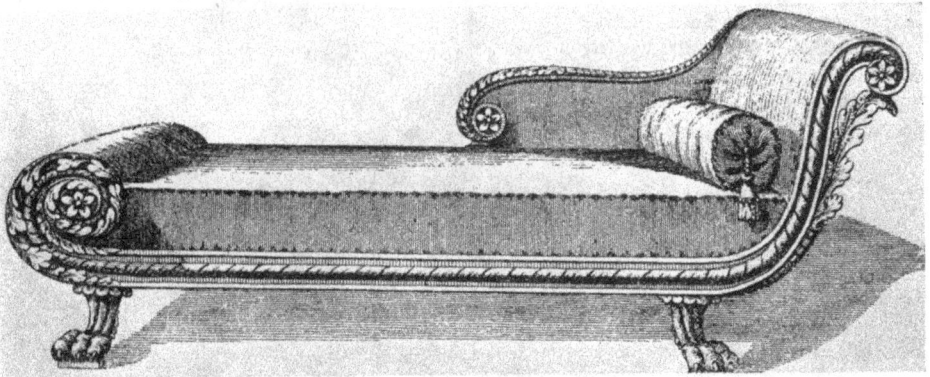

PLATE 60. *Above:* Gothic sofa and easy chair in the drawing-room at Eaton Hall, Cheshire. The house, built for Lord Grosvenor by William Porden between 1804 and 1812, was decorated and furnished in the fashionable tradition of the Gothic taste, before the earnestness of the Gothic revivalists changed its character. From *Views of Eaton Hall*, by J. C. Bucklet (1826).

Right: A Regency low chair, japanned black, decorated with brass twist moulding. *Circa* 1810–20. Low chairs of this type were popular for at least half a century, and a rather corpulent variation of the design was later known in the furniture trade as a "Spanish" chair. (See Hope's design on page 181.,
In the author's possession.

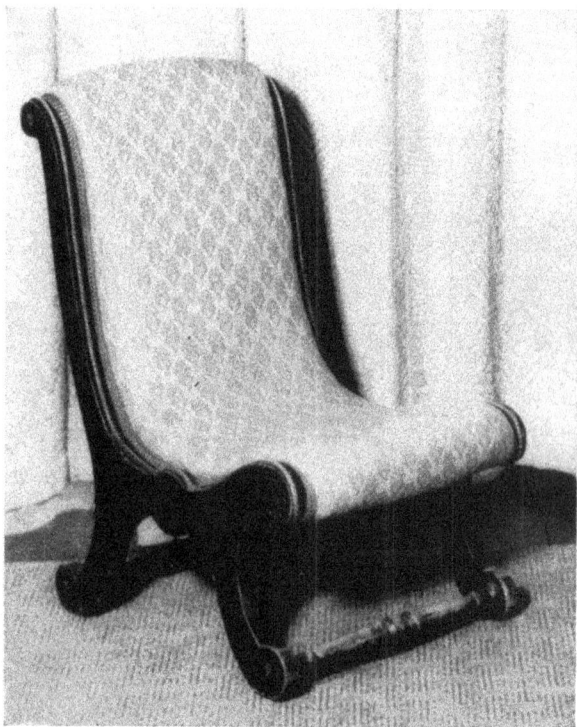

PLATE 61. *Above:* Two examples of Victorian elegance. *Left:* Papier mâché cane-seated drawing room chair, in black, with painted decoration and mother-of-pearl inlay. *Circa* 1850. *In the possession of Mrs Grace Lovat Fraser. Right:* Walnut bedroom chair, with turned legs, a waisted back, and the centre and yoke rails formed from cusps and foils. *Circa* 1860–70. *In the possession of Mrs John Gloag.*

Below, right: A lady's chair, with a black japanned frame, spoon back and turned front legs. The upholstery has a red Berlin wool background with multi-coloured bead embroidery, shading into grey and dark green *Circa* 1850–60. *In the possession of Mrs Grace Lovat Fraser.*

PLATE 62. *Above:* Pair of ladder-back rush-seated turned chairs, one in brown oak (on the left), one in yew. (*In the possession of Mr and Mrs John Gloag.*) Compare these modern examples with the mid-fourteenth-century prototype at the top of plate 12. Made in 1924 and designed by Sir Gordon Russell, they are more robust in form than the chair by Ernest Gimson, shown to the *right*. Gimson followed the Morris tradition of chair-making, using slender spindles for legs, stretchers, and back uprights, which were continuous with the back legs. See illustration of Morris rush-seated chairs on page 256.

PLATE 63. Three examples of Windsor chair. *Above, left:* Late eighteenth or early nineteenth century hoop-back, with spur stretcher, turned legs, and interlaced pierced back splat: yew, with an elm seat. *Above, right:* Mid-nineteenth century, heavily-built North country type with decorative turned spindles supporting the arms, which are continuous with the yoke rail. Up to the level of the yoke rail, the chair closely resembles the smoker's bow type (see page 189), built up at the back, to allow the hoop and six spindles to be socketed, while the pierced back splat passes through the yoke rail and links seat and hoop. Yew with an elm seat. *In the author's possession.* *Right:* The simplest form of hoop-backed chair, without a back splat. The "White Wycombes" of the early nineteenth century were generally of this type. (See pages 186, 190, and 195.)

PLATE 64. Two designs by the late Ernest Race, R.D.I., PP.S.I.A. *Left:* An easy chair, which received a Design Centre award in 1959. *Copyright: The Council of Industrial Design. Below:* An upholstered settee, designed in 1947, and an early example of Ernest Race's use of a welded steel rod frame for upholstery. Manufacturer: Race Furniture Limited.

INDEX

Where page numbers are given in italics, thus, *136*, they refer to a caption.

K

For Product Safety Concerns and Information please contact our EU
representative GPSR@taylorandfrancis.com
Taylor & Francis Verlag GmbH, Kaufingerstraße 24, 80331 München, Germany

9 781032 367606